IMAGES
of America

DUPLIN COUNTY

On the Cover: Duplin County residents gather under a produce shed advertising the 1936 Coastal Plain Strawberry Festival, described as "The Biggest Week in the History of this Section." The photograph was taken along Railroad Street in downtown Wallace. The 1922 Farmers Bank & Trust building can be seen in the background. (Courtesy of the State Archives of North Carolina.)

IMAGES
of America

DUPLIN COUNTY

Andrew C. Cole

ARCADIA
PUBLISHING

ISBN 978-1-4671-0871-3

Published by Arcadia Publishing
Charleston, South Carolina

Printed in the United States of America

Library of Congress Control Number: 2022938573

For all general information, please contact Arcadia Publishing:
Telephone 843-853-2070
Fax 843-853-0044
E-mail sales@arcadiapublishing.com
For customer service and orders:
Toll-Free 1-888-313-2665

Visit us on the Internet at www.arcadiapublishing.com

To my grandparents,
and to the residents of Duplin County
past, present, and future.

Contents

Acknowledgments

In many ways, this compilation of historic images of Duplin County is the result of my lifelong interest in history, a seed that was planted in me decades ago as I dug through my grandparents' old photo album, captivated by their tales of life "back then."

This book is by no means intended to be an in-depth history of Duplin County, but rather a brief overview of its cultural heritage told by photographs. It is intended to be a look back at the past, a glimpse of days gone by.

This publication would not have been possible without the generosity and support of several individuals within Duplin County and the surrounding region. For starters, I would like to express my gratitude to local historian Leon "Sonny" Sikes of Rose Hill for sharing with me his extensive collection of photographs and for providing additional context to those images when needed.

I would also like to thank Roland Edwards of Beulaville for setting aside time to invite me into his home to talk about local history and make use of his photograph collection for this publication. A thank-you is also due to the Bratcher family for allowing me to pull images from their family albums.

Furthermore, a debt of gratitude is owed to both Anne S. Taylor of the Faison Museum and Ken Dilda of the Mount Olive Area Historical Society for opening the doors of their respective institutions to share not only their photograph collections with me but also their invaluable knowledge of the area.

Special thanks also go out to the State Archives of North Carolina, particularly Vann Evans, for assisting me throughout my quest for historic images. I would also like to thank Laura Jones and the Duplin County Library System for offering me its support, as well as the Wilson Library at the University of North Carolina (UNC) Chapel Hill for the use of its images.

Last, but certainly not least, I would like to thank my wife, Jade, for the steady stream of encouragement bestowed upon me through the years and my daughter, Rosalie, for the additional motivation.

INTRODUCTION

Long before colonists established the borders of what was to become Duplin County, the region was a vast expanse of towering longleaf pines and blackwater streams. Native American tribes such as the Tuscarora inhabited the region, as did wild animals such as bears and wildcats.

During the 18th century, the area saw settlement by its first Europeans—the Welsh—followed closely by people of English, Scots-Irish, Swiss, German, and African descent.

In 1750, a bill "to divide the upper part of New Hanover County, into a County and Parish" passed through the General Assembly in New Bern. The new county would be named in honor of English nobleman Sir Thomas Hay, Lord of Dupplin, a member of the English Board of Trade and Plantations who served in several capacities within the British government. Duplin County was officially formed.

During the American Revolution, many of Duplin's residents pursued independence from Great Britain. During the battle of Moore's Creek on February 27, 1776, Patriot forces lost only one man, Pvt. John Grady of Duplin County. The Loyalists were defeated at Moore's Creek, and today, a monument towering 18 feet tall honors Grady on the battlefield.

In August 1781, a clash between British forces and Whig militia took place at Rockfish Creek, just a mile south of present-day Wallace. Though the Patriots were defeated during the skirmish, they would ultimately secure their independence after British general Charles Cornwallis surrendered his army in Yorktown a couple of months later, thus beginning a new chapter in Duplin's history.

In 1818, the Grove Settlement, or Duplin Courthouse, was renamed Kenansville after local Patriot leader Gen. James Kenan. A vocal opponent of the British Stamp Act, in 1765, Kenan led a group of volunteers to Wilmington to air their grievances. He would later serve in the Colonial Assembly and then in the Provincial Congress from 1774 to 1776. A natural leader, Kenan served as colonel of the Duplin Militia during the Revolutionary War and was promoted to the rank of brigadier general at the war's conclusion. He became one of the original trustees of the University of North Carolina at Chapel Hill and served as a member of the state Constitutional Convention in 1788 and 1799. James Kenan died in 1810. The town of Kenansville was officially incorporated in 1852 and is still the county seat today. Here, the vestiges of the county's humble beginnings can still be seen in historic sites such as Liberty Hall and the Cowan Museum.

Duplin's early residents took advantage of the near-endless supply of pines by creating a bustling naval stores industry. Locals produced pitch, pine tar, turpentine, and other supplies for shipbuilding and floated them down the Northeast Cape Fear River to the port at Wilmington. By the mid-19th century, distilling turpentine was a major industry in Duplin County. However, as more land was cleared and the number of longleaf pines decreased, residents slowly shifted their focus from the naval stores industry to farming.

By the 1840s, the establishment of the Wilmington & Weldon Railroad along Duplin's western edge further transformed the landscape. Towns such as Warsaw, Magnolia, Wallace, Rose Hill, Calypso, and Faison thrived along its tracks and became home to vibrant produce markets.

Through the years, Duplin County has held onto its agricultural heritage, and today it is one of the nation's leading producers of livestock.

In 1852, the prominent African American educator Ezekiel Ezra Smith was born in Duplin County. After graduating from Shaw University in 1872, E.E. Smith, as he would become known, took on the role of principal at a school in nearby Goldsboro. In 1883, Smith became the head of the Fayetteville State Normal School, which is currently Fayetteville State University. Involved in the politics of his time, Smith was eventually appointed resident minister and general consul to the Republic of Liberia by Pres. Grover Cleveland.

Duplin County was also home to the father of the state community college system. A native of Rose Hill, Dr. William Dallas Herring was born in 1916. Beholden to the philosophy that an education should be accessible to everyone, Herring joined the Duplin County Board of Education in 1951 and was soon made chairman. Herring was appointed to the state Board of Education in 1955 and was once again made chairman, a position he would hold for more than 20 years. During this time, he oversaw the development of North Carolina's system of technical education institutes, a forerunner to the state's community colleges. In 1963, the General Assembly established the North Carolina Community College System.

Over the years, some of the county's residents have found themselves thrust onto the world stage. Many found themselves on foreign soil, helping decide the world's fate in battles from Europe to Asia. Nineteen of Duplin's sons, including brothers Lane and Joseph Hargrove, were killed during the Vietnam War. Others, such as Woodrow Weeks, had their lives tragically cut short in the fighting around Normandy, while Emanuel Pickett, a Wallace police officer and North Carolina National Guardsman, was sadly lost during the war in Iraq. Outside of the county courthouse, one can find monuments recognizing the sacrifices of Duplin's veterans. Today, the county has a proud military legacy, with the town of Warsaw hosting what is believed by many to be the oldest consecutively-held Veterans Day celebration in the nation.

Over the course of nearly three centuries, Duplin's borders have shifted, and the landscape has changed. Businesses within the county have come and gone, as have historical figures and old homes. The cultural legacy they have created, however, lives on in the residents who call Duplin County home today.

One

Communities

A patchwork of small towns and rural hamlets, the communities of Duplin County, though connected by a shared history, each have their own distinctive stories.

Situated on the western side of the county, communities such as Calypso, Faison, Bowdens, Warsaw, Magnolia, Rose Hill, Teachey, and Wallace owe much of their history to the establishment of the Wilmington & Weldon Railroad. Other communities farther east, such as Chinquapin, Hallsville, and Sarecta, sprang up near the banks of the Northeast Cape Fear River. Most of Duplin's communities have historical ties to agriculture, though their crops varied.

Each community of Duplin County had its own schools, churches, social hot spots, and local leaders. Kenansville, near the center of the county, takes its name from a prominent Patriot leader and serves as the county seat. Meanwhile, Beulaville, toward the county's eastern edge, takes its name from the Beulah Baptist Church and can trace its roots to the local timber industry.

Scattered throughout the county are unincorporated towns and crossroad communities such as Greenevers, Albertson, White Flash, Beautancus, Pin Hook, and Potters Hill. Each of these communities represents a thread in the fabric that binds Duplin County together.

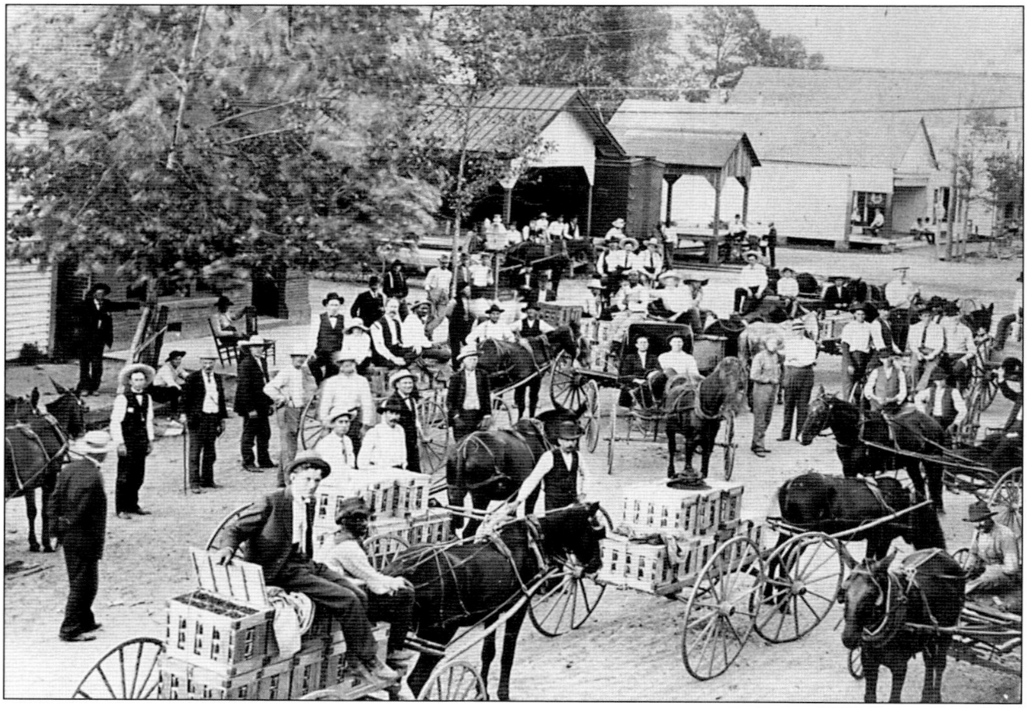

Throughout the 20th century, strawberries played an important role in Duplin County's agricultural heritage. This 1908 photograph, taken in Wallace along Main Street and Railroad Street looking east, shows farmers transporting their crops to market. (Courtesy of Leon Sikes.)

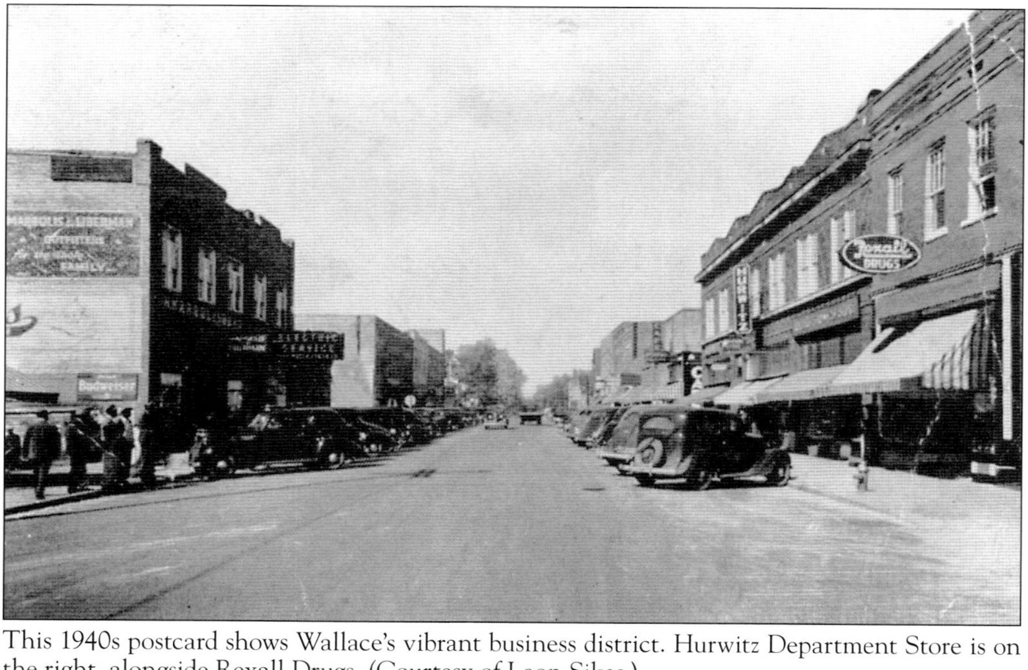

This 1940s postcard shows Wallace's vibrant business district. Hurwitz Department Store is on the right, alongside Rexall Drugs. (Courtesy of Leon Sikes.)

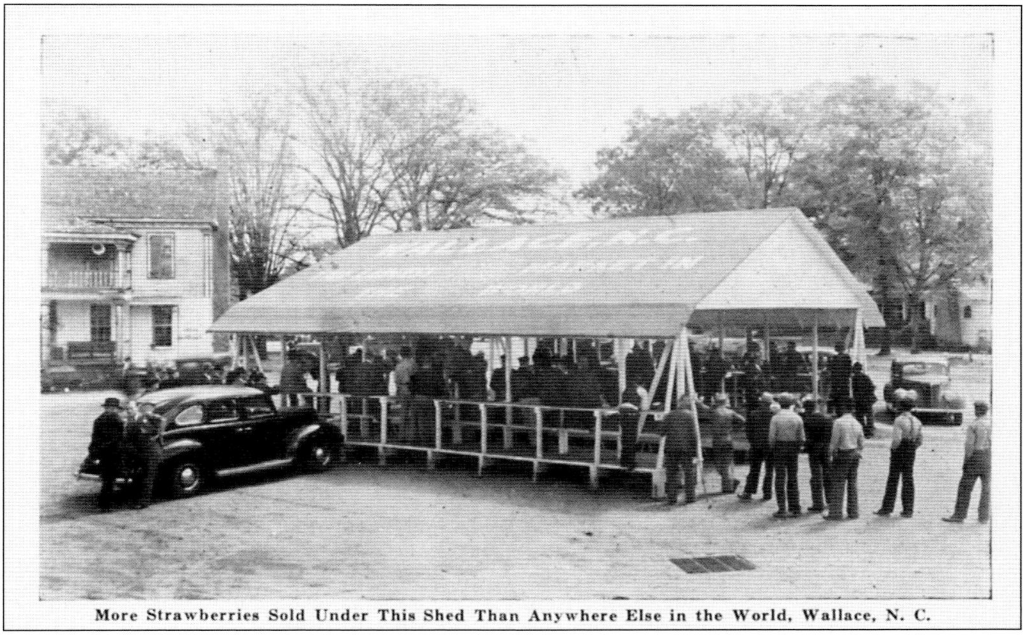

The flourishing strawberry industry was a source of pride for many in the Wallace community. This 1930s postcard makes the claim "More Strawberries Sold under this Shed than Anywhere Else in the World." Inscribed on the produce shed's roof is a message proclaiming Wallace the largest strawberry market in the world. (Courtesy of UNC Chapel Hill's Wilson Library.)

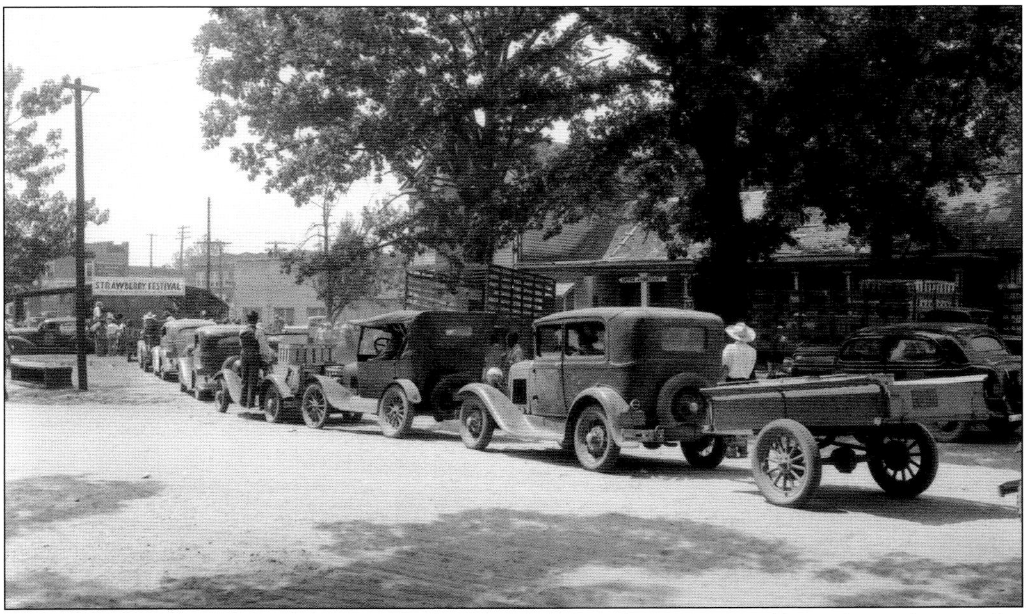

Festivalgoers line up for the 1936 Strawberry Festival in downtown Wallace. According to the *Wallace Enterprise*, "a program is featured each night along with entertaining and educational vaudeville acts and stage presentations." The newspaper also stated that the six-day festival would conclude with the "awarding of a 1936 Chevrolet Coach to the holder of the lucky ticket." (Courtesy of the State Archives of North Carolina.)

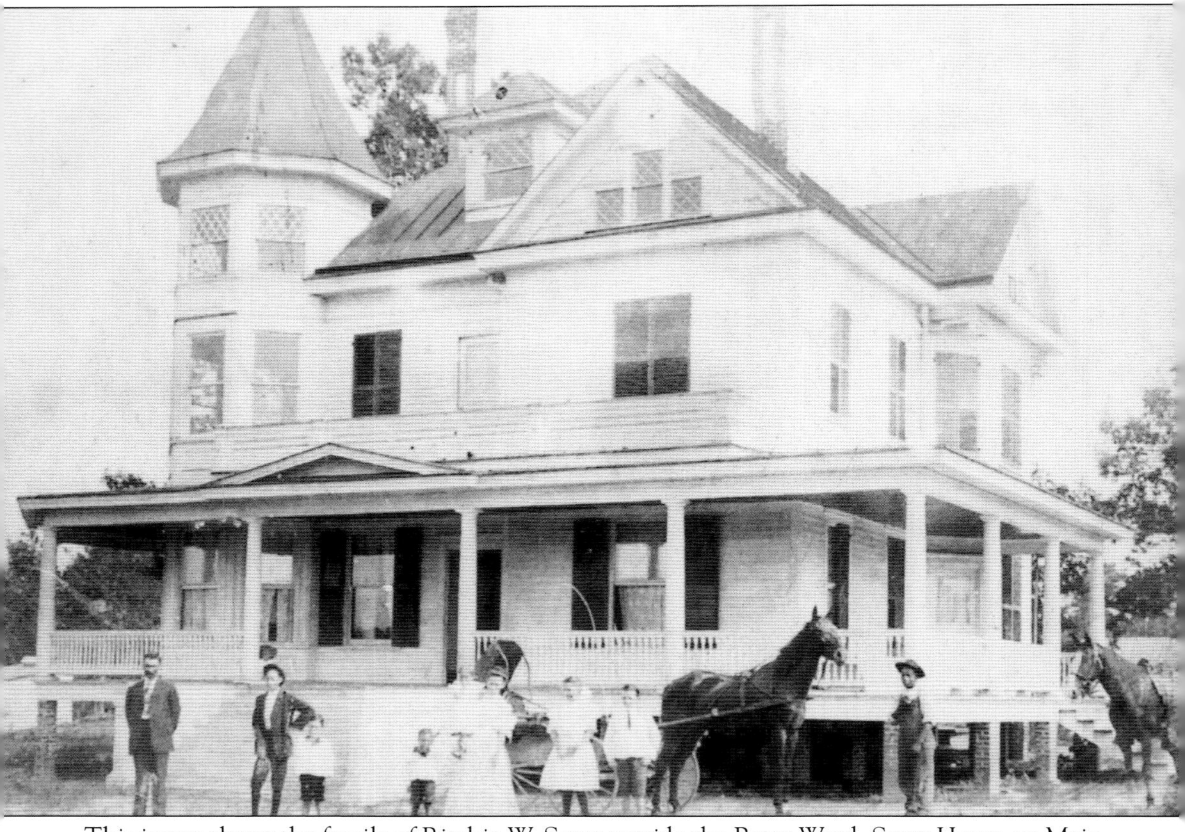

This image shows the family of Ritchie W. Scott outside the Betty Ward–Scott House on Main Street in Wallace. The Scott family was one of the first to live there, moving into the home around 1908. The family eventually sold the house to George and Betty Ward. (Courtesy of Leon Sikes.)

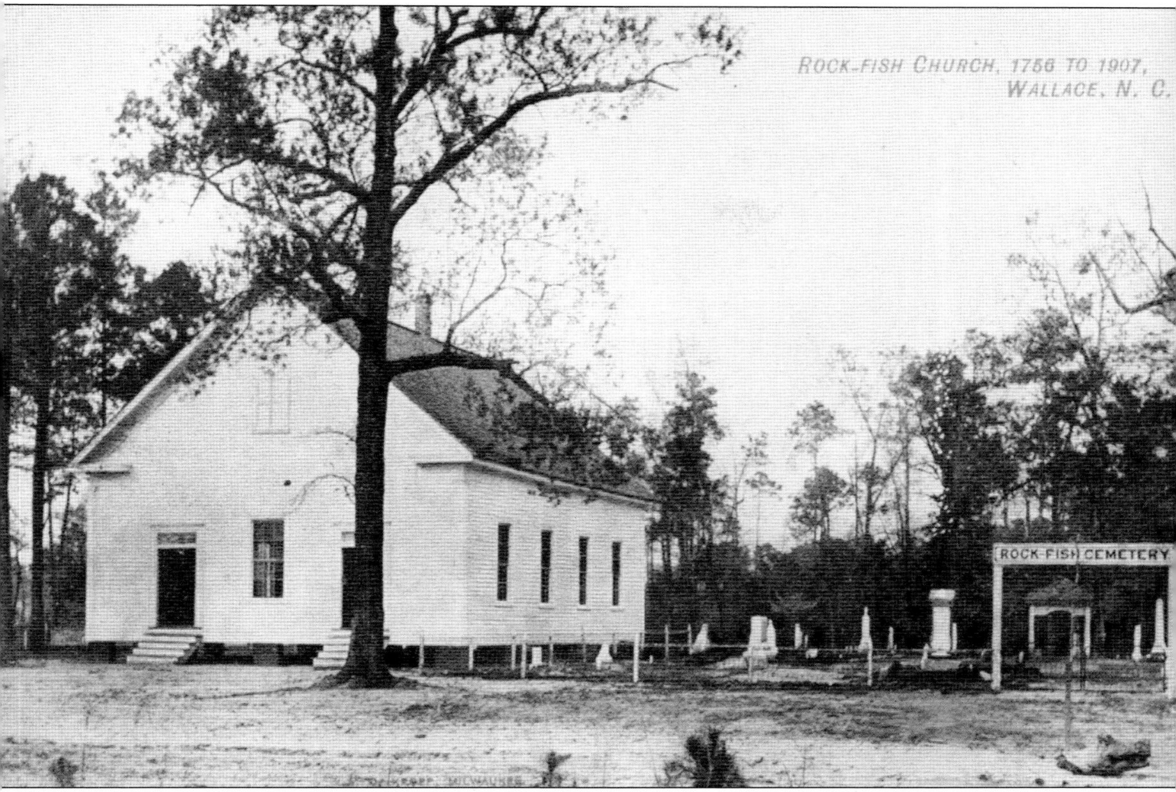

This postcard reveals how the Rock-Fish Church near Wallace looked in 1907. Organized by Presbyterians in 1756, its early ministers included Hugh McAden and Robert Tate. (Courtesy of UNC Chapel Hill's Wilson Library.)

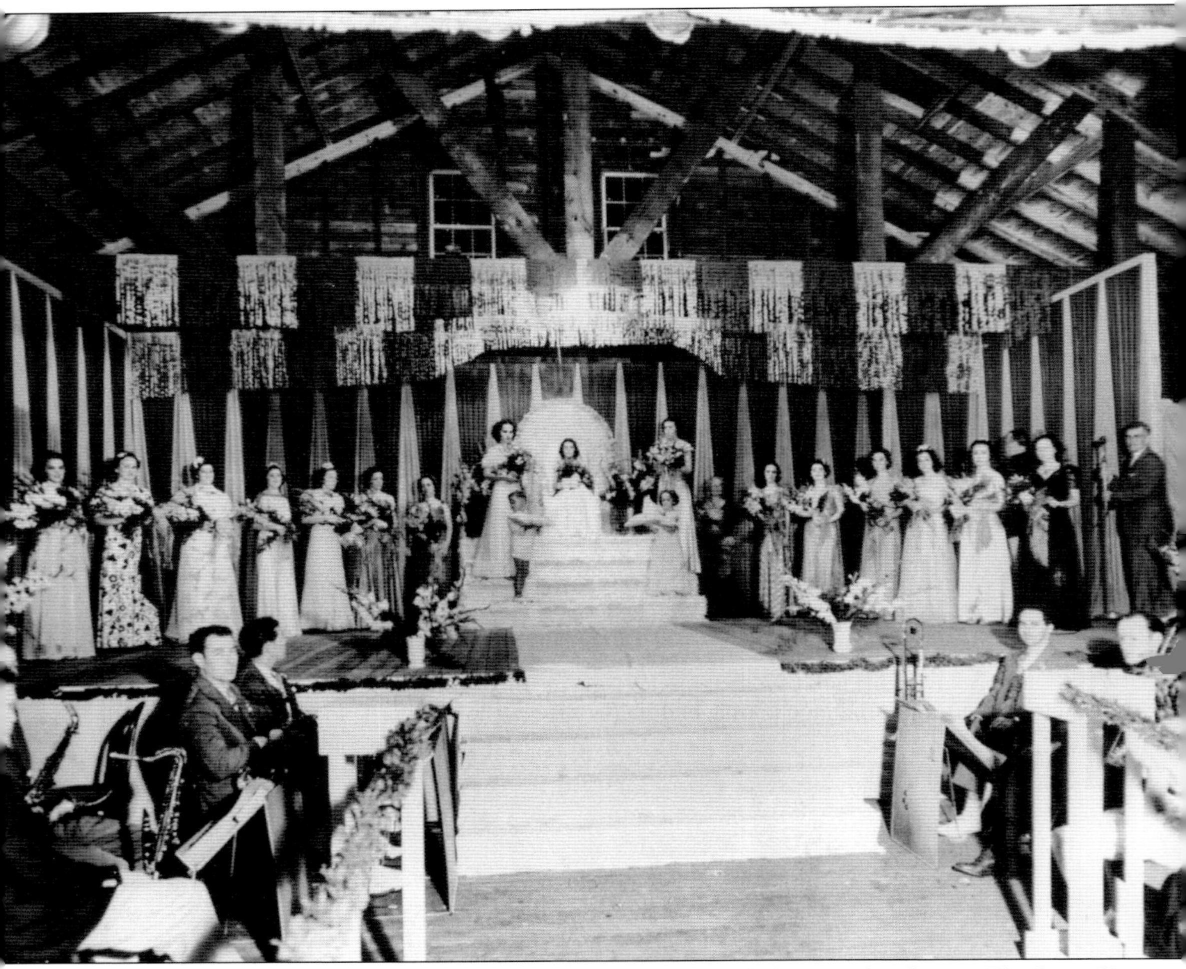

The 1937 queen of the Strawberry Festival takes her rightful place on the throne. The June 17, 1937, *Wallace Enterprise* reported that Dorothy Wysong was dubbed festival queen that year. (Courtesy of Leon Sikes.)

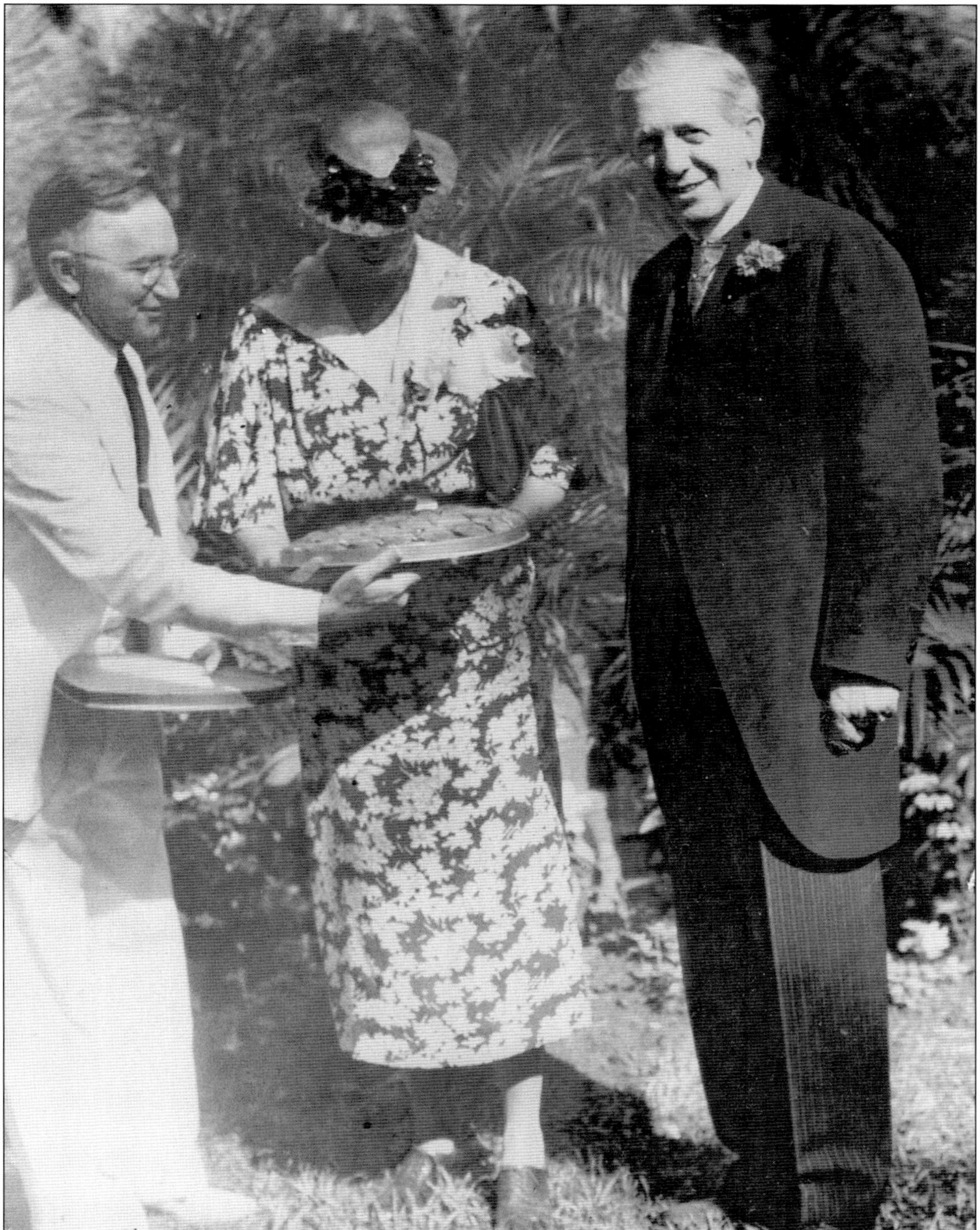

In 1937, the Strawberry Festival attracted the attention of First Lady Eleanor Roosevelt, seen here alongside North Carolina governor Clyde Hoey (right) and the mayor of Wallace, J. Aubrey Harrell. Roosevelt wrote of her visit to eastern North Carolina in her nationally syndicated newspaper column *My Day*, where she noted that "A very lovely box of strawberries was presented to me which represented a development obtained by two hundred crosses of various varieties. This berry was called three-thirty-seven, not having yet been given a name, and they offered to name it after me." (Courtesy of Leon Sikes.)

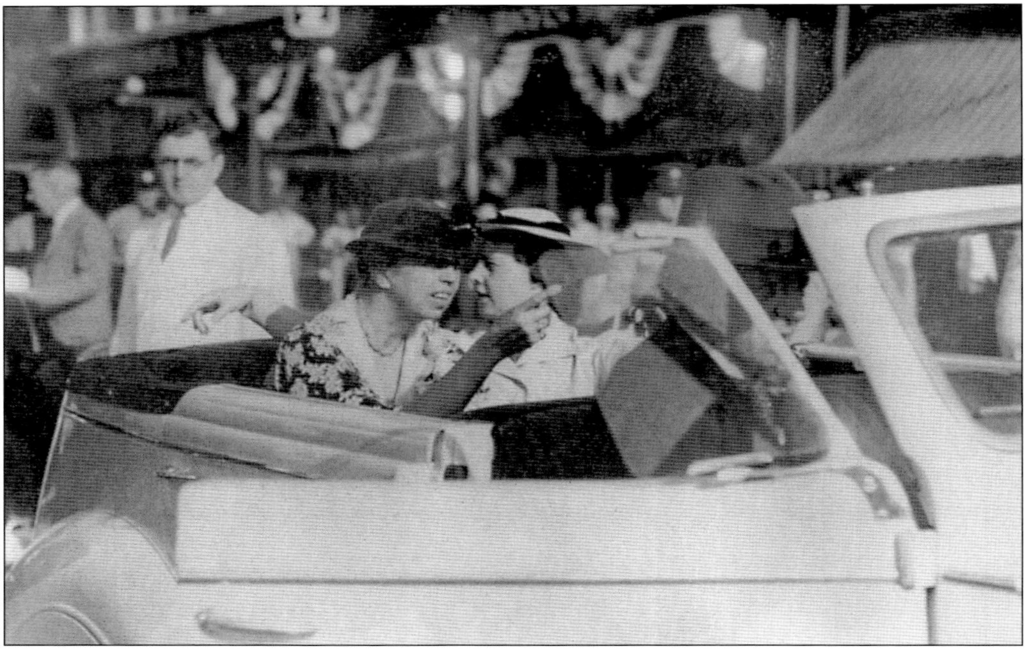

First Lady Eleanor Roosevelt tours Wallace during the 1937 Strawberry Festival. During her visit, she also toured the Penderlea homestead, a New Deal–era resettlement project in neighboring Pender County. (Courtesy of Leon Sikes.)

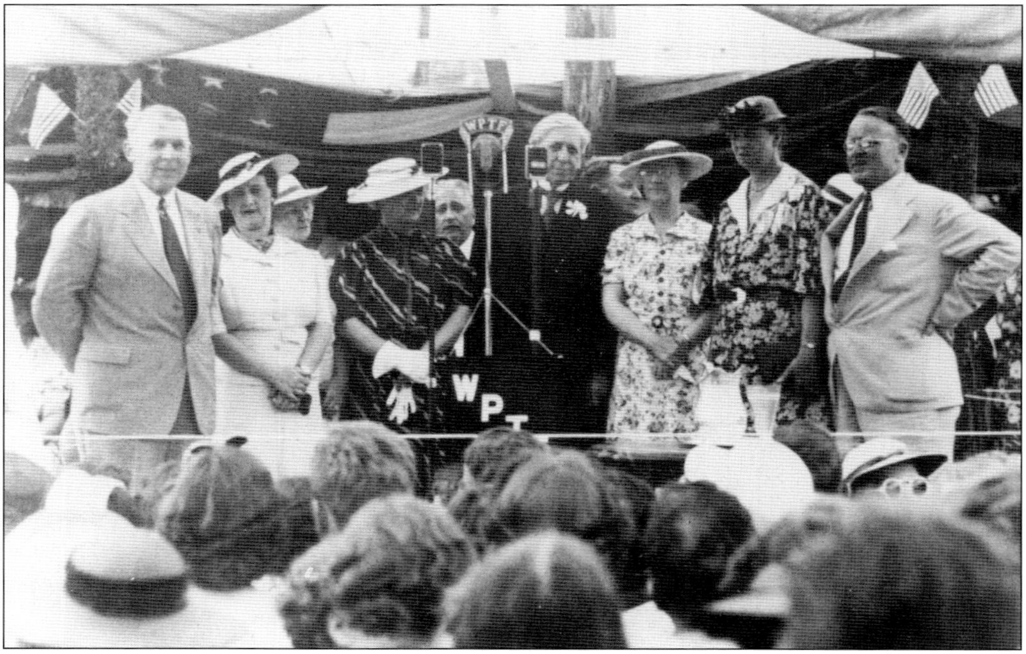

Roosevelt (second from right) poses with Governor Hoey (center), Mayor Harrell (far right), and Dr. John Robinson and his wife (far left) during the 1937 Strawberry Festival. The *Wallace Enterprise* stated that the occasion marked the first time that "a First Lady has set foot on Duplin County Soil." (Courtesy of Leon Sikes.)

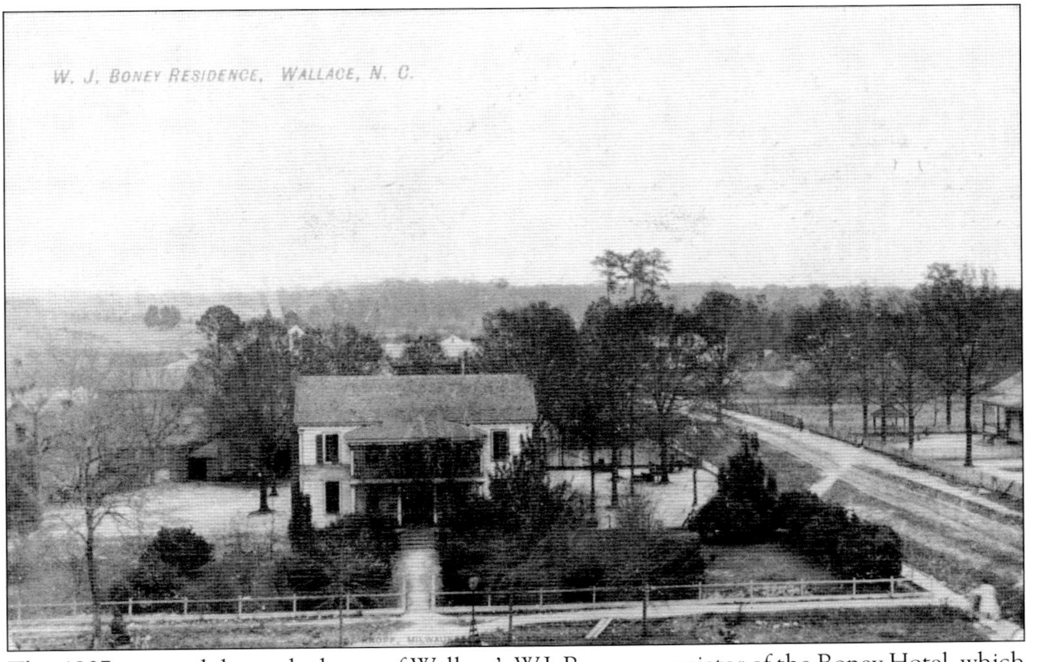

This 1907 postcard shows the home of Wallace's W.J. Boney, proprietor of the Boney Hotel, which was later known as Pine View. (Courtesy of UNC Chapel Hill's Wilson Library.)

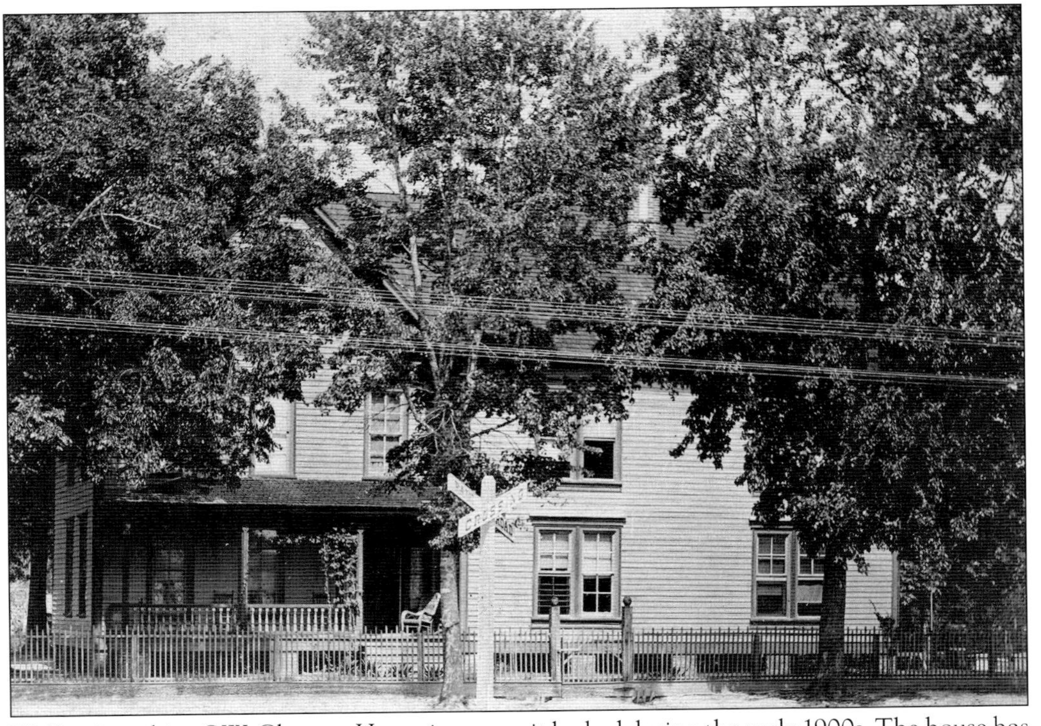

Wallace's striking S.W. Clement House is seen as it looked during the early 1900s. The house has since been lost to time. (Courtesy of the State Archives of North Carolina.)

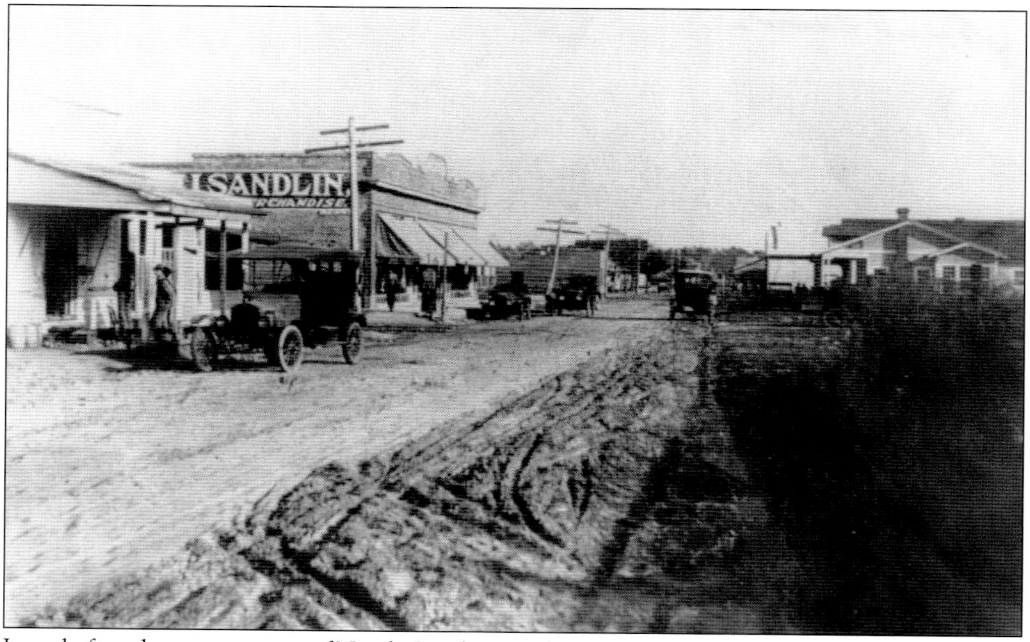

Long before the construction of North Carolina Highway 24, Beulaville's Main Street was nothing more than a dirt road lined by a few homes and shops. This photograph shows Main Street in Beulaville as it looked during the 1920s. Built in 1917, I.J. Sandlin's General Merchandise is in the background. One of the foremost businesses in town, the store served as a one-stop shop for Beulaville residents for years. (Courtesy of Roland Edwards.)

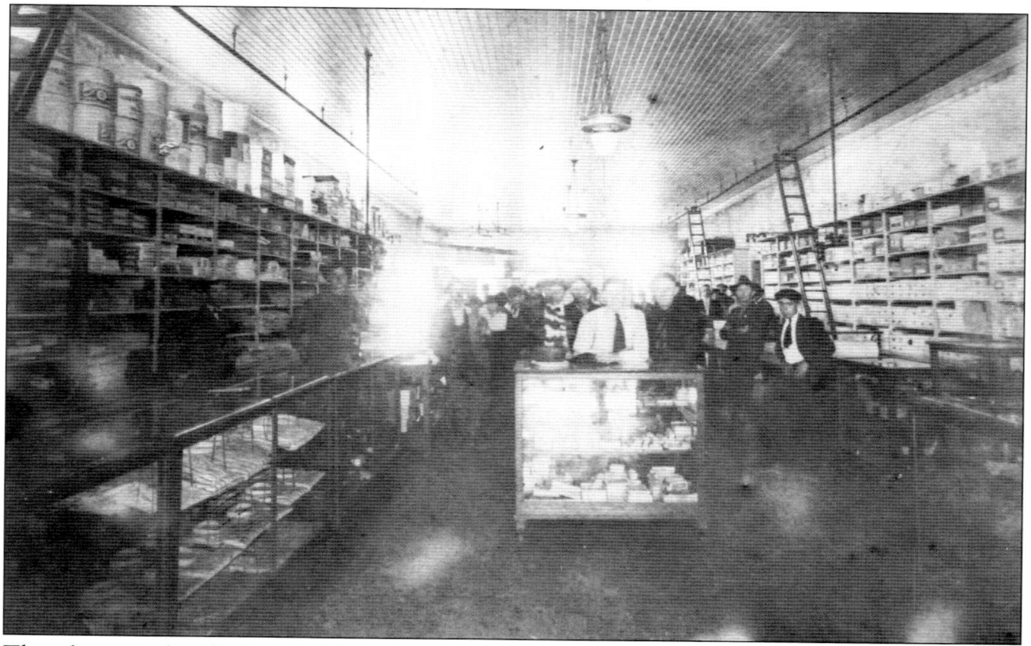

This photograph, taken on November 26, 1921, shows a group of men gathered inside I.J. Sandlin's store in Beulaville, indicating the shop was much more than a business, it was also a place for gathering socially. Note the wide variety of wares in stock. (Courtesy of Roland Edwards.)

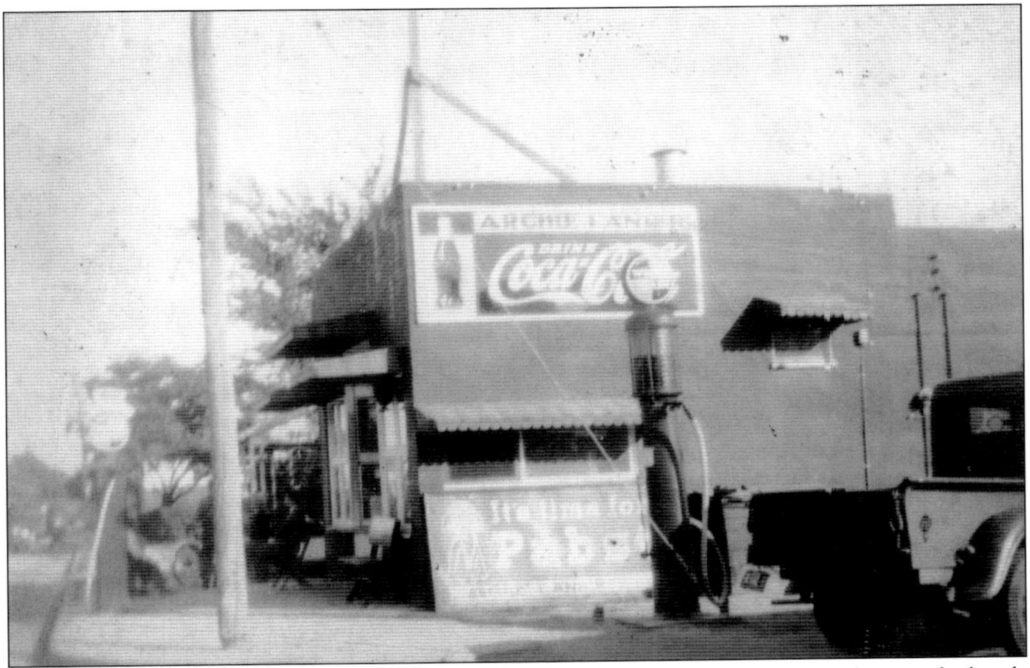

Also located on Beulaville's main drag was Archie Lanier's store. It became a popular spot for locals to grab a hot dog and soda. In this photograph, men can be seen relaxing out front. (Courtesy of the Bratcher family.)

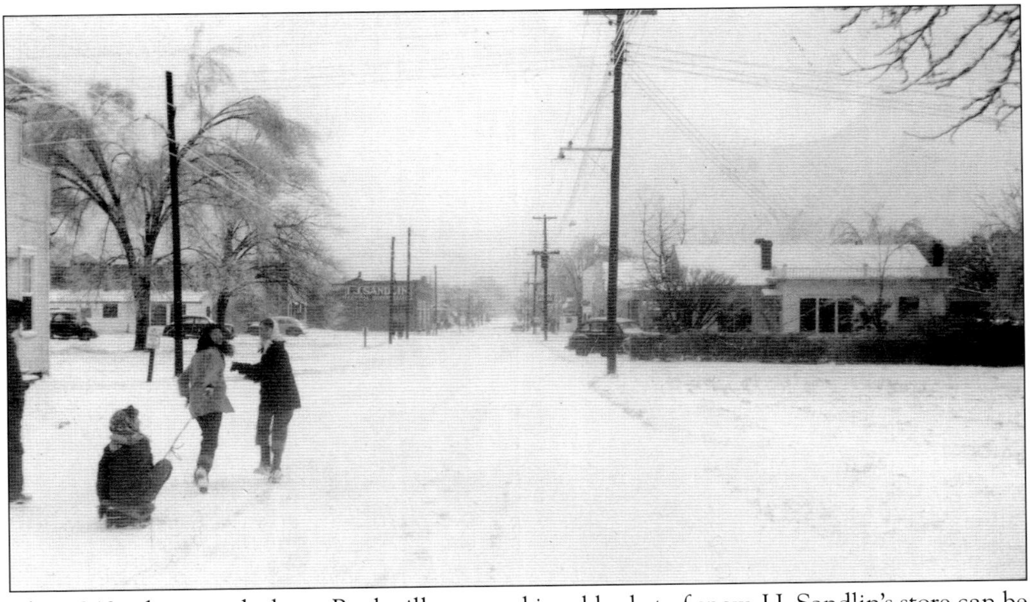

This 1940s photograph shows Beulaville covered in a blanket of snow. I.J. Sandlin's store can be seen in the background. Snow being somewhat uncommon in this region of North Carolina, many residents are enjoying the wintry occasion. The photographer is looking down Beulaville's Main Street, what is now the four-lane North Carolina Highway 24. (Courtesy of the Bratcher family.)

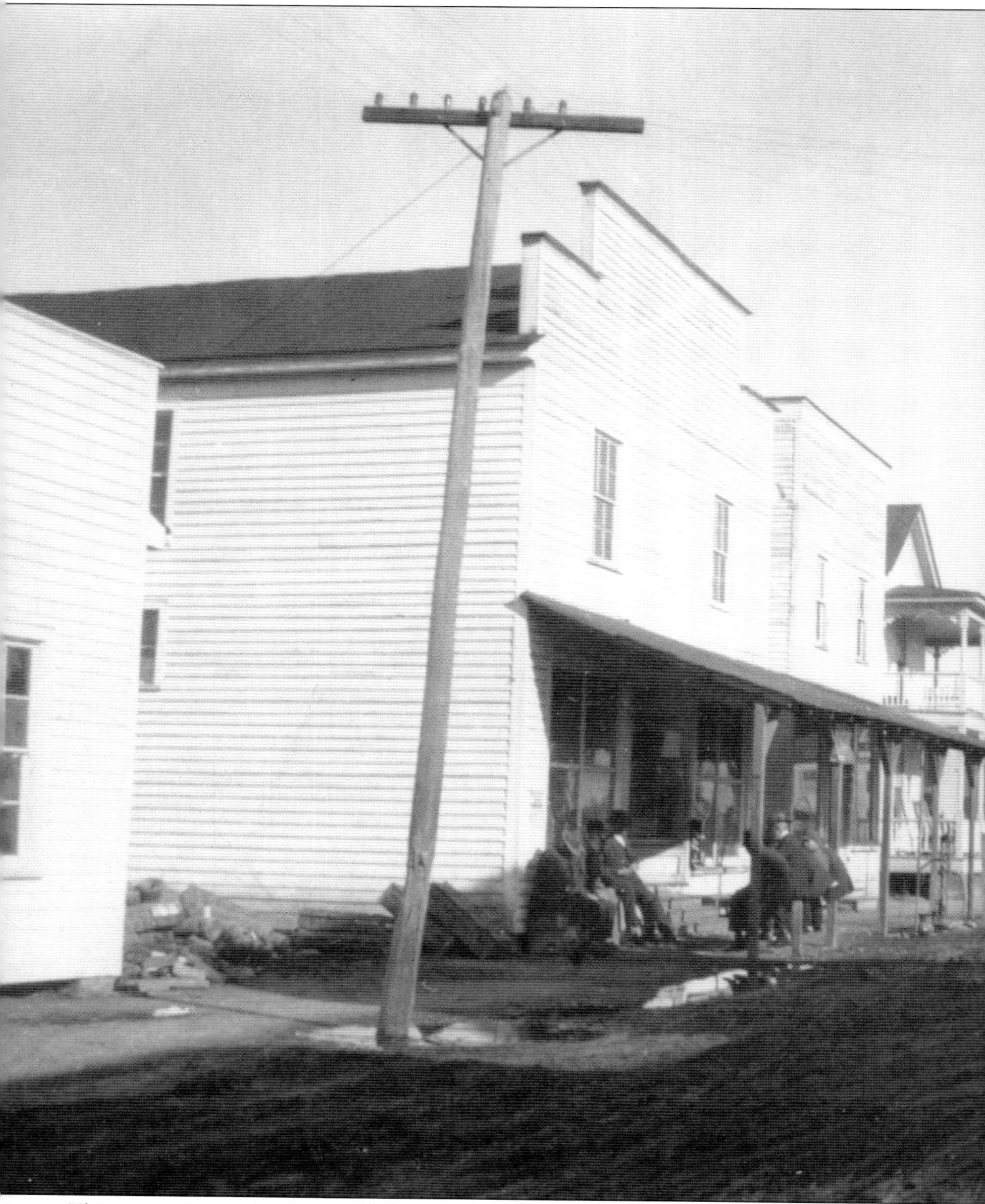

This image shows what Beulaville looked like between 1910 and 1915. The white, two-story building at the end of the street to the right was the original Beulaville School. The structure

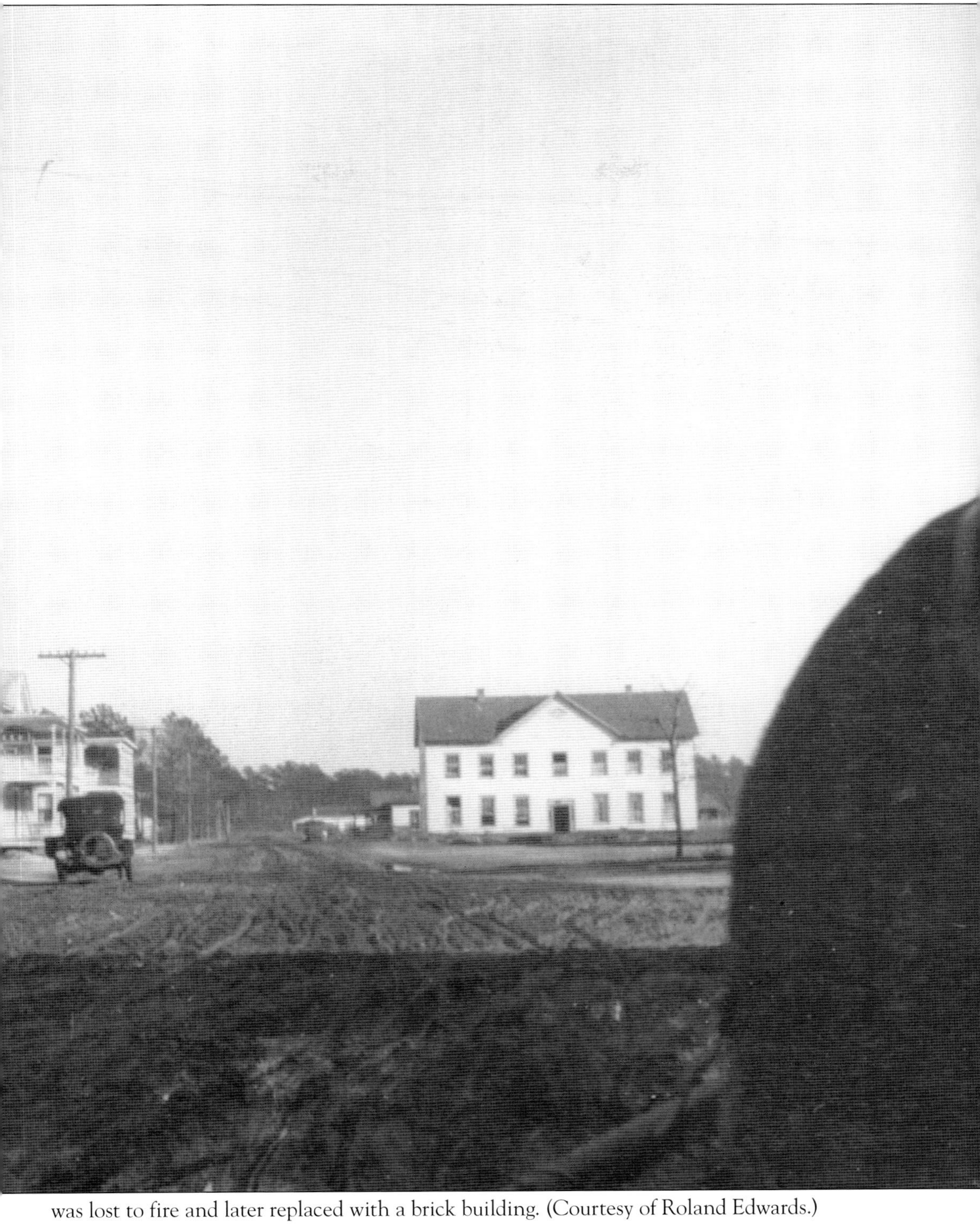

was lost to fire and later replaced with a brick building. (Courtesy of Roland Edwards.)

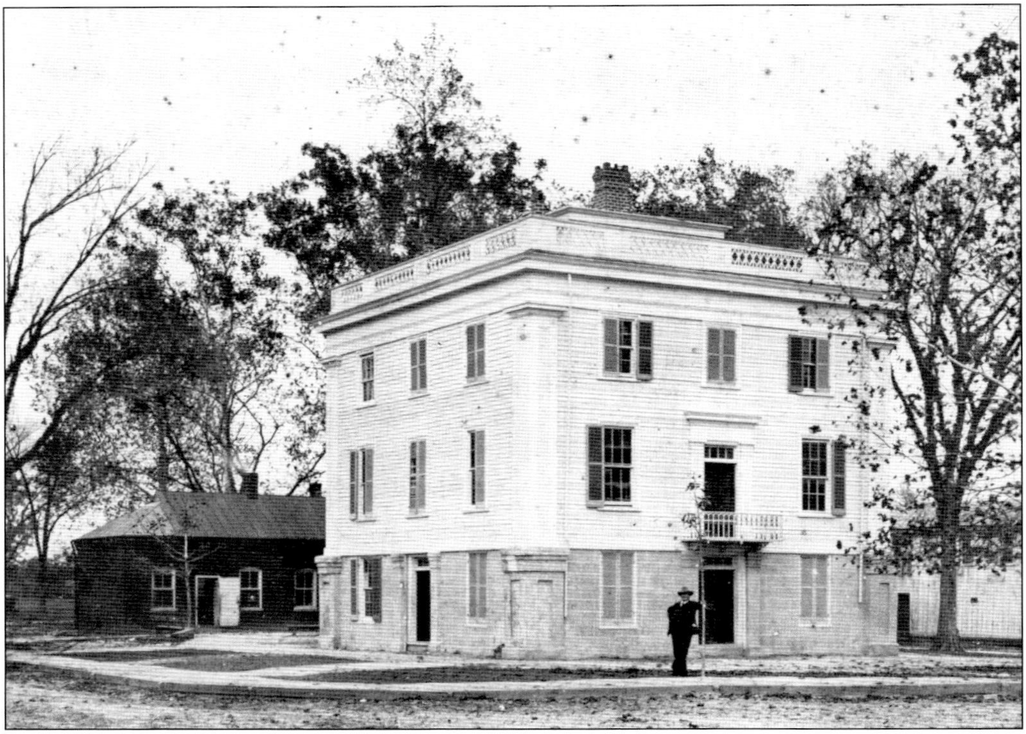

Originally known as the Grove Settlement during the 18th century, it was not until 1818 that the town of Kenansville was renamed in honor of Revolutionary War leader and prominent Duplin resident James Kenan. The town became the county seat and hosted the Duplin County Courthouse and other facilities for local government. Here, a man stands outside the 1818 Duplin County Courthouse in 1911. This structure was remodeled during the 1840s. (Courtesy of the State Archives of North Carolina.)

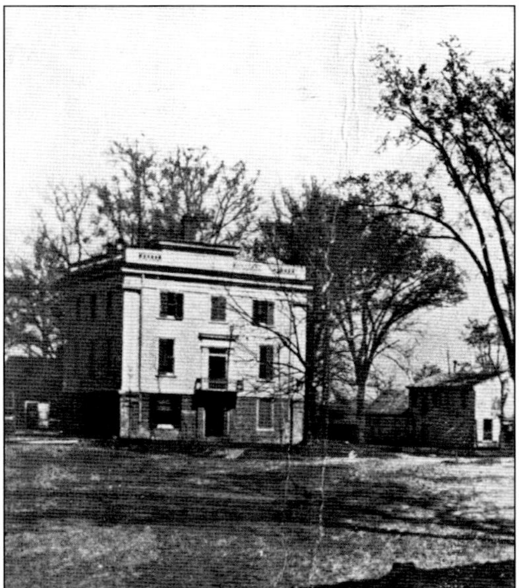

This postcard shows the 1818 Duplin County Courthouse in Kenansville. Addressed to Mrs. S.L. Patterson of Caldwell County, North Carolina, it reads, "Sept. 9th, 1907—The trees are beautiful here & it is a quaint old town. The school is promising this year. With love for yourself & cousin Mollie. L. Lenoir." The postcard was likely sent by someone affiliated with the James Sprunt Institute. (Courtesy of UNC Chapel Hill's Wilson Library.)

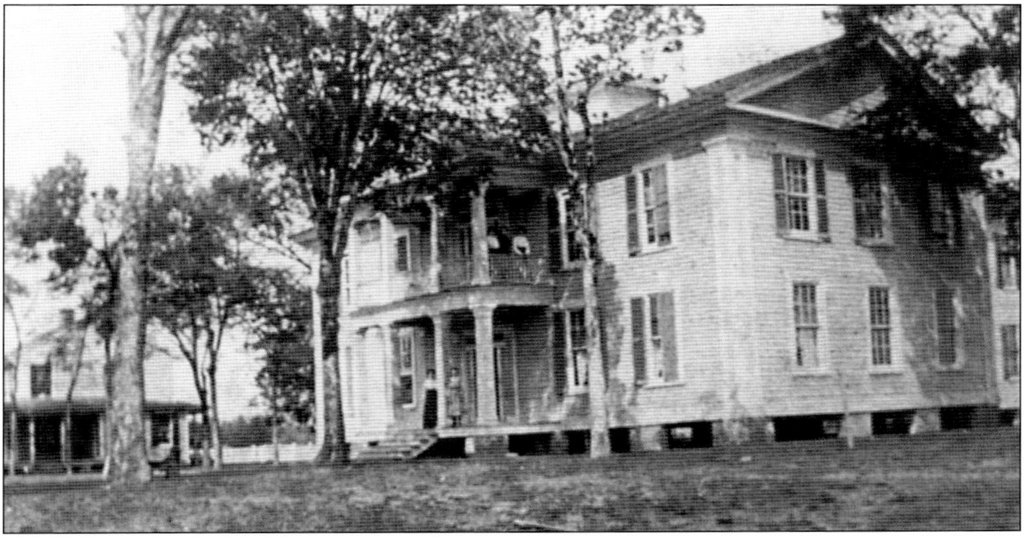

Named in honor of educator, botanist, county official, and Presbyterian minister James Menzies Sprunt, the James Sprunt Institute operated outside Kenansville from 1897 to 1923. After emigrating from Scotland during the mid-19th century, Sprunt worked at Duplin's Grove Academy and was later appointed president of the Kenansville Female Seminary. This was prior to serving in the Confederate army as a chaplain. Sprunt died in 1884. James Sprunt Community College is named in his honor. (Courtesy of Leon Sikes.)

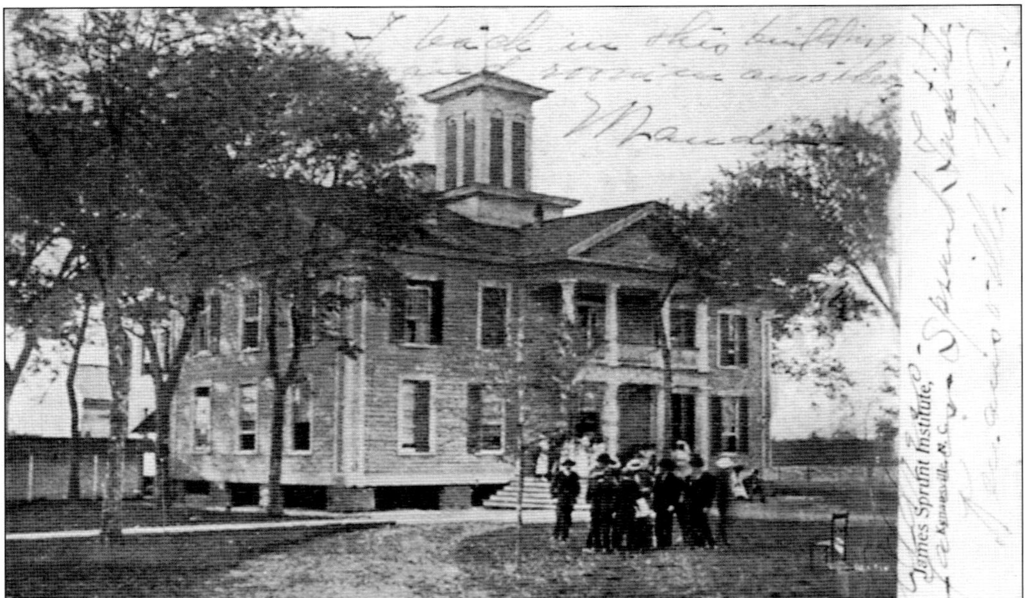

This 1908 postcard shows students gathered outside the James Sprunt Institute. Addressed to Mrs. Will Stickley of Augusta County, Virginia, the front of the card reads, "I teach in this building and room in another. The back reads, "Hello Rose: How are you, Willie & Paul? When are you going on your trip? I like N.C. alright. Am awfully interested in my work—My! It's hot down here. I am about fifty miles from the sea coast. Send me a card & tell me how you are. I am fat & fine." (Courtesy of UNC Chapel Hill's Wilson Library.)

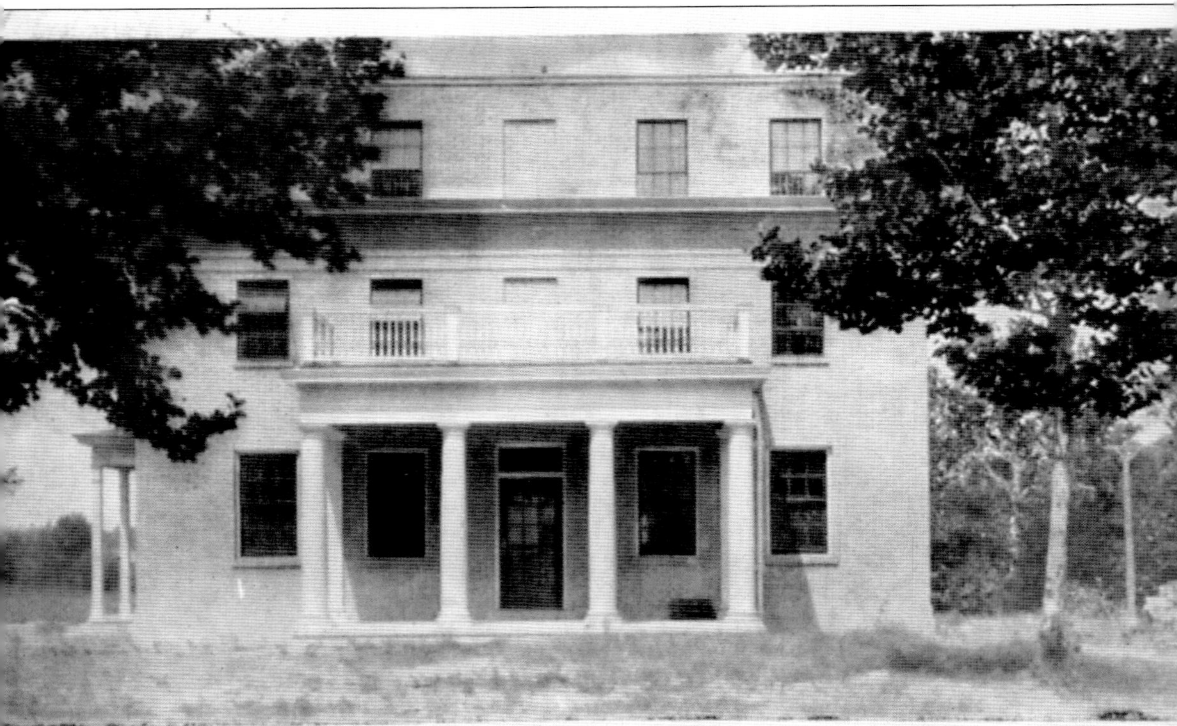

Duplin County Jail, Kenansville, N. Car.

This 1940s postcard shows what was once the Duplin County Jail. This building was constructed by the Works Progress Administration, a New Deal program created by Pres. Franklin Roosevelt with the aim of creating jobs for millions of struggling Americans during the Great Depression. (Courtesy of UNC Chapel Hill's Wilson Library.)

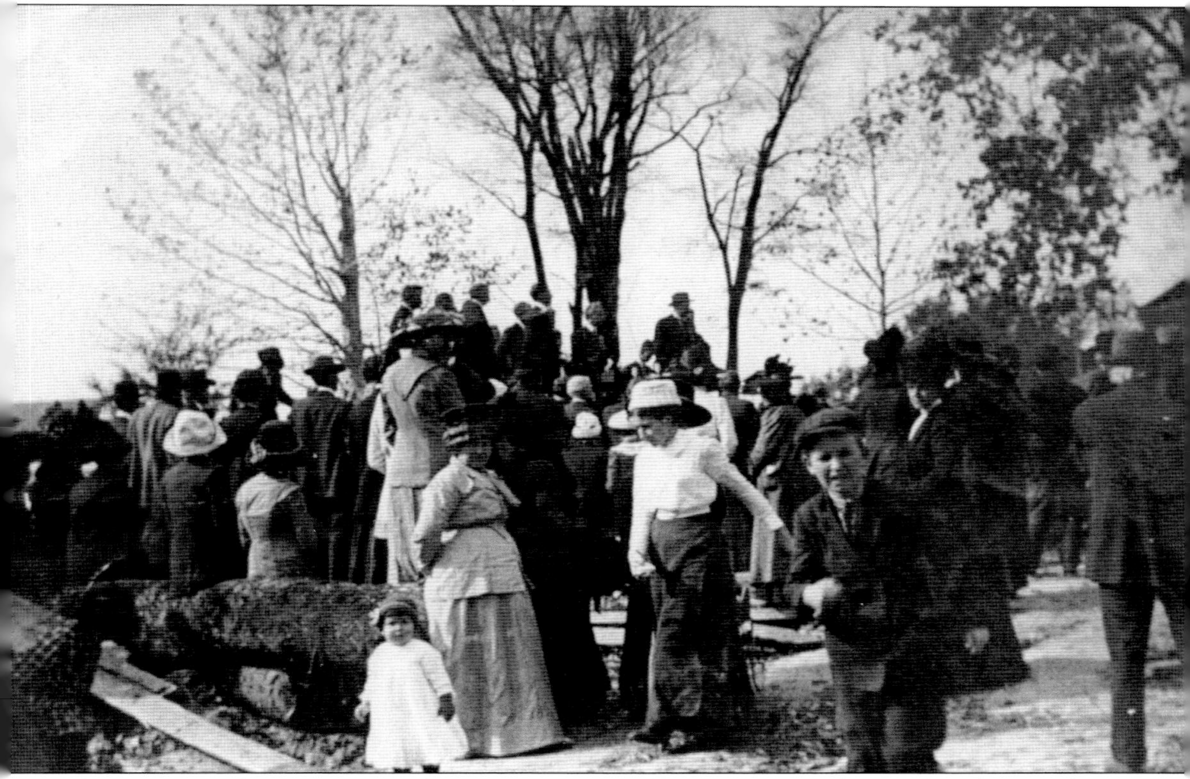

The current Duplin County Courthouse was constructed between 1911 and 1912. This photograph shows a scene from the laying of its cornerstone on November 17, 1911. The woman in the white hat is believed to be Ada Quinn Brinson, and the woman on the left is thought to be Dolly Quinn Stroud. The little girl in the foreground is Lorena Brinson Vestal. (Courtesy of Leon Sikes.)

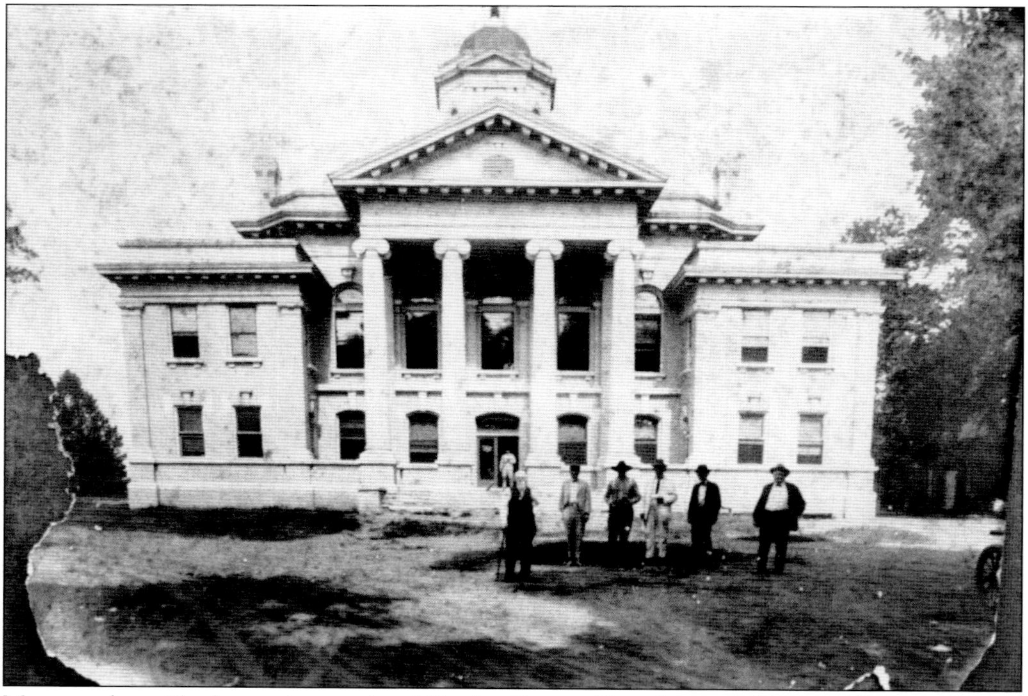

Men stand outside the newly completed Duplin County Courthouse in Kenansville around 1913. Aside from an annex building added in 1959, the exterior of the structure has remained relatively unchanged. (Courtesy of Leon Sikes.)

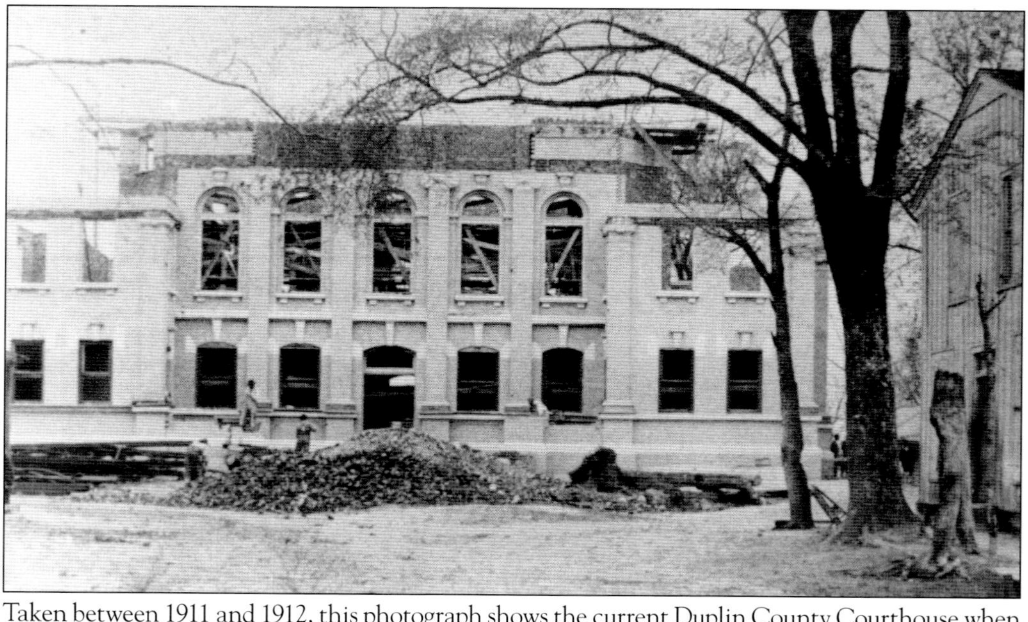

Taken between 1911 and 1912, this photograph shows the current Duplin County Courthouse when it was under construction. The Charlotte-based architectural firm Wheeler and Stern designed the structure, which became the centerpiece of downtown Kenansville. (Courtesy of Leon Sikes.)

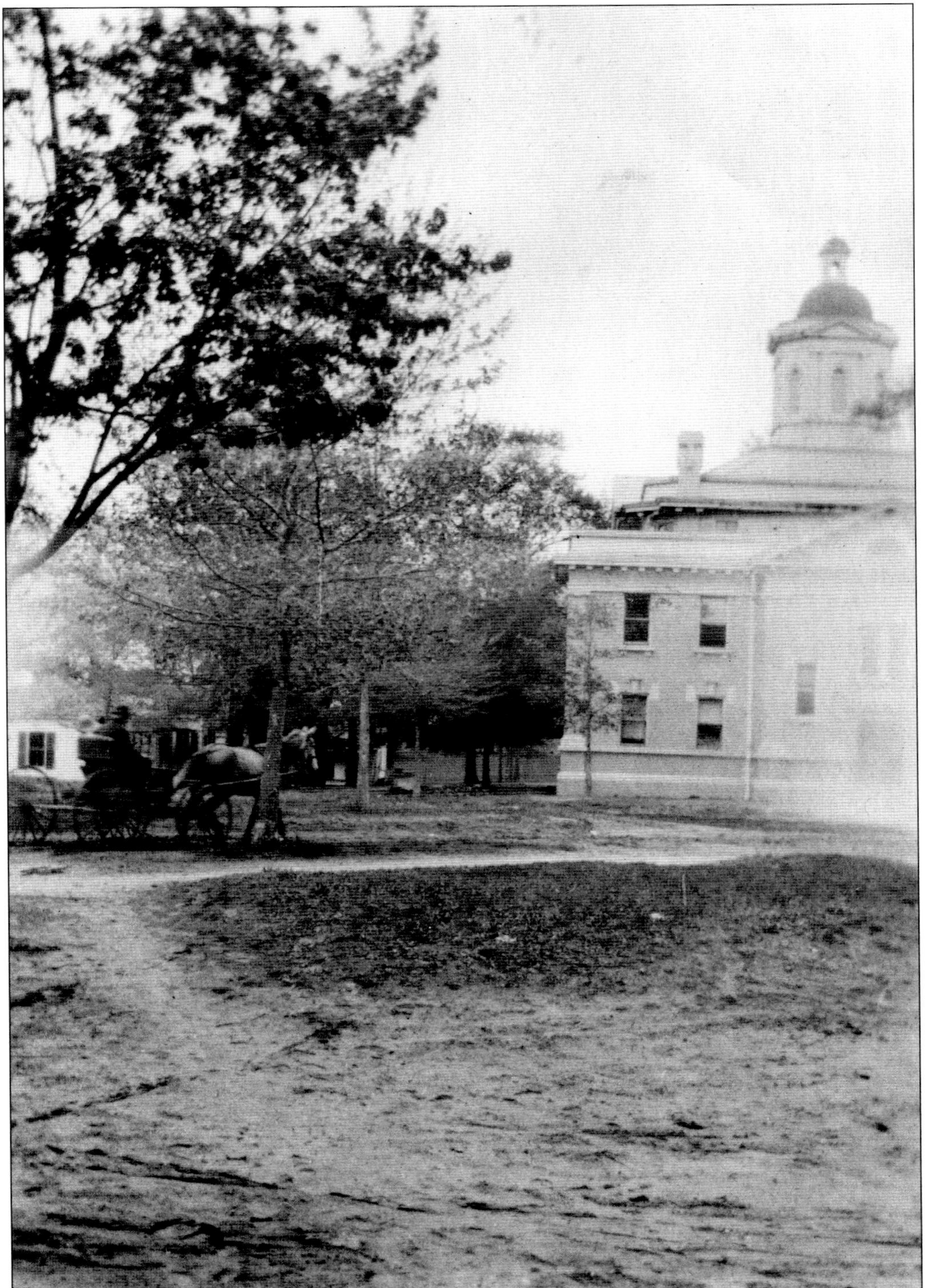

A man in a horse and buggy rides across the green of the Duplin County Courthouse in Kenansville. The photograph is dated April 19, 1918. (Courtesy of the State Archives of North Carolina.)

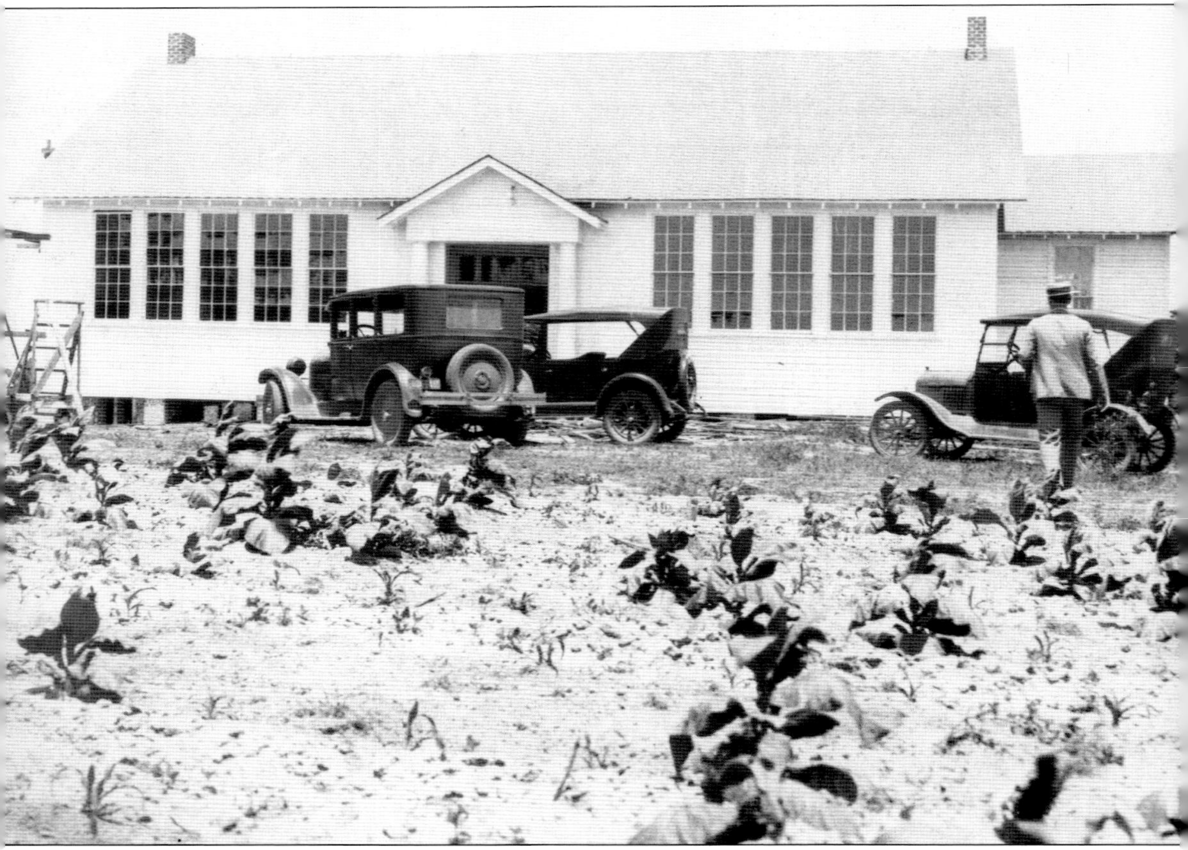

This photograph shows the Kenansville School, an African American school constructed by the Rosenwald Fund. A joint effort between Booker T. Washington of the Tuskegee Institute and Julius Rosenwald, philanthropist and president of Sears, Roebuck and Co., these Rosenwald schools helped provide educational opportunities to African Americans in the rural, segregated regions of the United States. Seven Rosenwald schools were constructed in Duplin County. (Courtesy of Leon Sikes.)

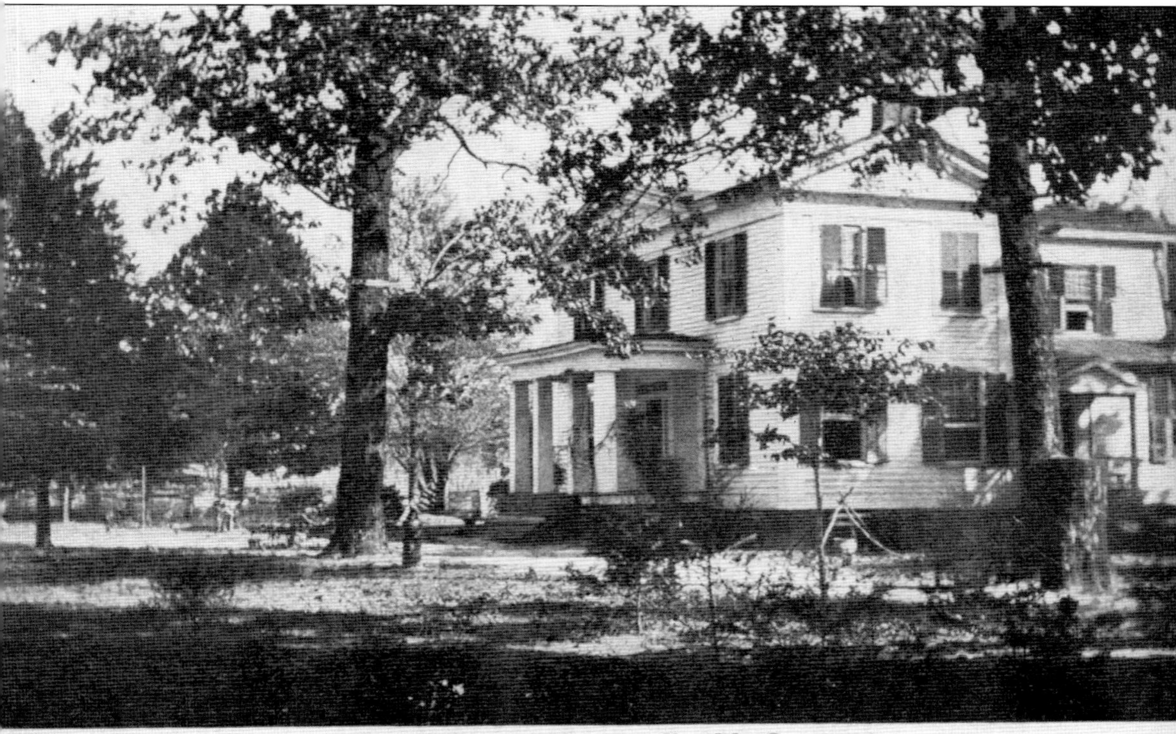

Kenan Home, Kenansville, N. C.

The present Liberty Hall in Kenansville was built by Thomas Kenan, son of Duplin County icon Gen. James Kenan, during the early 19th century. The stately home housed generations of the Kenan family and was the site of the marriage of Mary Lily Kenan to multimillionaire Henry Flagler in 1901. The original Liberty Hall, constructed during the 1700s, was at Turkey Branch in what is now Sampson County but was lost to fire. (Courtesy of UNC Chapel Hill's Wilson Library.)

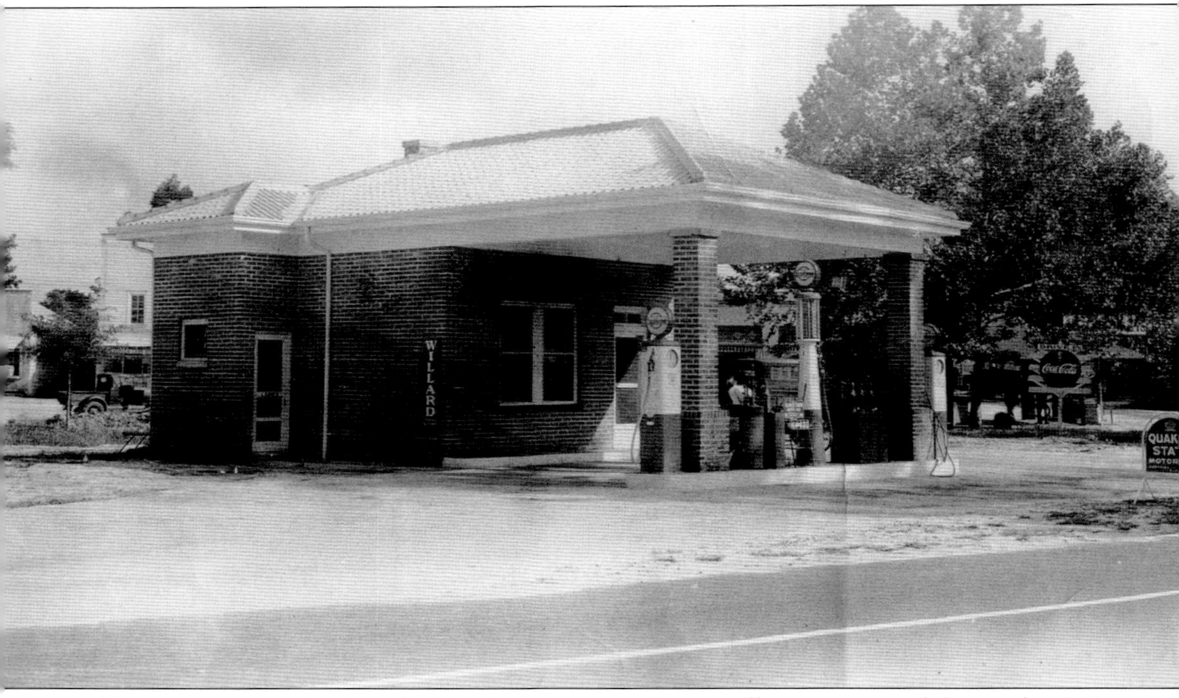

This image shows the Standard Oil fuel station in Kenansville as it appeared during the 1930s. Note the gravity-fed visible Essolene gas pump. A hand-operated pump moved gasoline into the clear cylinder on top, allowing customers to view how much fuel they were purchasing. (Courtesy of Leon Sikes.)

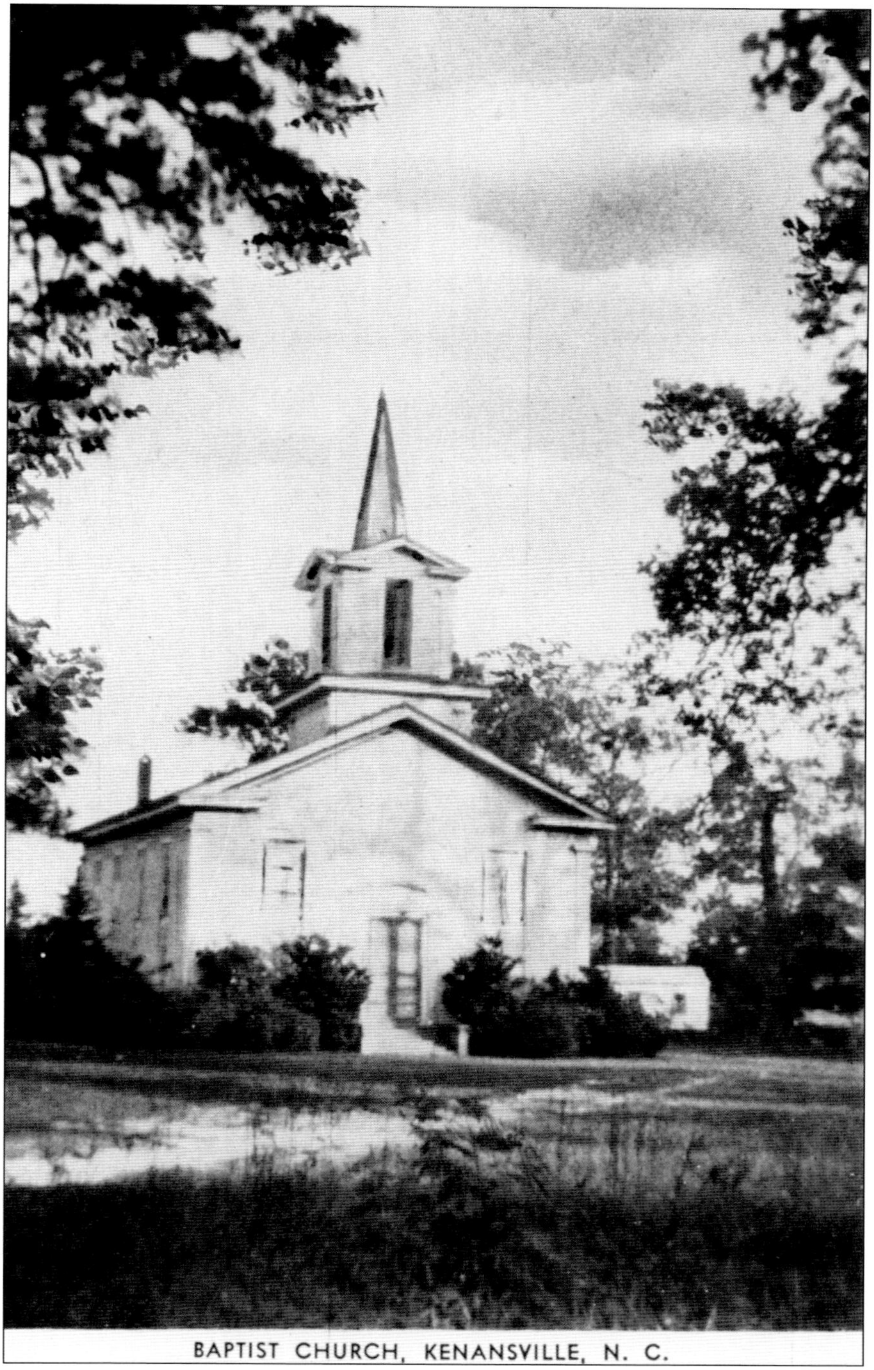

Its chapel dating to 1859, the Kenansville Baptist Church is one of the more prominent historical structures in town. The church's congregation was first formed in 1837 following a meeting by members of the Baptist Church of Christ at the Kenansville Masonic Lodge. The present-day church sits on land donated by Daniel C. Moore in 1839. This postcard shows how the church looked in 1910. (Courtesy of UNC Chapel Hill's Wilson Library.)

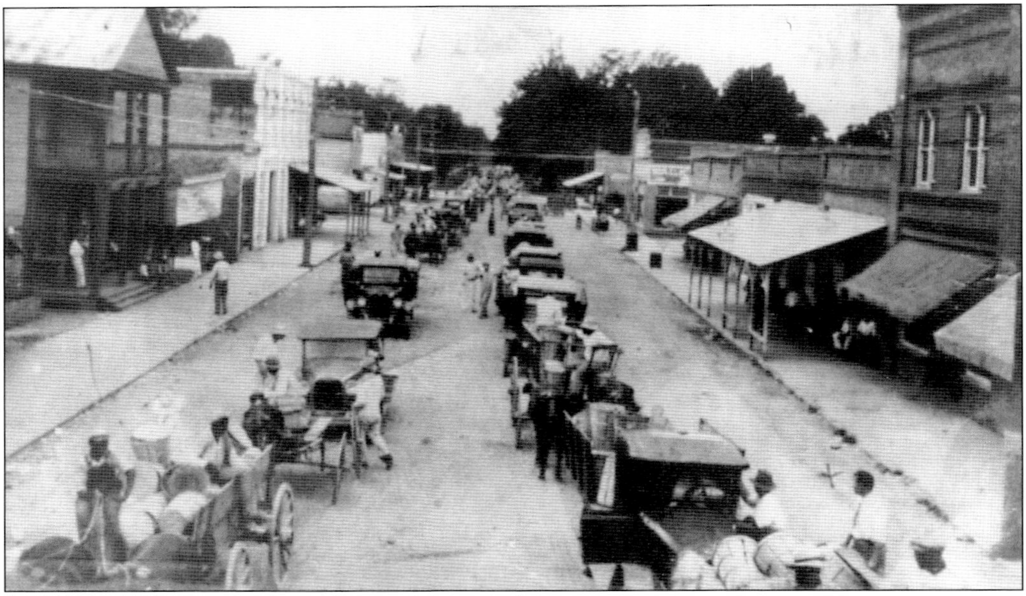

Farmers bringing their produce to market line the streets of Faison around 1910. Like other Duplin communities during this era, Faison had its own bustling produce market and a long history rooted in agriculture. (Courtesy of the Faison Museum.)

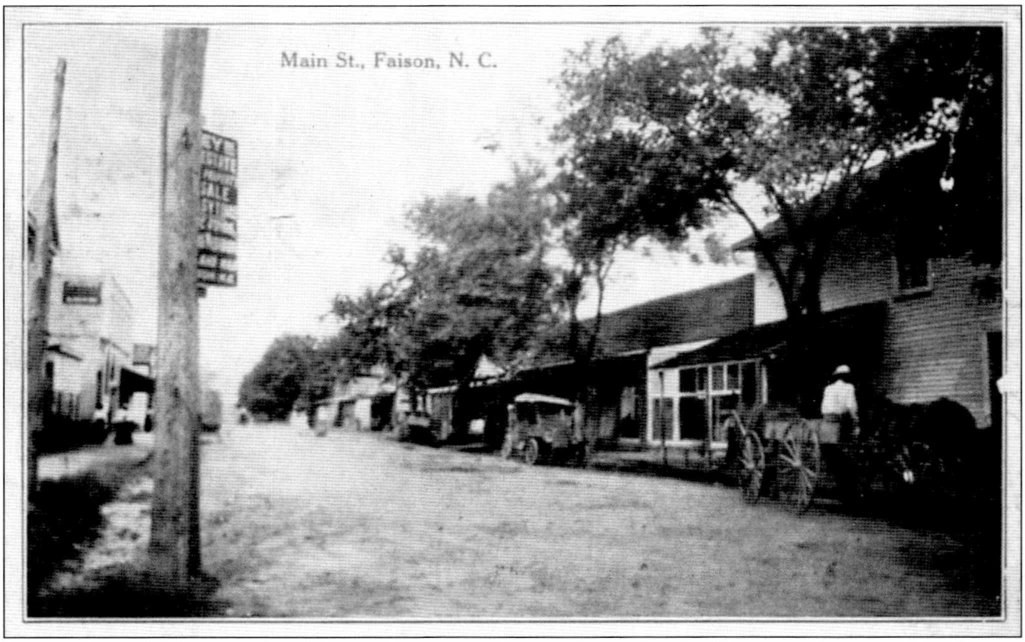

This 1915 postcard offers a glimpse of Faison's Main Street on an ordinary day. A combination of storefronts, cars, and horse-drawn wagons can be seen along the unpaved street. (Courtesy of UNC Chapel Hill's Wilson Library.)

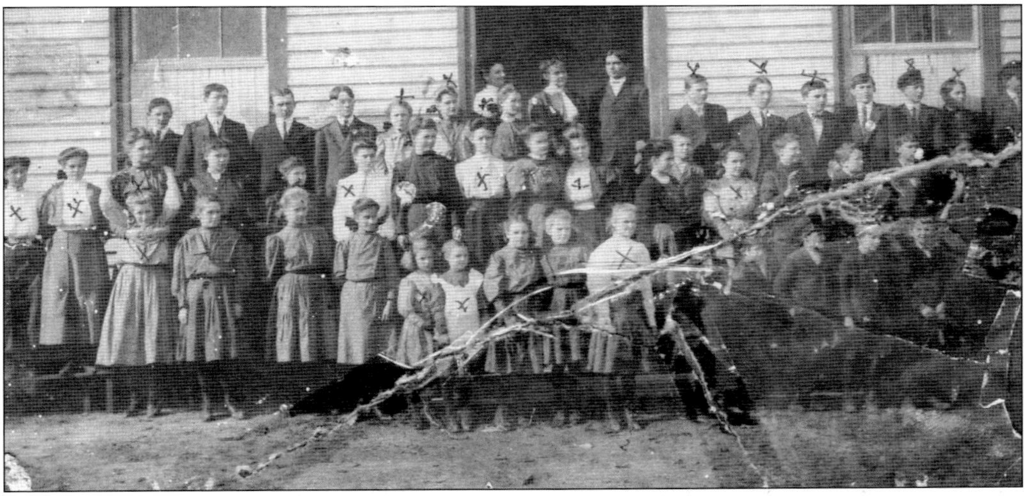

Students of the Faison Academy pose outside the school in 1904. The young boys in the front row are, from left to right, Robert Witherington, DeVane Faison, Virginius Williams, Marcus Rose, Eddis Taylor, Paul Armstrong, Elias Faison, and James Faison. The girls are, from left to right starting at the back, Ruth Faison, Estelle King, Martha Faison, Anna Pierce, Ida May Taylor, Bettie Taylor, Lizzie Cooper, Viola Bowden, Fonnie Sewell, Kate Clifton, Floy Johnson, Laura Murphey Faison, Frances Clifton, Bessie Perrett, Ethel McCullen, Mary Parrett, Eva Grant, Marguerite Shine, Eva Faison, Bessie Southerland, Hattie May Hollingsworth, Edna Shine, Elinor Southerland, and Marie Faison. The boys in the back row are believed to be ? Shine, Francis Wells, Faison Witherington, Frank Taylor, Rolland Williams, Sam Taylor, Henry Faison, Percy Clifton, Tom Taylor, Henry Cooper, Albert Hall, and Perry Konegay. Standing in the doorway are, from left to right, Winnie Faison, Josie Sewell, and unidentified. (Courtesy of the Faison Museum.)

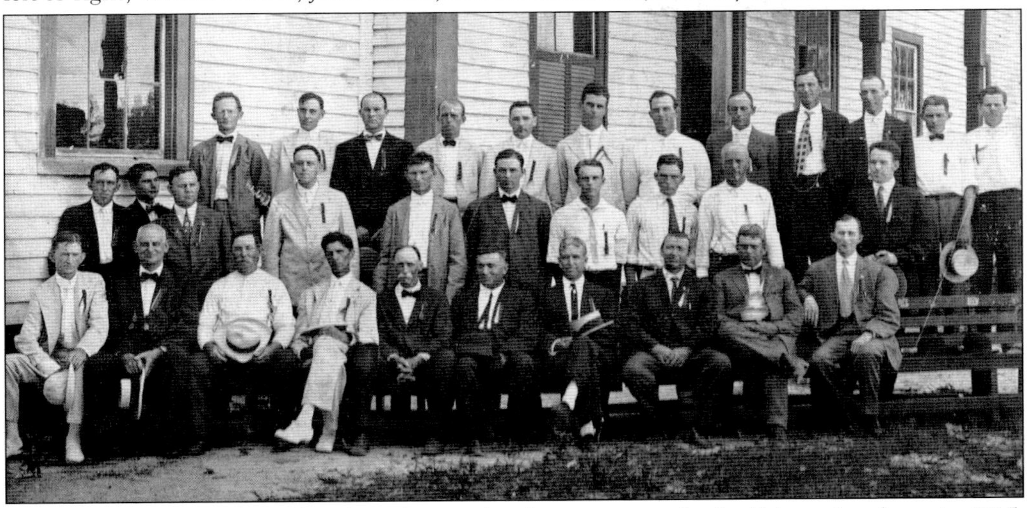

Members of the Knights of Pythias fraternal order pose outside the Faison Academy in 1915. From left to right are (first row) two unidentified, Luther Taylor, Isham Hines, Paul Armstrong Sr., ? Westbrook, unidentified, Howard Faison, Vance Blount, and Frank DeVane; (second row) Henry Shine, B.F. McColman, Frank James, Oscar Taylor, Tomp Hines, Add Hawley, James Faison, Robert Witherington, Enoch McCullen, and John Shine; (third row) Marshall Williams, John Howard, ? Jinnette, Tom Shine, Rolland Williams, Joyce Gibbons, Ross Ireland, William Thompson, Moseley Bowden, J.C. Ball, Tim Williamson, and Leon Taylor. (Courtesy of the Faison Museum.)

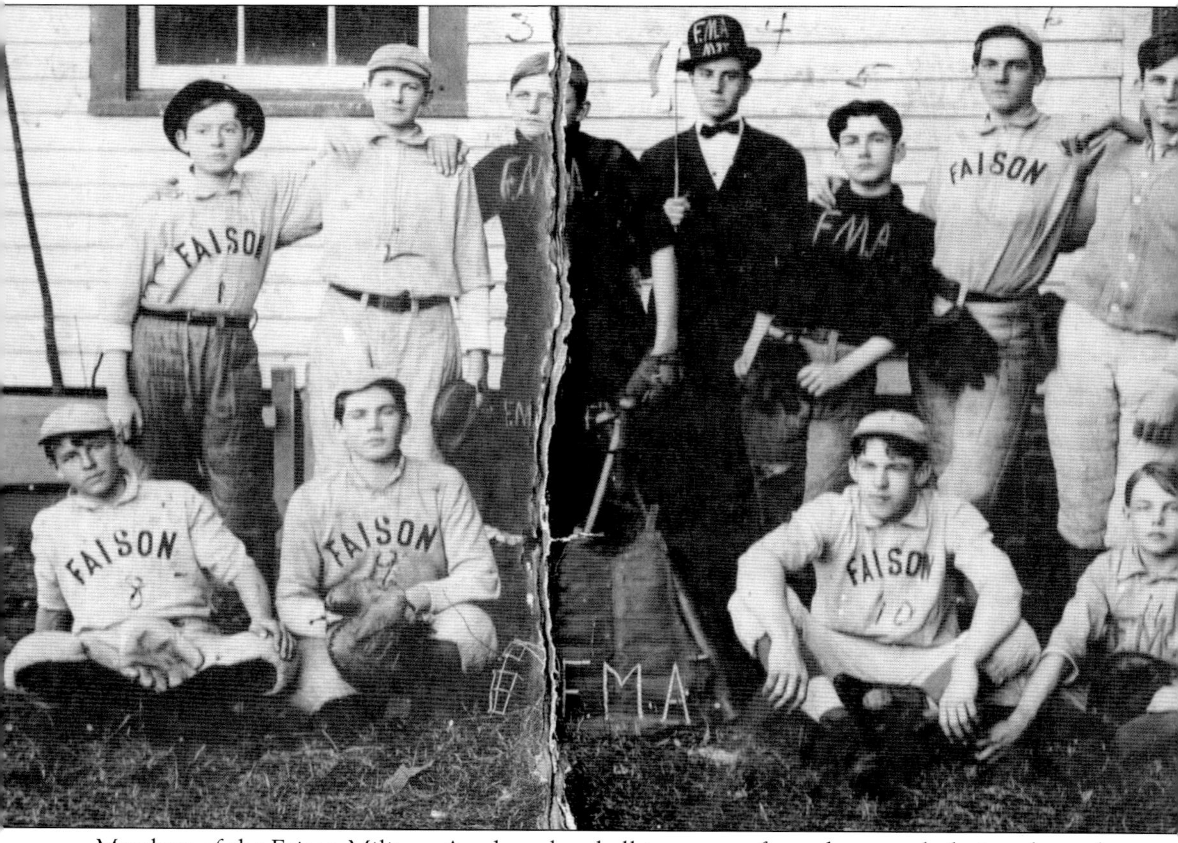

Members of the Faison Military Academy baseball team pose for a photograph during the early 1900s. From left to right are (first row) George Trust, Robert Witherington, John Shiver, and James Faison; (second row) George Hall, Marshall Williams, DeVane Faison, John Howard, Norwood Whitman, Leo Clifton, and Henry Faison. (Courtesy of the Faison Museum.)

Many of the communities on the western side of Duplin County developed in part due to the Wilmington & Weldon Railroad line (originally the Wilmington & Raleigh Railroad), which ran through towns such as Calypso, Faison, Bowdens, Warsaw, Magnolia, Rose Hill, Teachey, and Wallace. This image shows a train between the Calypso and Faison portion of the route during the 1920s. (Courtesy of the Faison Museum.)

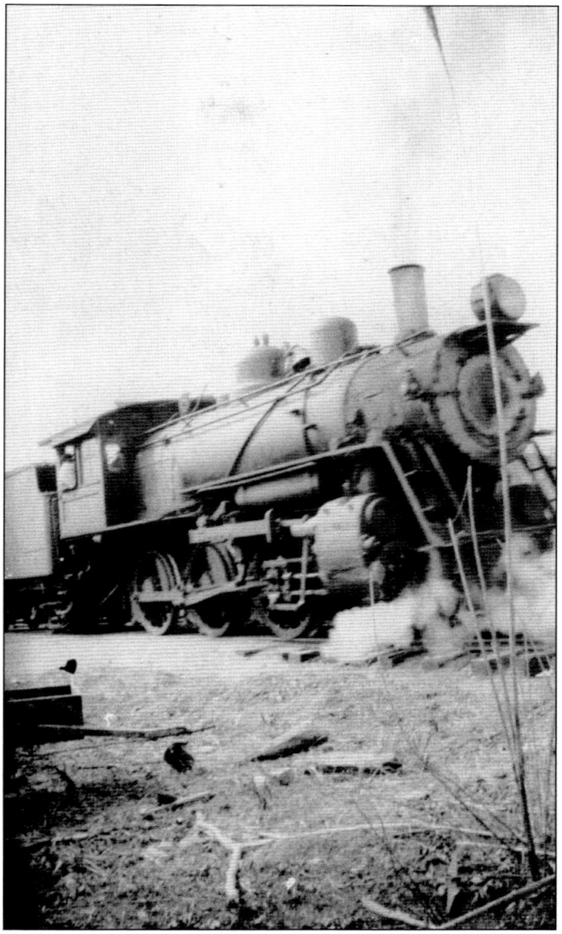

The Wilmington & Weldon played a major role in the Civil War by transporting much-needed supplies for the Confederacy to the port of Wilmington. In the decades following the war, the railroad made it easier for local farmers to ship their produce to wider markets, further reducing the need for steamboats along the Northeast Cape Fear River. Following the merger of several companies around 1900, the Wilmington & Weldon became part of the Atlantic Coast Line Railroad. (Courtesy of the Faison Museum.)

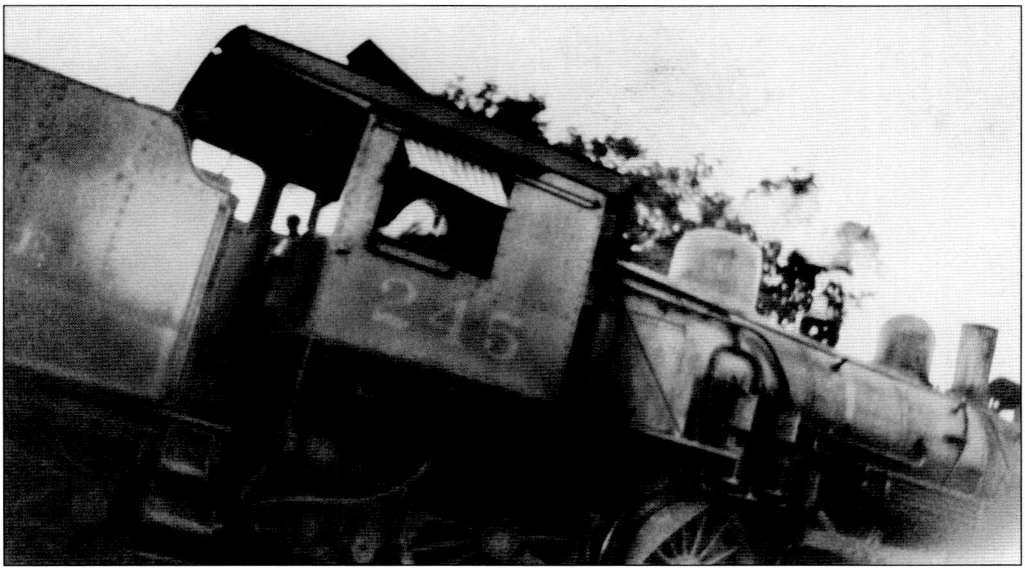

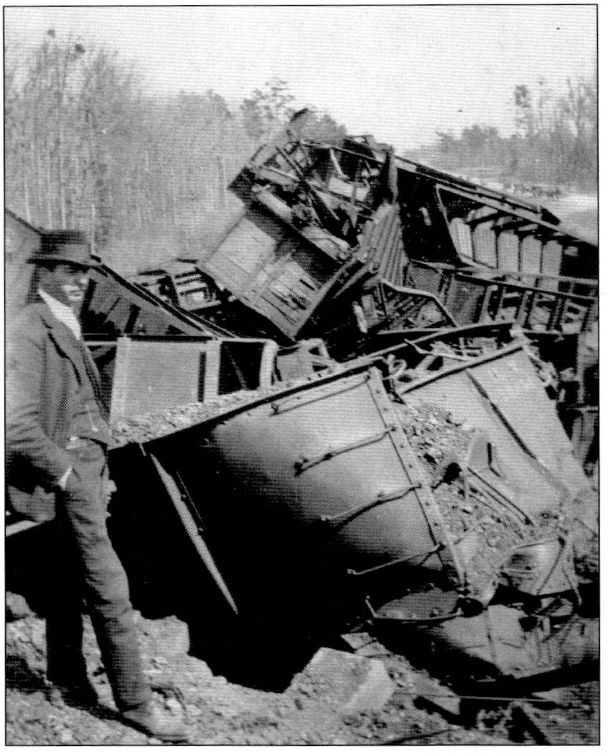

A man stands beside the aftermath of a train derailment between Faison and Calypso in 1924. (Courtesy of the Faison Museum.)

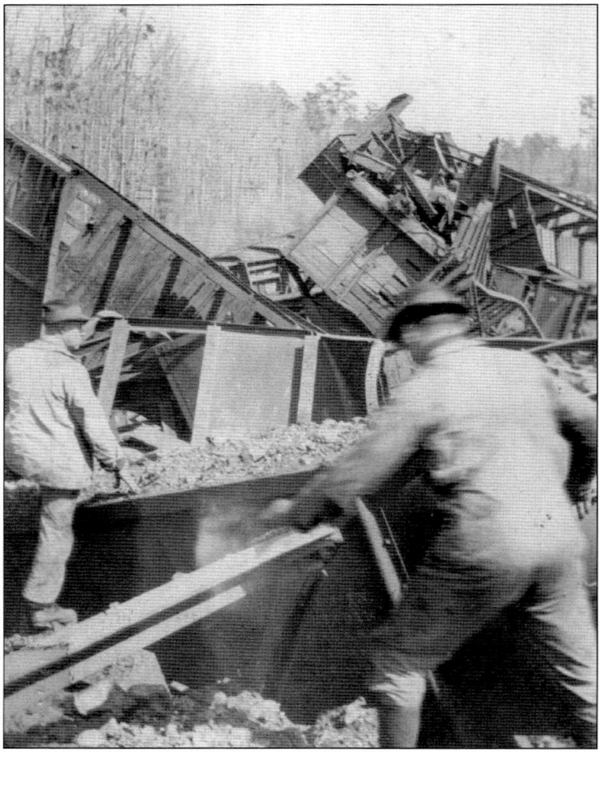

Workers sort through the aftermath of the 1924 train derailment outside of Faison. The wreck occurred as a southbound train traveled over the trestle at Goshen Swamp. Miraculously, no one was killed during the accident. (Courtesy of the Faison Museum.)

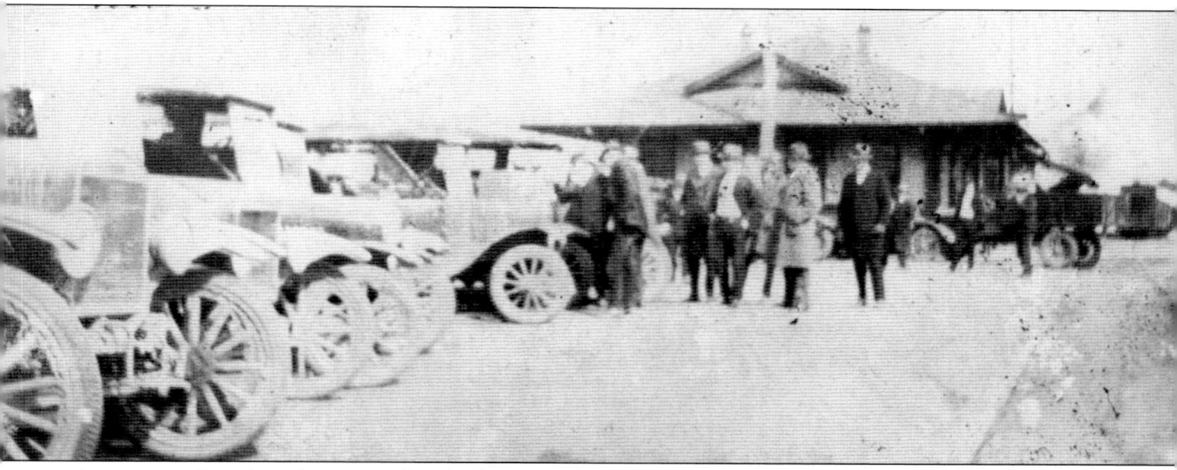

A group gathers beside a row of parked cars at the Faison train depot around 1920. Constructed in 1888, the depot was originally on Main Street but has since been relocated to Faison Park. Currently, it houses the town library and a small museum. (Courtesy of the Faison Museum.)

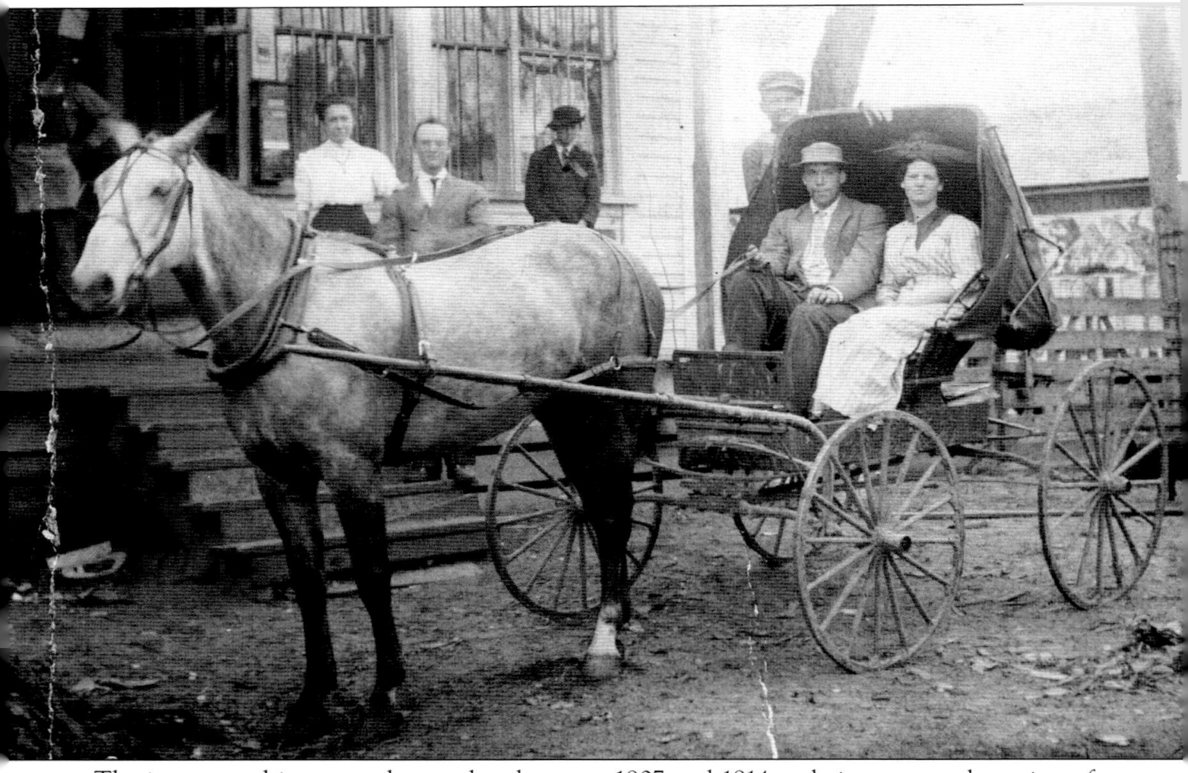

The image on this postcard was taken between 1907 and 1914 and gives an up-close view of a Faison storefront. (Courtesy of the Faison Museum.)

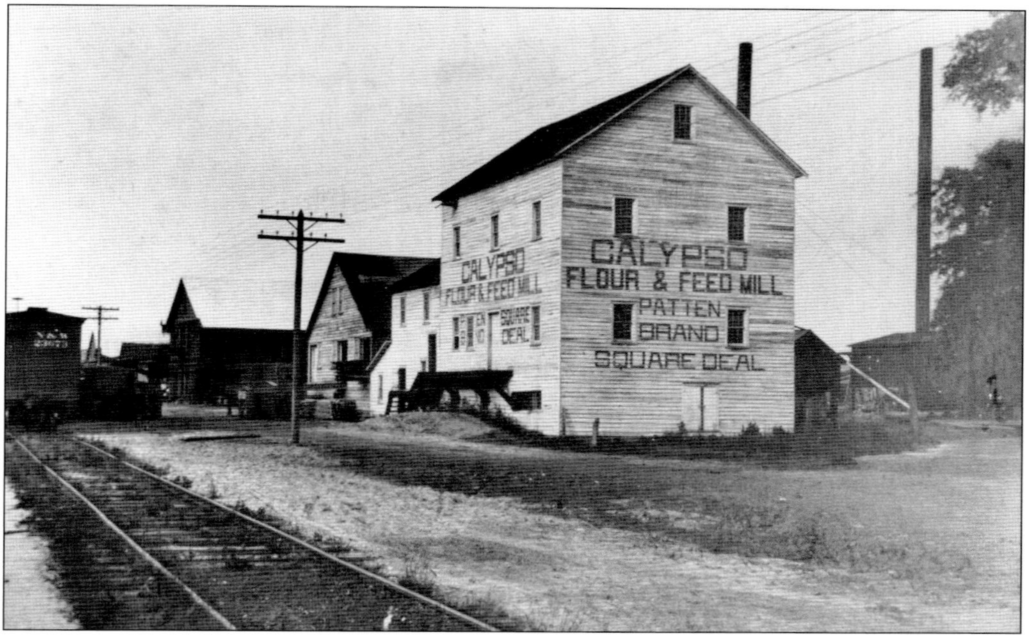

Settled around the 1890s, the town of Calypso was Duplin County's last stop heading north on the Wilmington & Weldon Railroad (later the Atlantic Coast Line Railroad) before entering neighboring Wayne County. Taken in 1905, this image shows the Calypso Flour and Feed Mill adjacent to the railroad line. (Courtesy of Leon Sikes.)

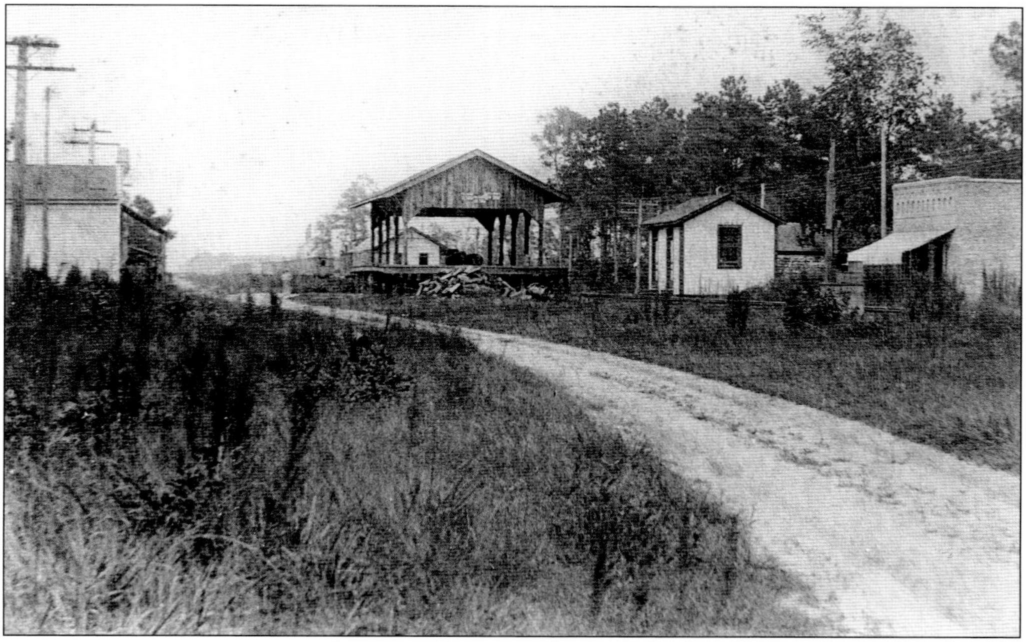

Calypso's railroad loading dock can be seen in the background of this 1910 photograph. Like most Duplin County communities, Calypso was centered around agriculture. The town suffered economically following the relocation of its produce market to nearby Faison. (Courtesy of Leon Sikes.)

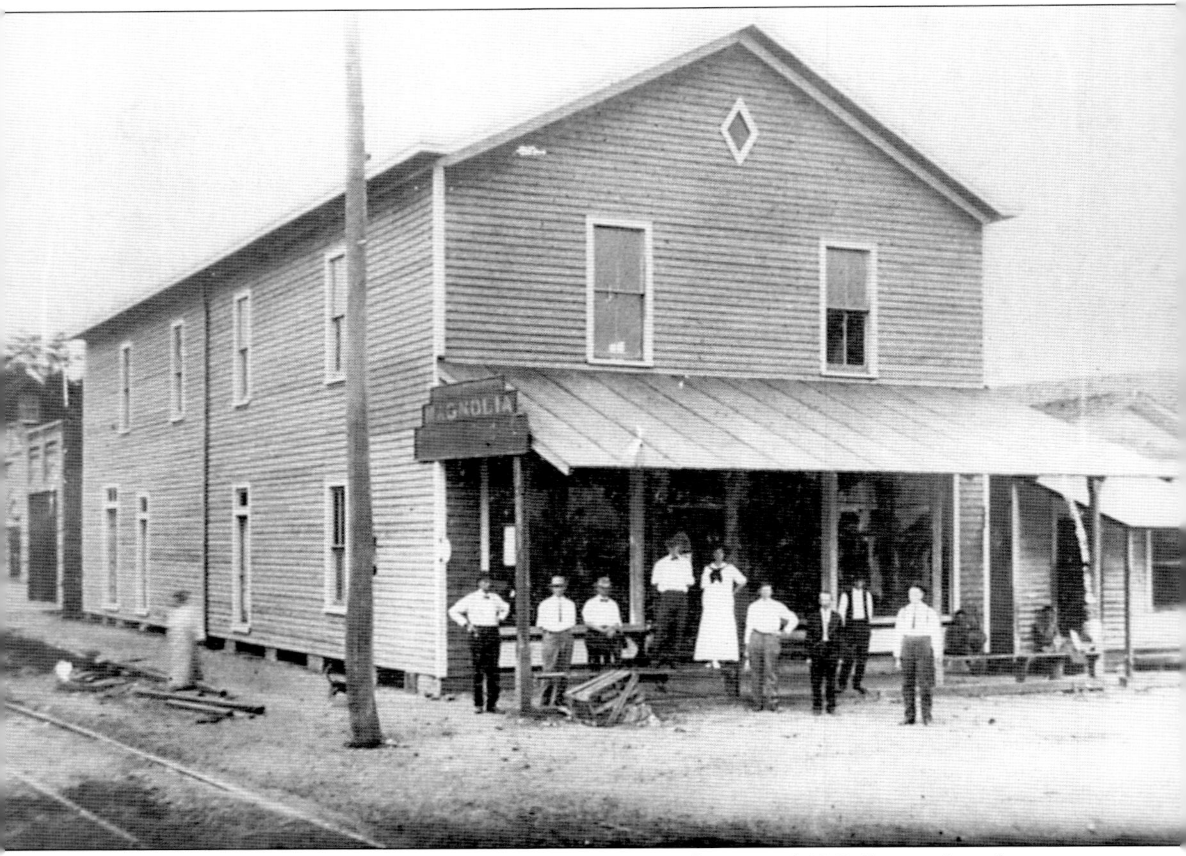

Residents gather outside Hiram Swinson's store in Magnolia around 1912. Located on the western side of Duplin County, the town of Magnolia formed along the tracks of the Wilmington & Weldon Railroad and was originally known as Stricklands Depot, later Stricklandville. (Courtesy of Leon Sikes.)

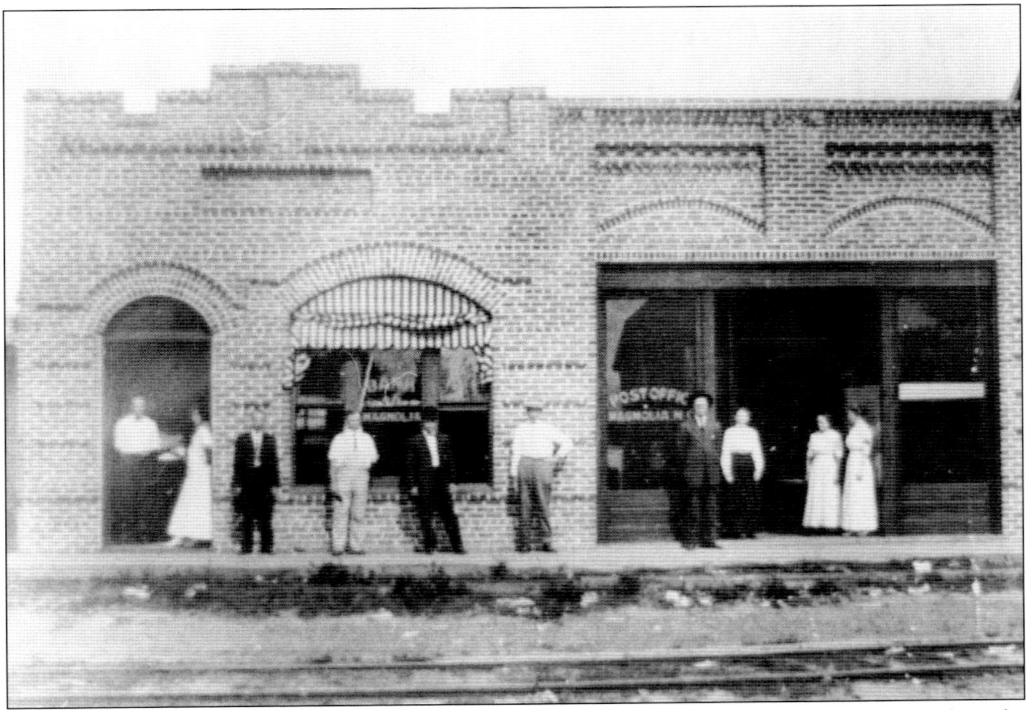

Magnolia residents pose in front of the town's bank and post office in 1911. The railroad tracks can be seen in the foreground. (Courtesy of Leon Sikes.)

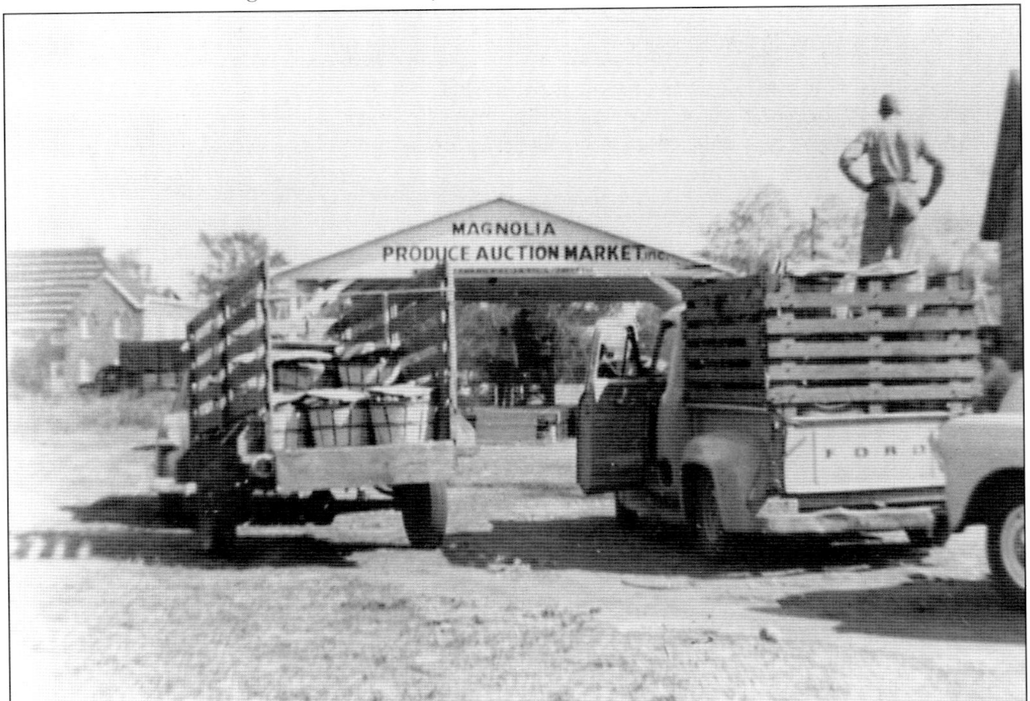

Farmers are hauling their potatoes to Magnolia's produce shed in 1954. (Courtesy of Leon Sikes.)

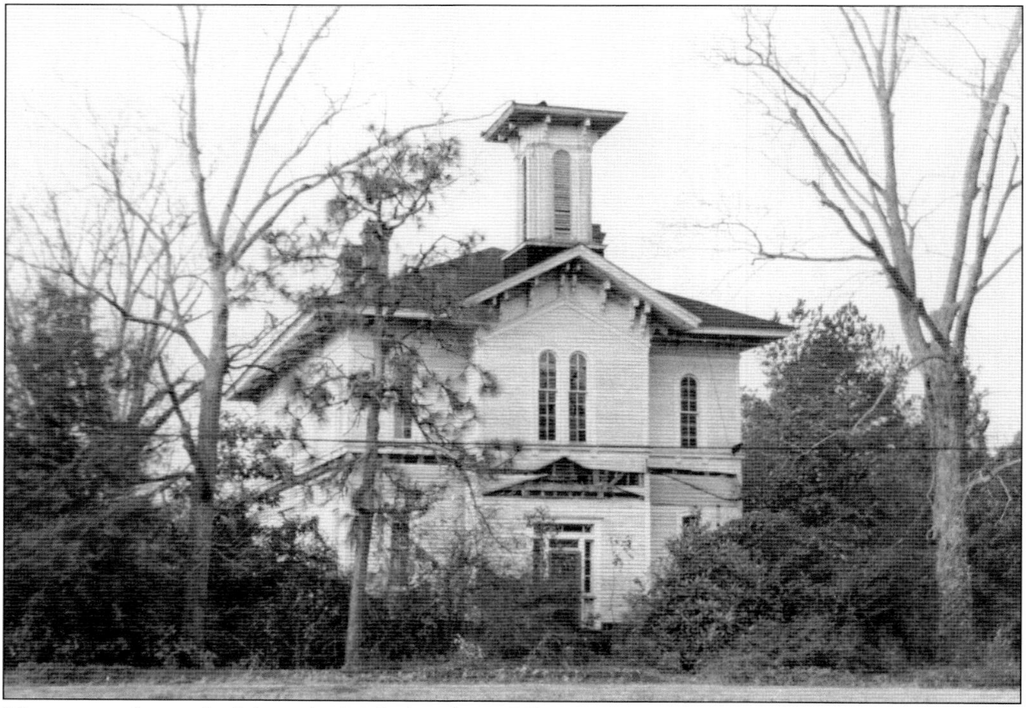

This image shows the Magnolia Male Academy following decades of wear and tear. Construction began on the structure in 1858, with classes first held there the following year. The building briefly served as Magnolia College during the late 19th century. (Courtesy of Leon Sikes.)

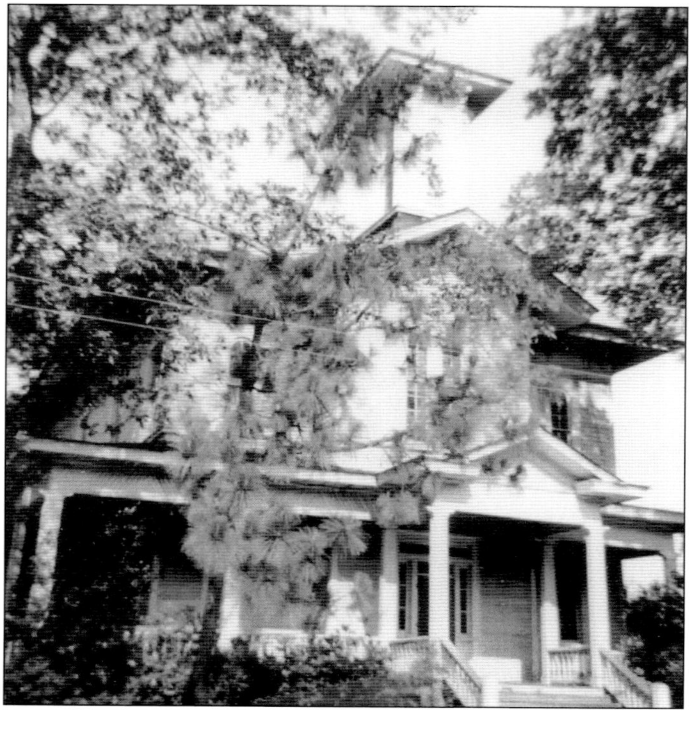

Another view shows the Magnolia Male Academy around 1951. Local nursery owner John F. Croom purchased the structure in the 1890s and used it to store flower bulbs prior to using it for a dwelling. (Courtesy of Leon Sikes.)

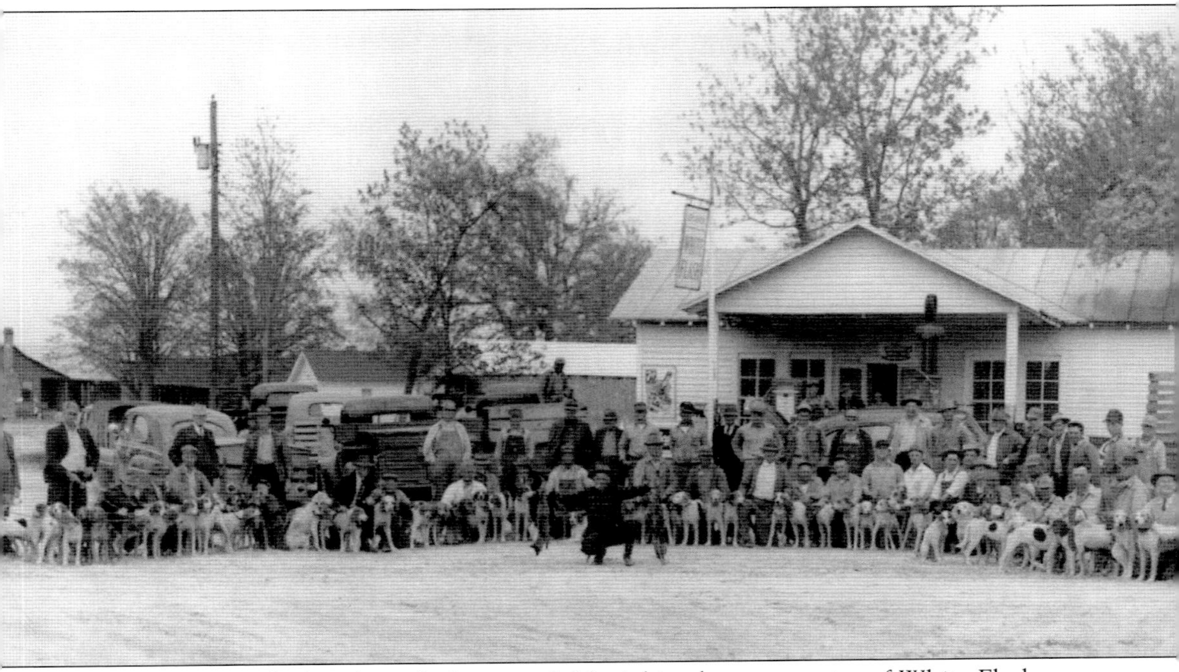

Hunters pose with their hounds during a field trial in the community of White Flash, near Albertson. Local lore suggests that the community took its name from the White Flash brand of gasoline sold at the local store. (Courtesy of Leon Sikes.)

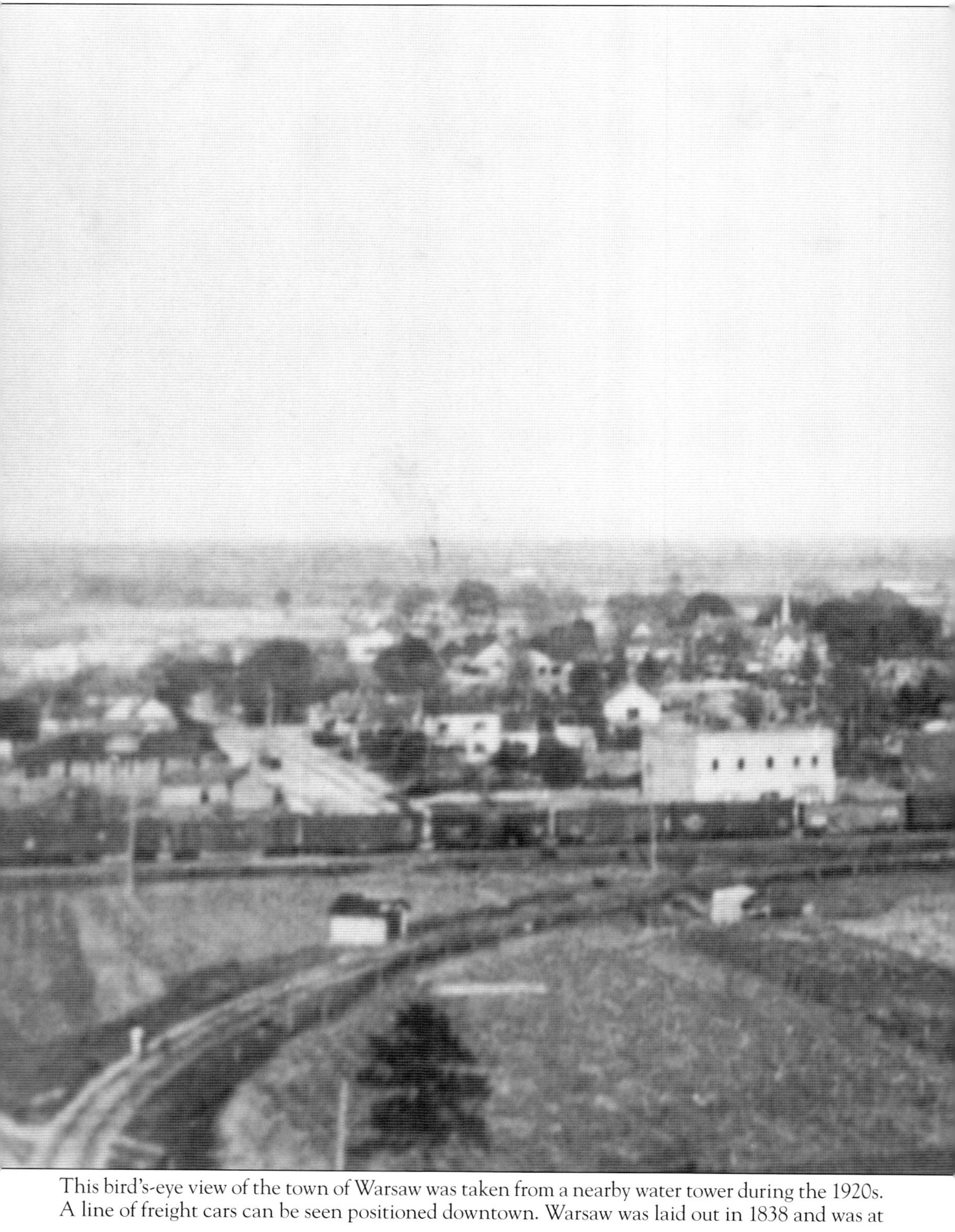

This bird's-eye view of the town of Warsaw was taken from a nearby water tower during the 1920s. A line of freight cars can be seen positioned downtown. Warsaw was laid out in 1838 and was at

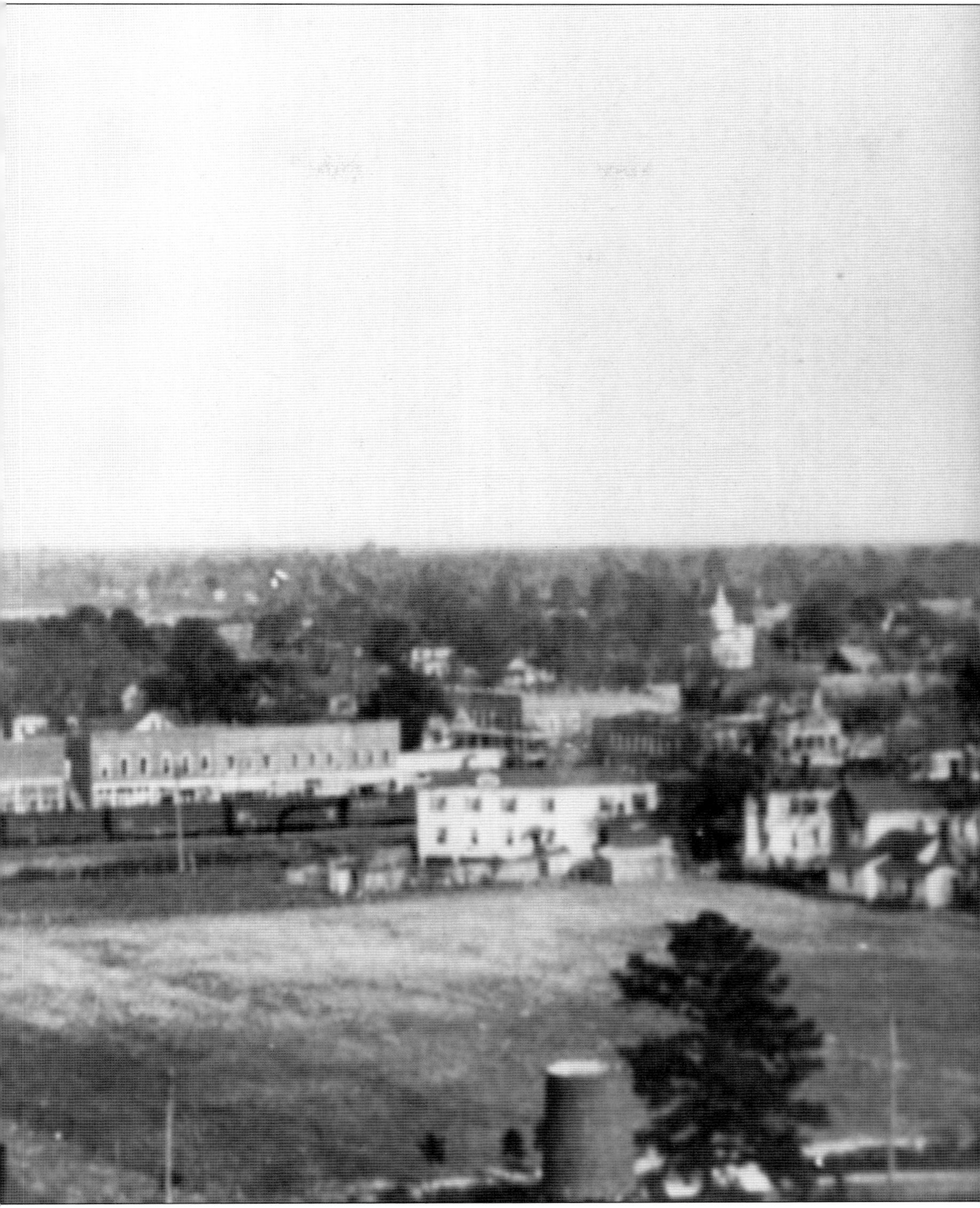

one time called Duplin Depot. (Courtesy of Leon Sikes.)

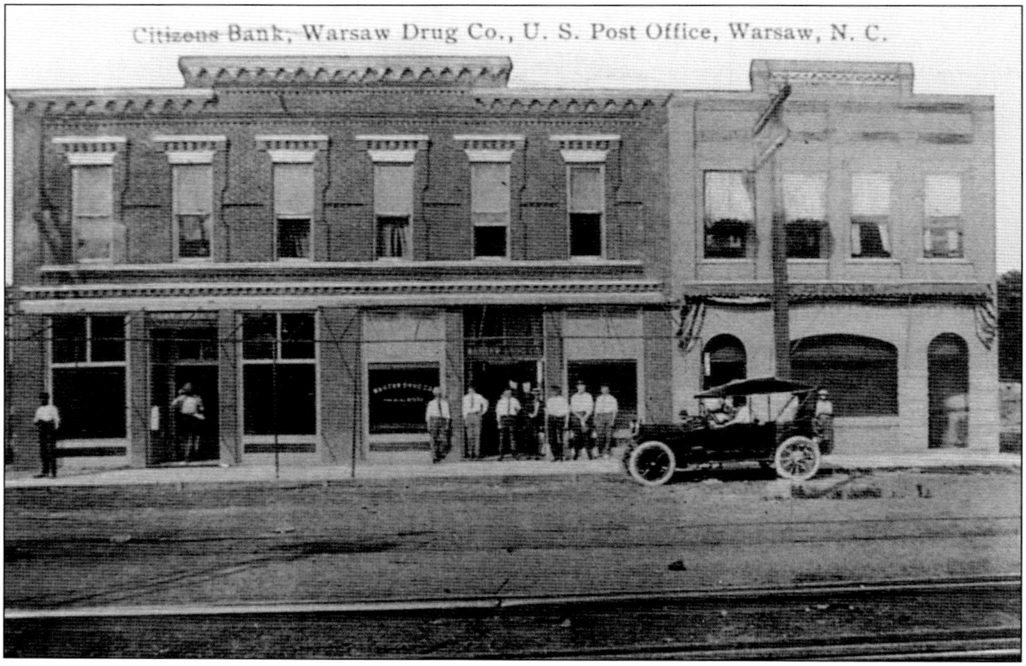

Men pose outside the Warsaw Drug Company in 1921. It is believed that the town eventually took its name from the book *Thaddeus of Warsaw,* which had gained popularity during the mid-19th century. (Courtesy of Leon Sikes.)

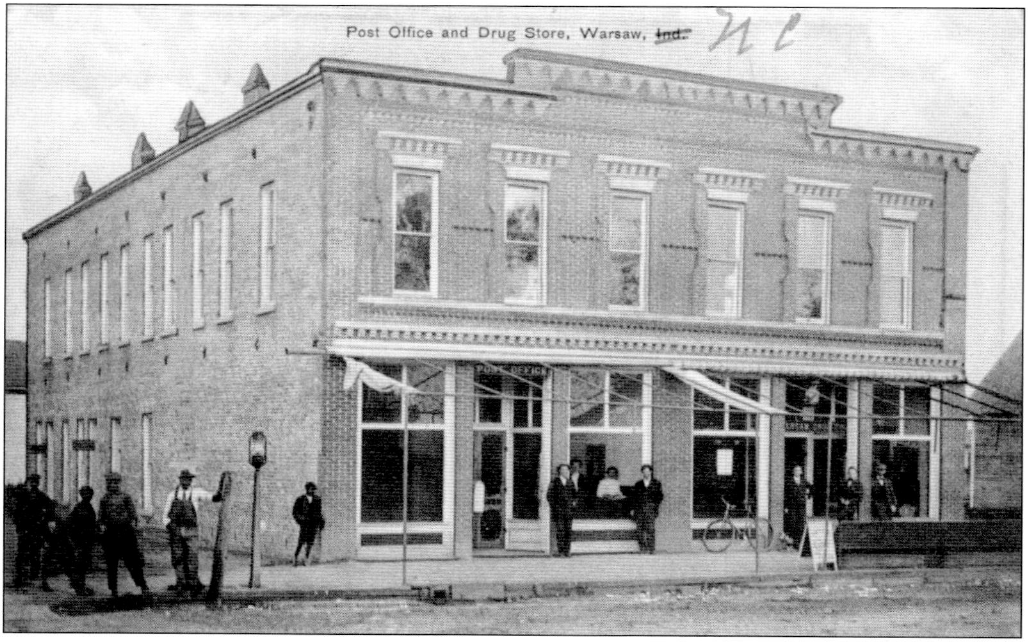

This 1909 postcard shows residents gathered outside the Warsaw Post Office and Drug Company. The business was originally called Sheffield Drug Store and was owned by Barney Sheffield. Note that the abbreviation of Indiana has been marked out and replaced with "NC." (Courtesy of UNC Chapel Hill's Wilson Library.)

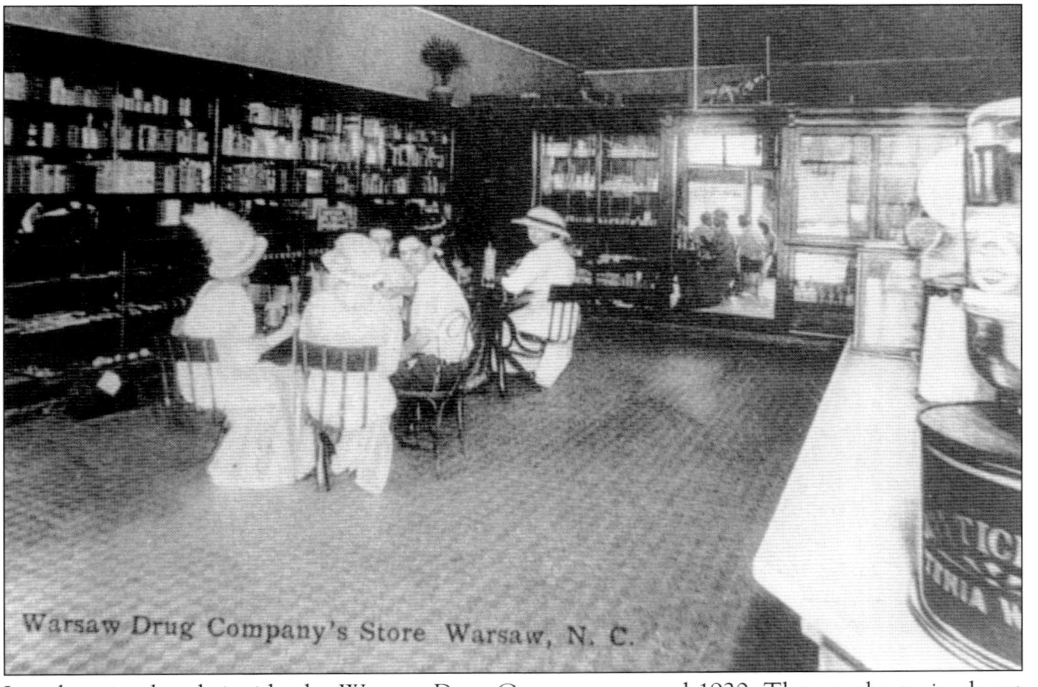

Locals enjoy lunch inside the Warsaw Drug Company around 1920. The nearby train depot attracted scores of farmers to Warsaw to ship their crops, thus giving a boost to local businesses. (Courtesy of Leon Sikes.)

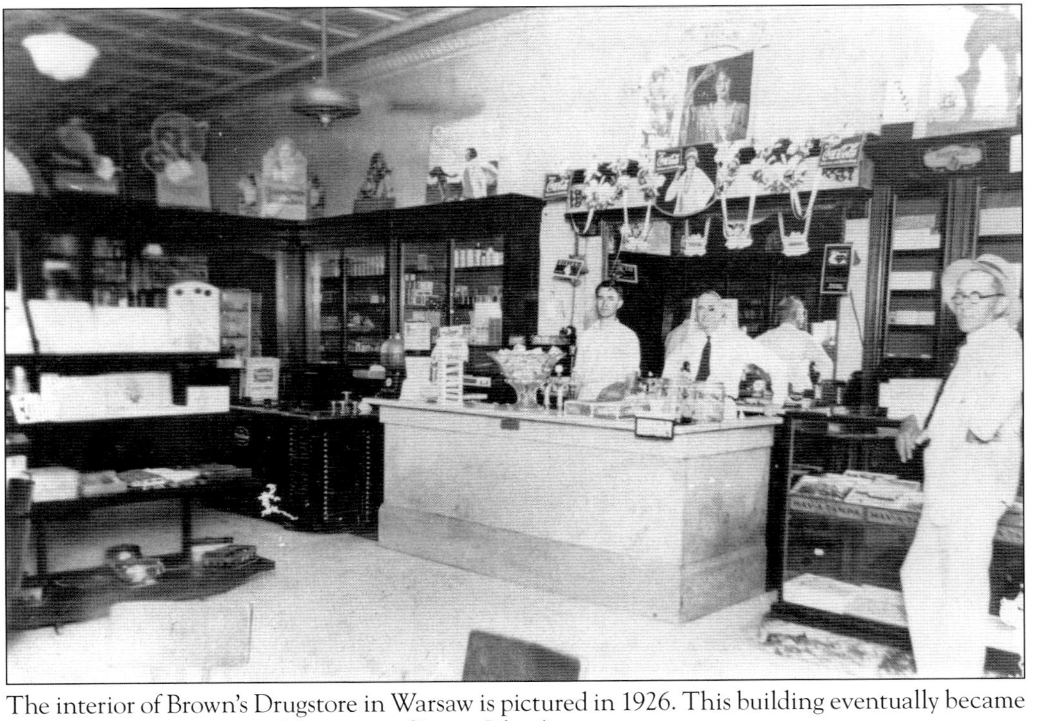

The interior of Brown's Drugstore in Warsaw is pictured in 1926. This building eventually became the Warsaw Drycleaners. (Courtesy of Leon Sikes.)

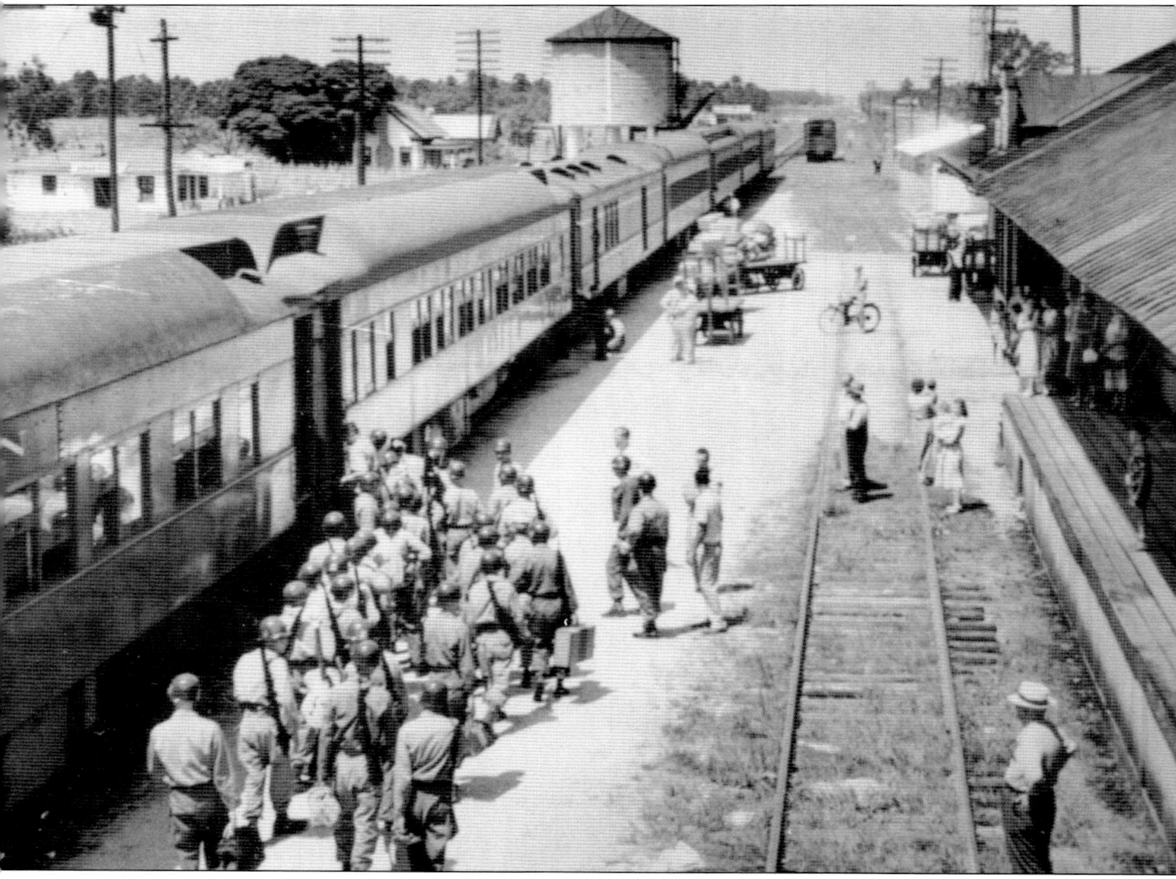

Soldiers are departing from the Warsaw train station in the 1940s. Today, Warsaw is believed to have the oldest continuous Veterans Day celebration in the country. (Courtesy of Leon Sikes.)

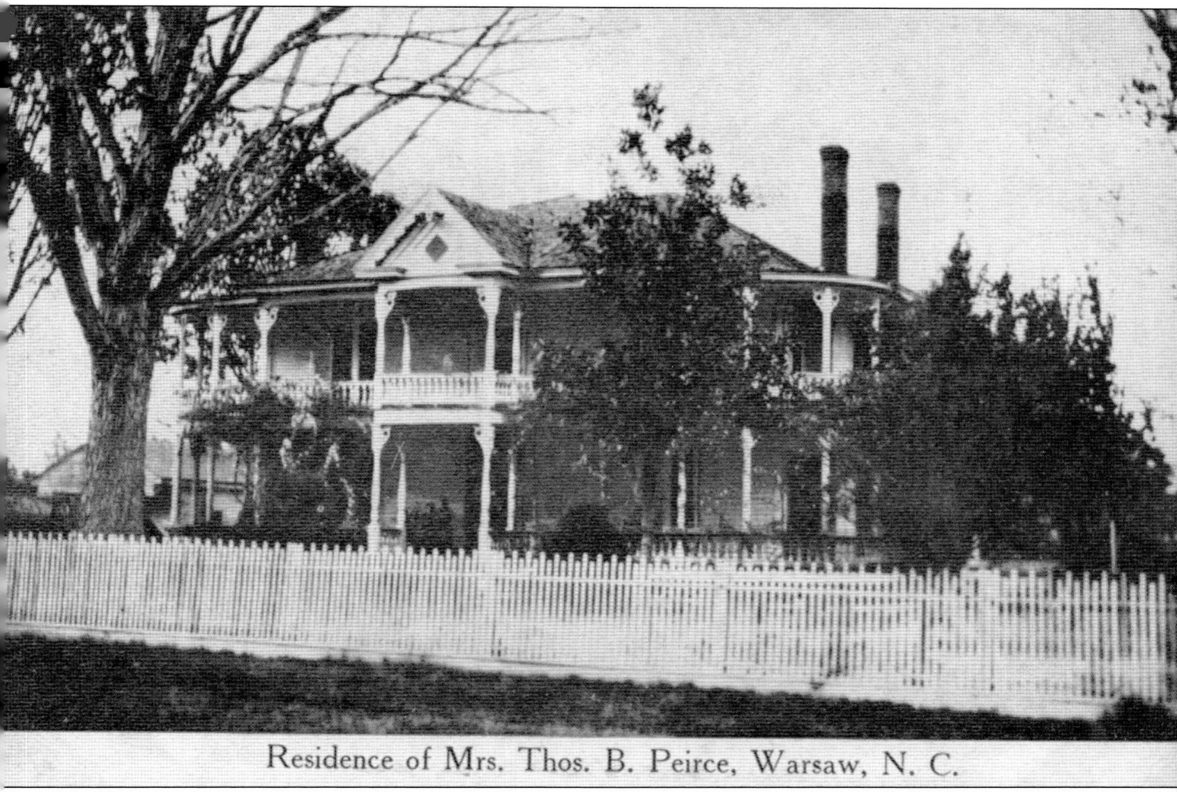

This historic postcard shows Thomas B. Peirce's home between 1905 and 1915. Construction began on the home during the 19th century approximately two miles outside of Warsaw. (Courtesy of UNC Chapel Hill's Wilson Library.)

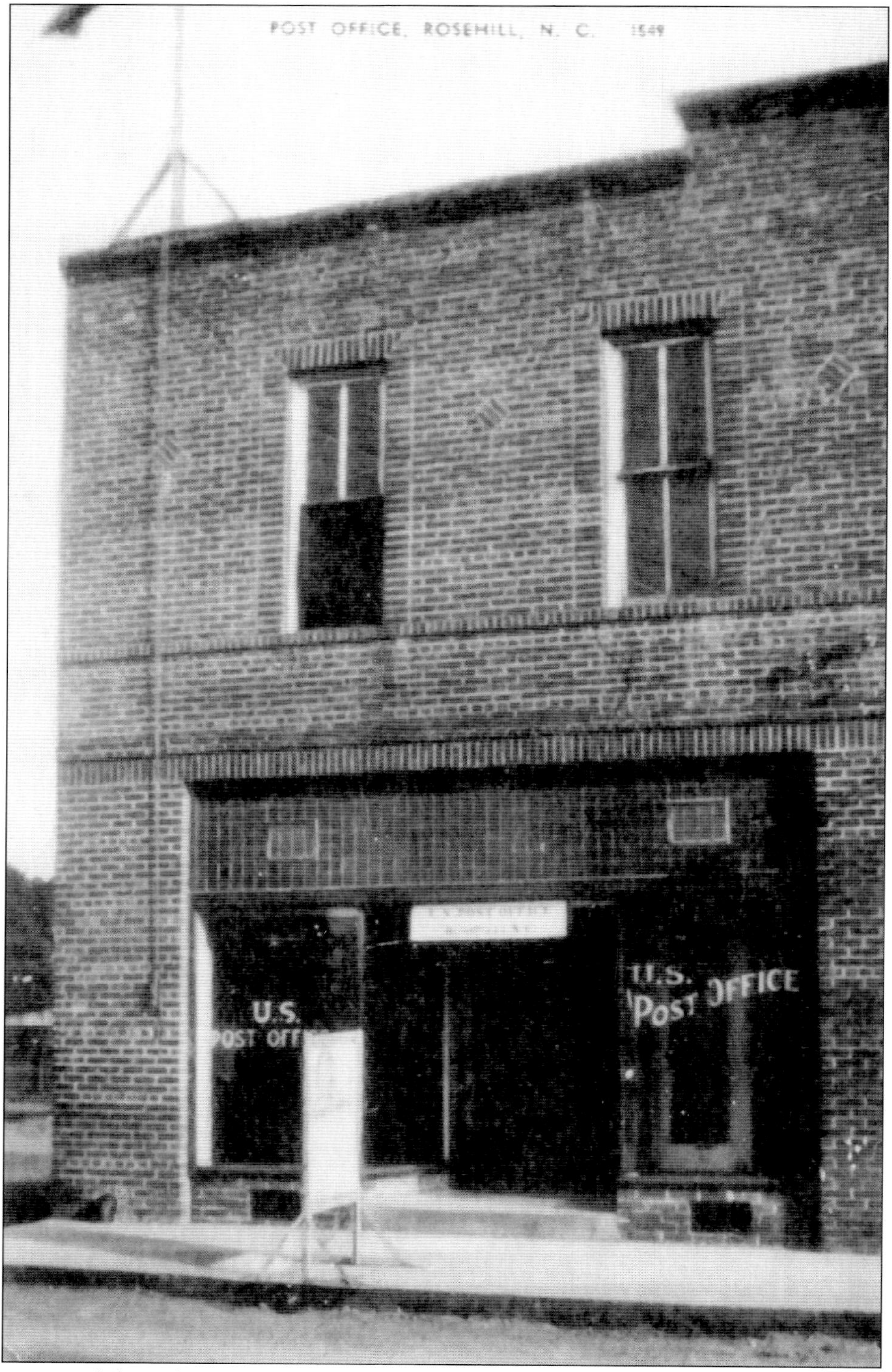

This postcard shows how the Rose Hill Post Office looked in 1952. Like its neighbor Wallace, Rose Hill had its own vibrant strawberry industry. (Courtesy UNC Chapel Hill's Wilson Library.)

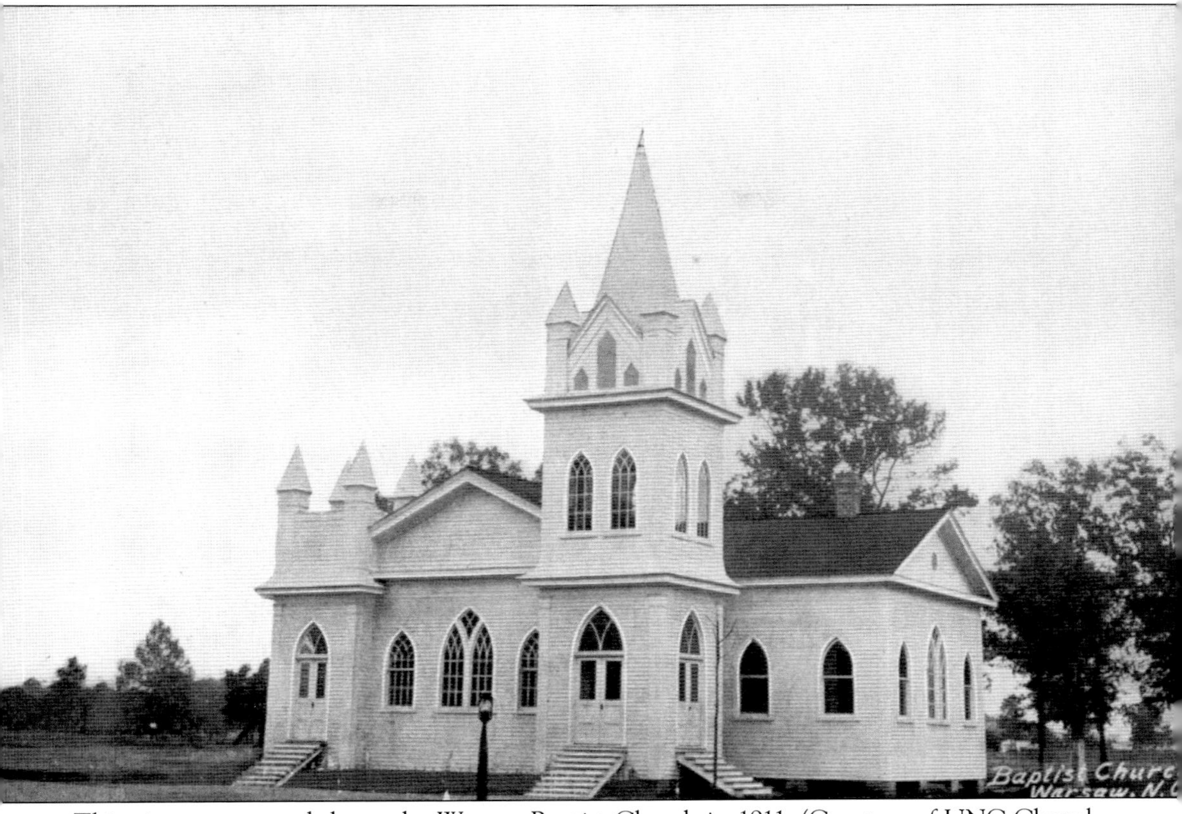

This vintage postcard shows the Warsaw Baptist Church in 1911. (Courtesy of UNC Chapel Hill's Wilson Library.)

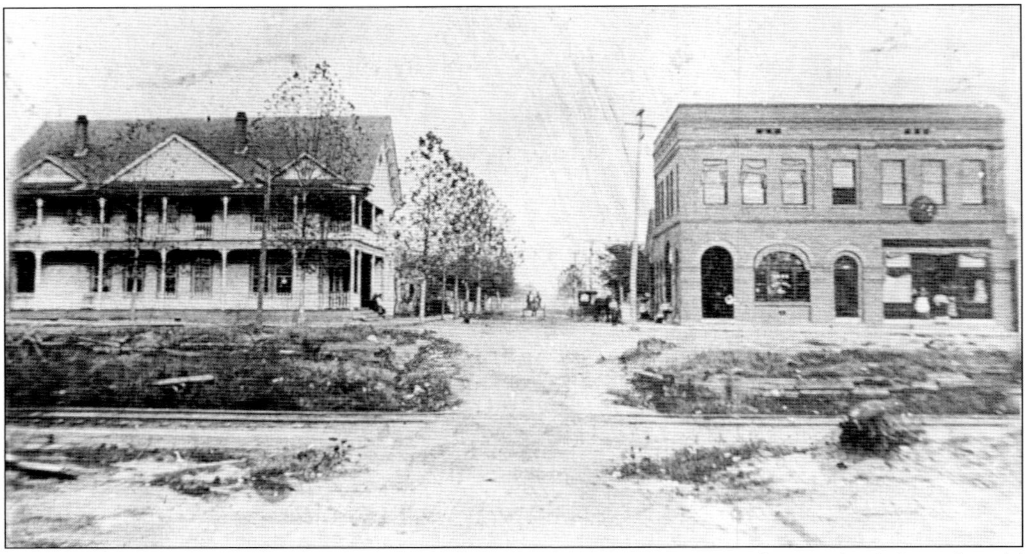

This 1906 photograph offers a view of East Main Street in Rose Hill. On the left is the old Overbrooke Hotel, where strawberry brokers lived during the season. Later, it was renamed the Strawberry Inn and eventually Rose Hill Hotel. Though the exterior appearance has been altered over the years, it still stands. (Courtesy of Leon Sikes.)

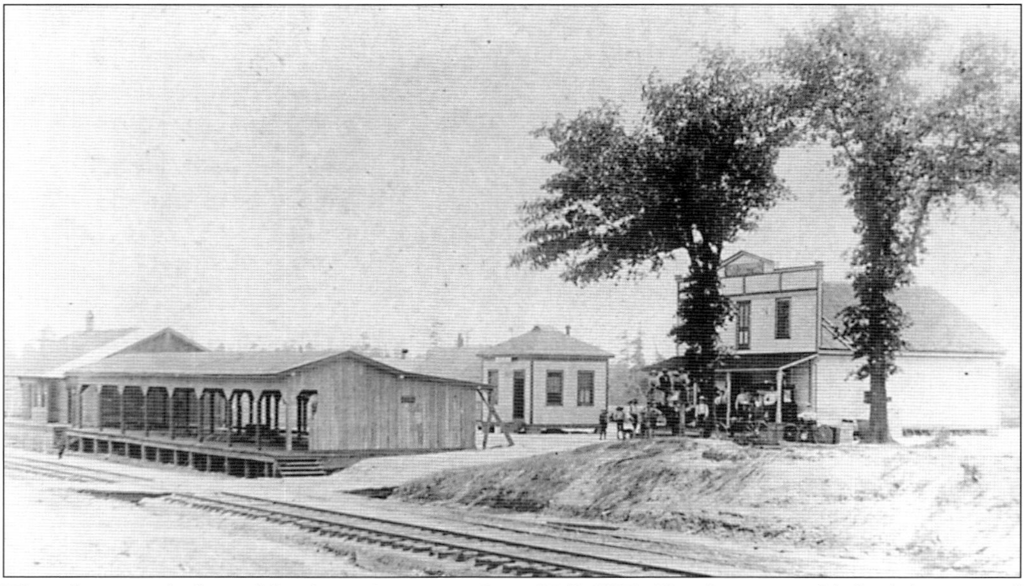

This photograph shows Henderson's store in Rose Hill. W.D. Henderson established the general store in 1898. He operated a store until the 1940s in various locations on the west side of the railroad. This building was moved at least one time and was eventually demolished. Following its destruction, a smaller building was used. (Courtesy of Leon Sikes and the late Lena Heyer.)

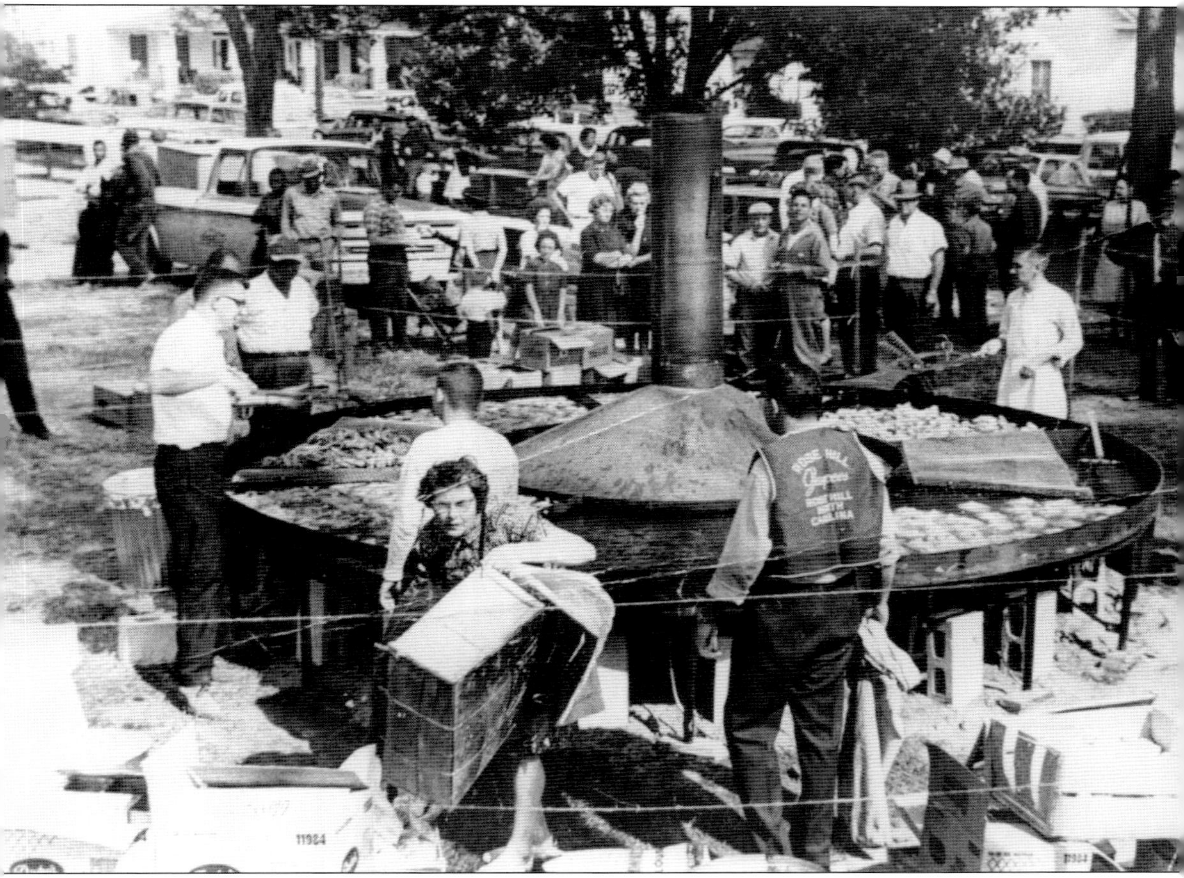

Rose Hill lays claim to the World's Largest Frying Pan, measuring 16 feet in diameter. The frying pan was first introduced in October 1963 during the Rose Hill Poultry Jubilee. It currently sits on the town square and is used to raise funds for charity. (Courtesy of Leon Sikes.)

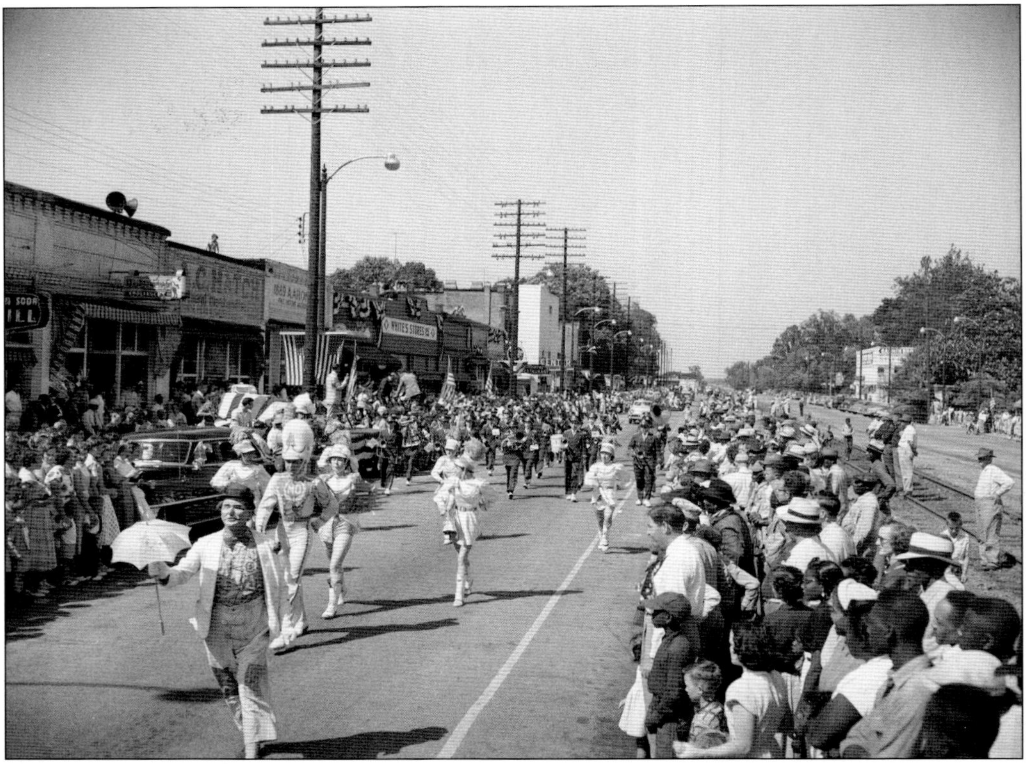

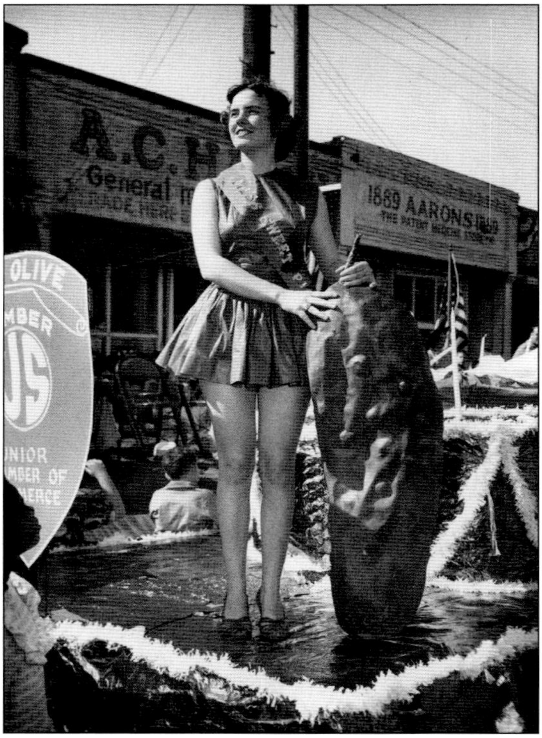

A tiny section of the Mount Olive community sits in Duplin County along its northern border with Wayne County. Being the home of the Mount Olive Pickle Company and sharing a similar agricultural heritage as Calypso and Faison in regards to cucumbers, the town held its first Pickle Festival in 1952. (Courtesy of the State Archives of North Carolina.)

Mary Dell Sutton was given the title of Miss Sweet Pickle that first year. Currently, the festival is known as the Carolina Pickle Festival. (Courtesy of the Mount Olive Historical Society.)

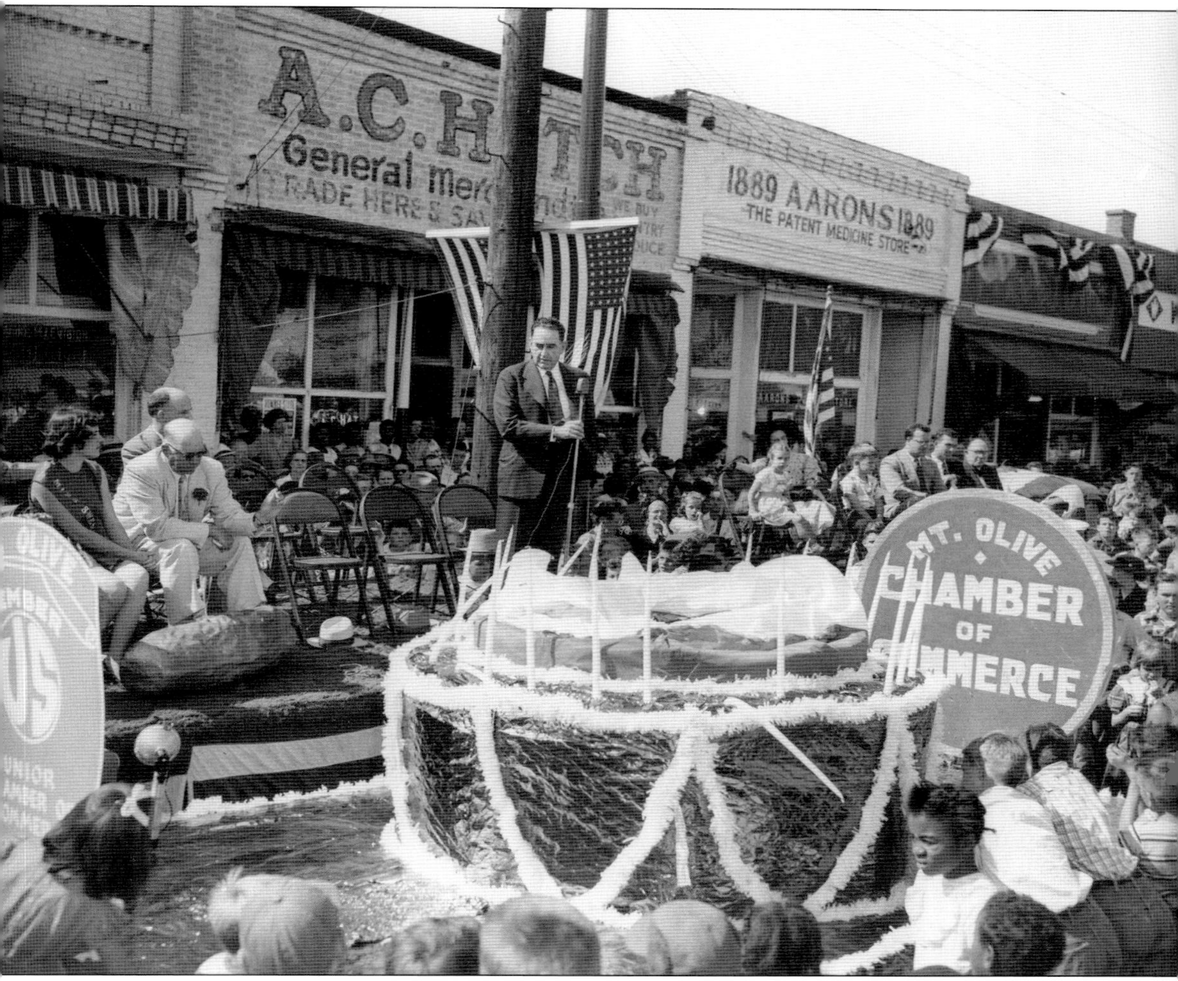

Gov. W. Kerr Scott makes a few remarks during the 1952 Mount Olive Pickle Festival. (Courtesy of the Mount Olive Historical Society.)

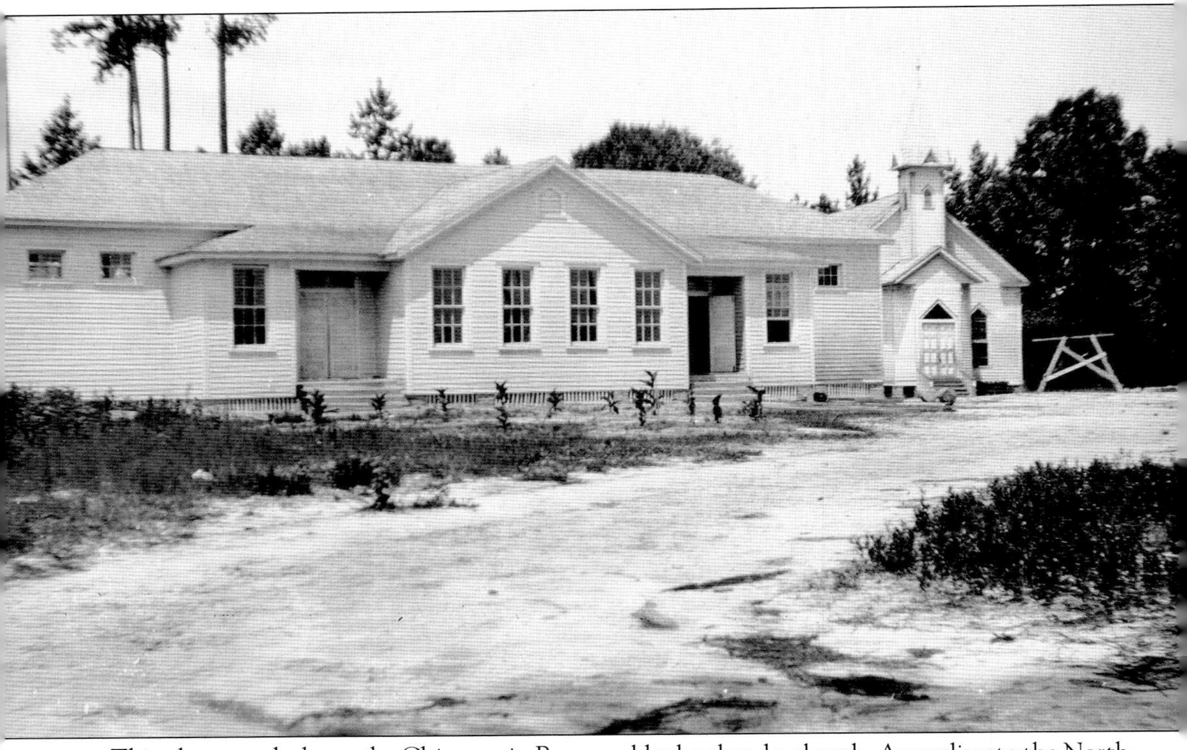

This photograph shows the Chinquapin Rosenwald school and a church. According to the North Carolina Department of Natural and Cultural Resources, it is believed that the Rosenwald Fund helped construct an estimated 5,300 schools between 1910 and 1932, with approximately 800 built in North Carolina, more than any other state. (Courtesy of the State Archives of North Carolina.)

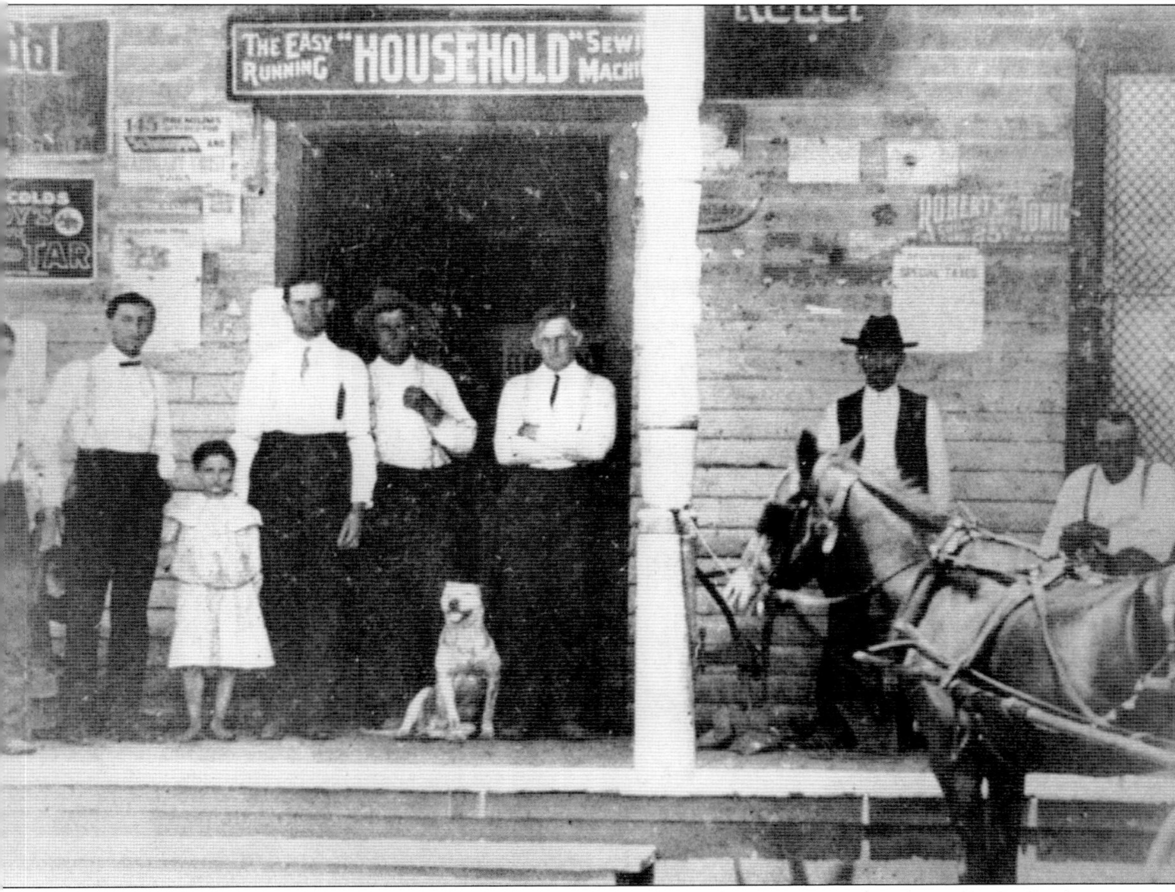

In this 1909 photograph, residents of Chinquapin gather on the front porch of G.B.D. Parker's general store. At left is L.L. Dail, third from left is Amy Bland, sixth from left is Will Herring, second from right is Bob Quinn, and seated at far right is store owner G.B.D. Parker. The mule's name is believed to have been Old Bill. (Courtesy of Leon Sikes.)

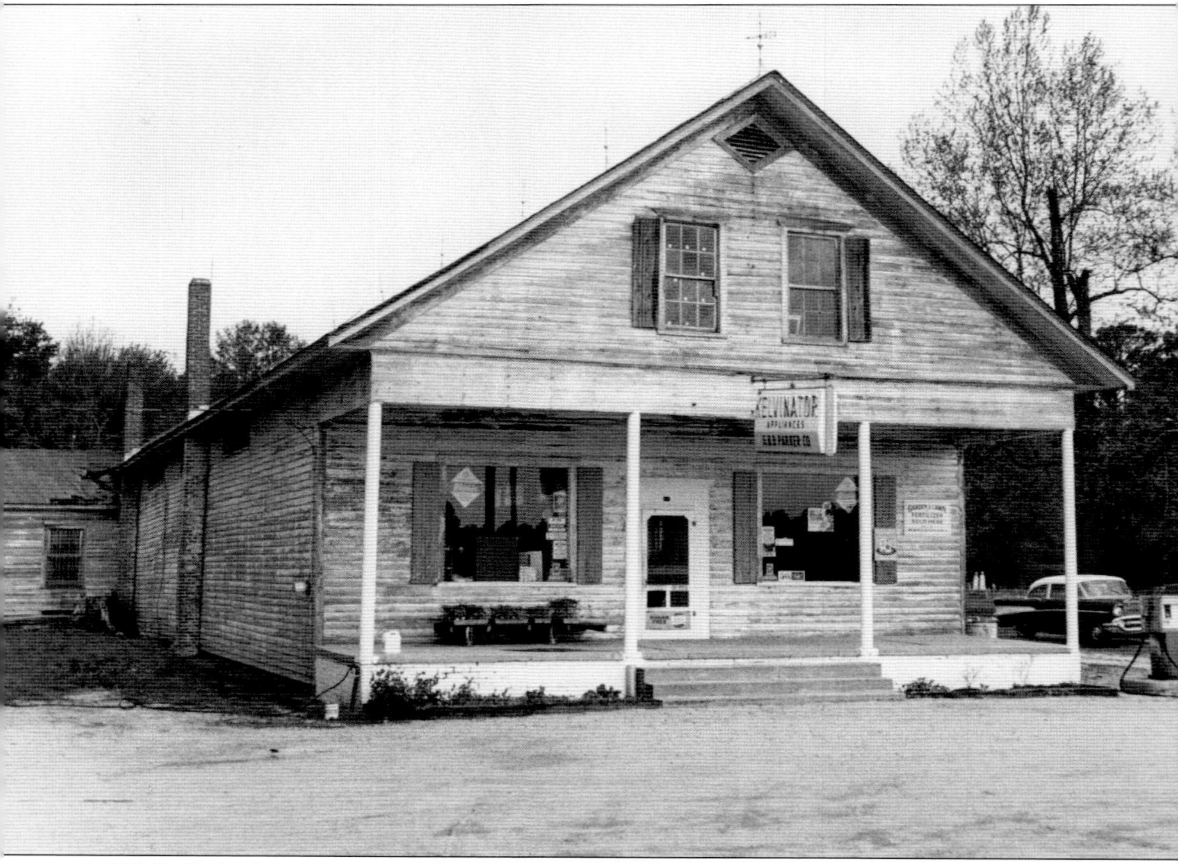

G.B.D. Parker's store is pictured in the early 1980s. (Courtesy of Leon Sikes.)

Two

Agriculture and Industry

Timber, cucumbers, livestock, tobacco, and strawberries once formed the backbone of Duplin County's economy. Many communities had their own markets where farmers and produce merchants would come together to conduct business. Families worked long hours together picking vegetables and looping tobacco, while some raised livestock such as turkeys and hogs. Helping drive these agricultural markets was the railroad, which allowed the county's products to be sold in wider markets. The railroad also helped create jobs for locals.

In its early days, Duplin had a bustling naval stores industry. Workers took advantage of the vast expanse of pine trees to make pitch, turpentine, pine tar, and rosin used in the shipbuilding industry. By the late 19th century, lumber companies had begun laying down miles of narrow-gauge railroad to extract timber from the surrounding forest. Many of these spur lines have long since been removed, but the county's railroad legacy remains evident in towns such as Wallace, Warsaw, Faison, Magnolia, and Calypso. Today, the CSX Transportation Company maintains a presence in the county.

Though farming practices have changed through the years, Duplin County's economy remains heavily dependent on agriculture, with locals now raising everything from livestock to muscadine grapes. Today, a new generation of farmers carries on Duplin County's long-cultivated agricultural legacy.

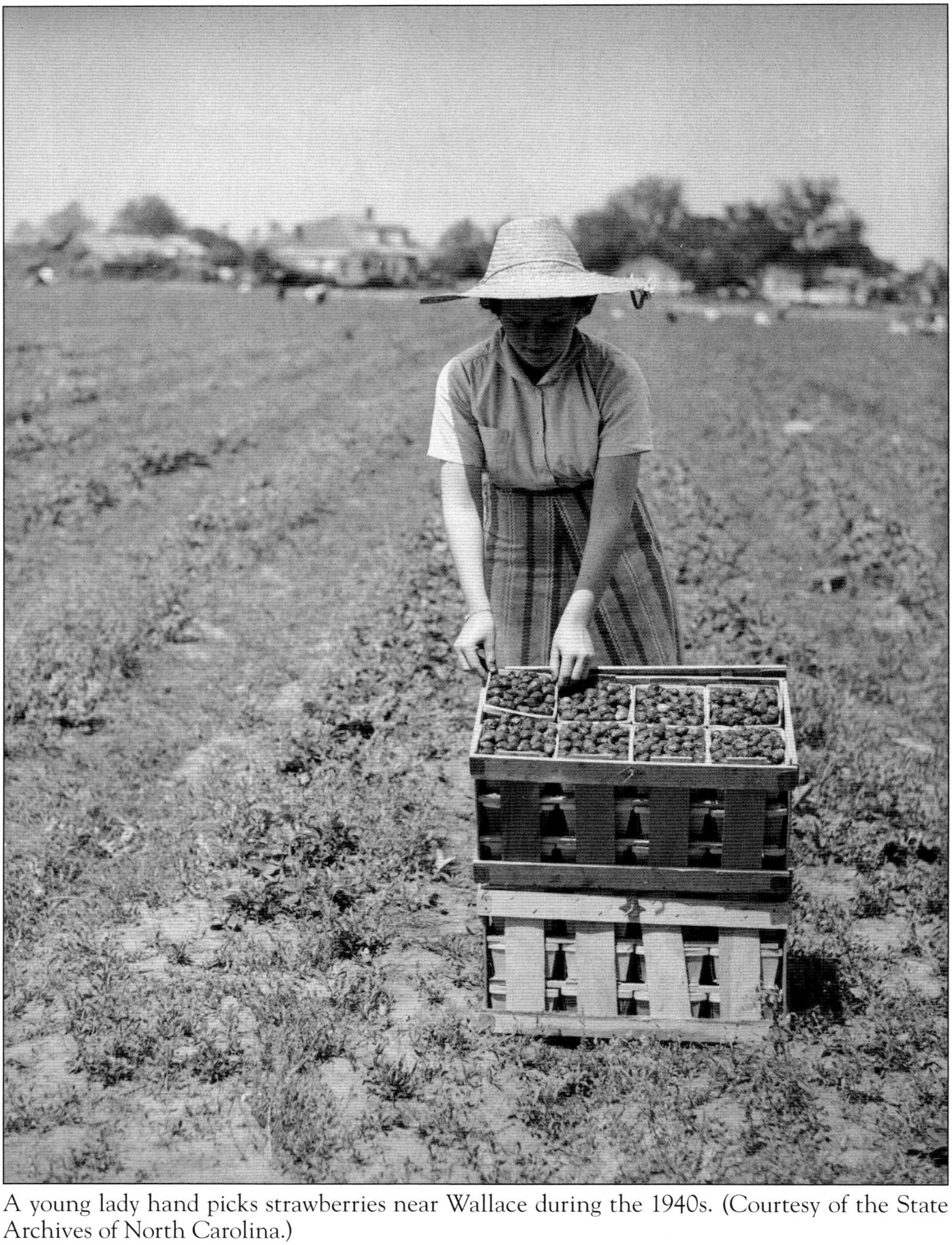

A young lady hand picks strawberries near Wallace during the 1940s. (Courtesy of the State Archives of North Carolina.)

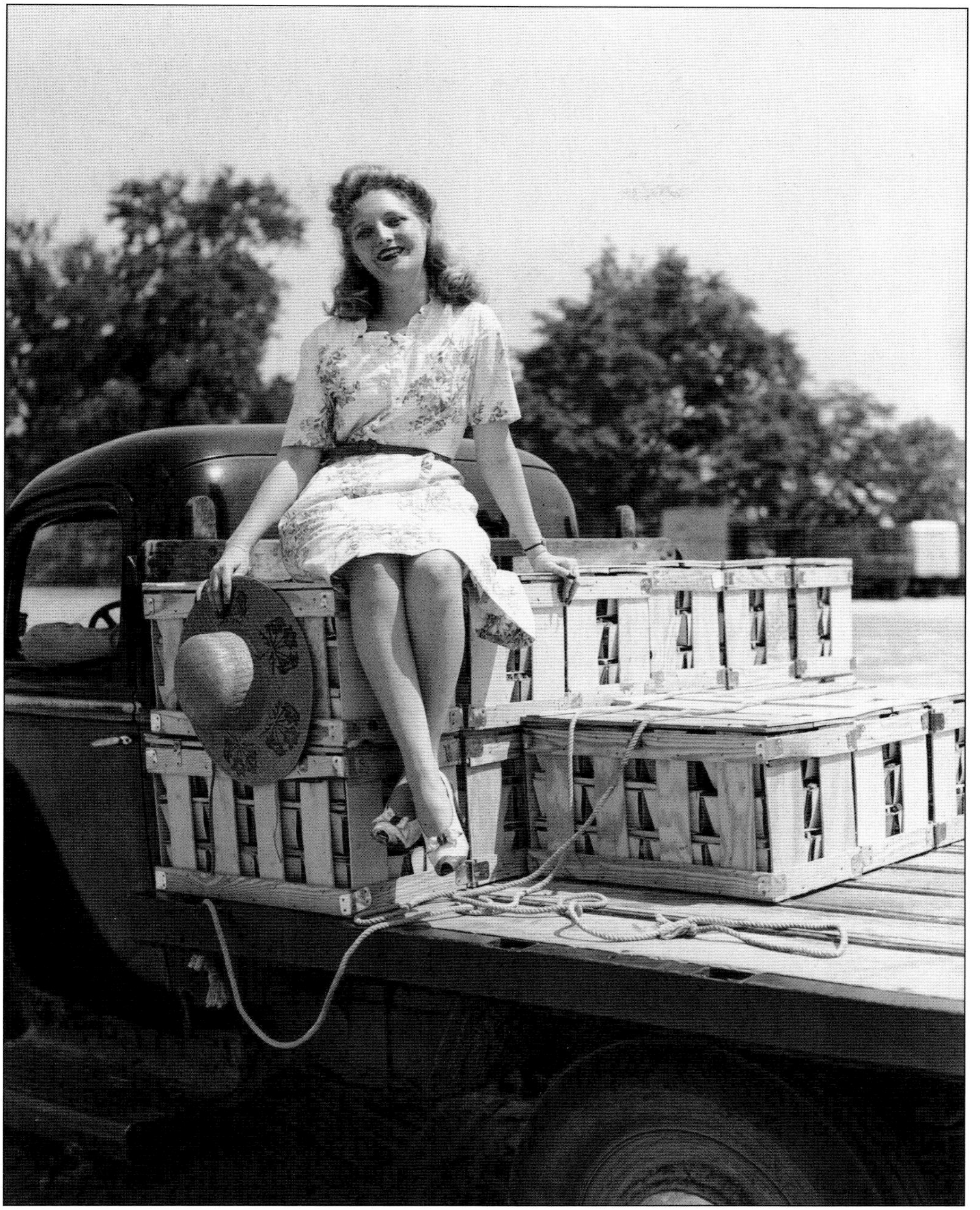

A woman poses on the back of a truck during picking time outside Wallace. Soon, this truck would transport its load of fresh strawberries to local produce sheds to be sold. (Courtesy of the State Archives of North Carolina.)

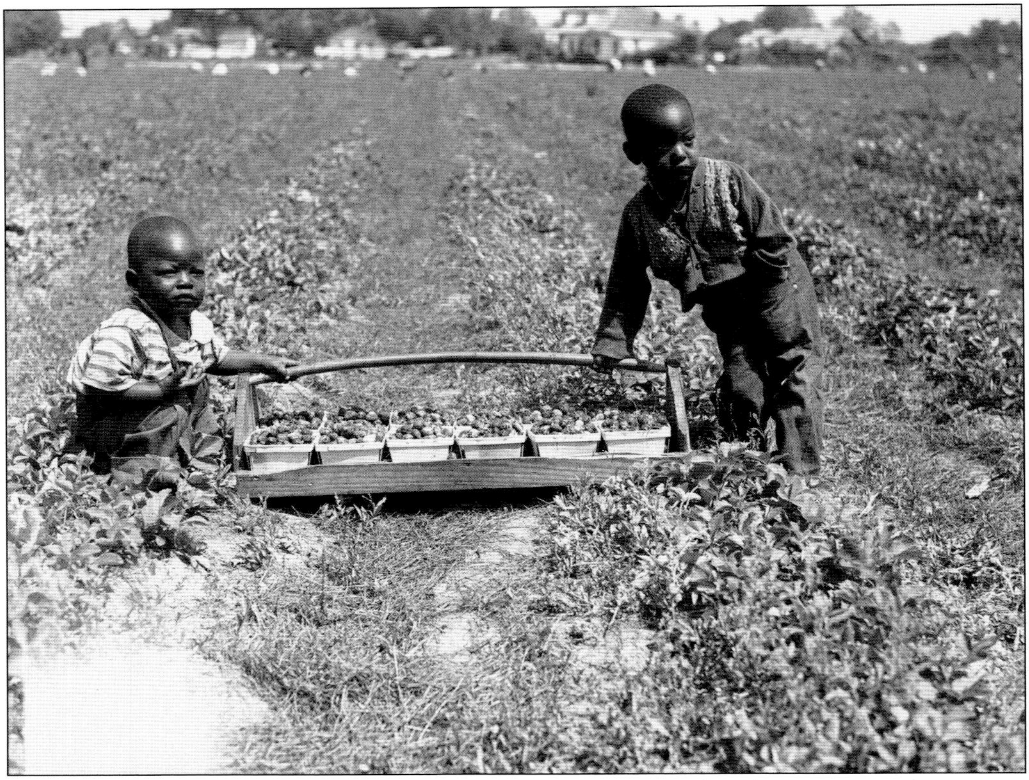

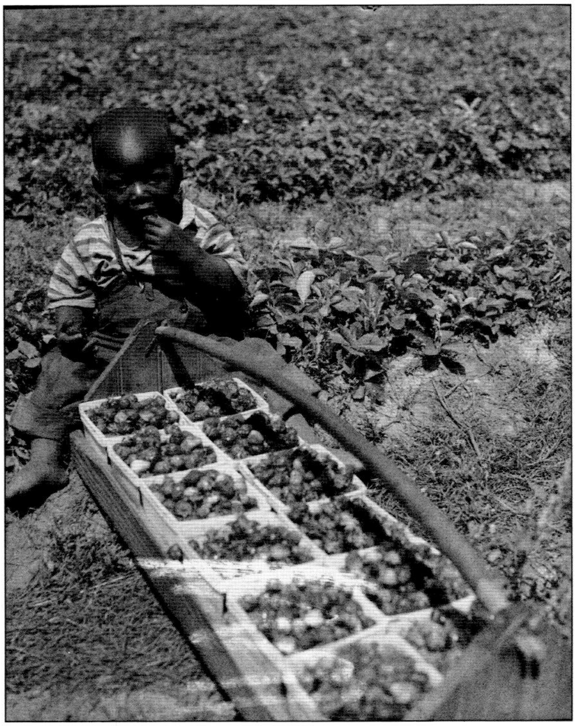

In agricultural communities, it was common for entire families to pitch in during harvest time. Here, two children lend a hand during a strawberry harvest near Wallace. (Courtesy of the State Archives of North Carolina.)

A child samples a strawberry during harvest time outside Wallace around 1940. (Courtesy of the State Archives of North Carolina.)

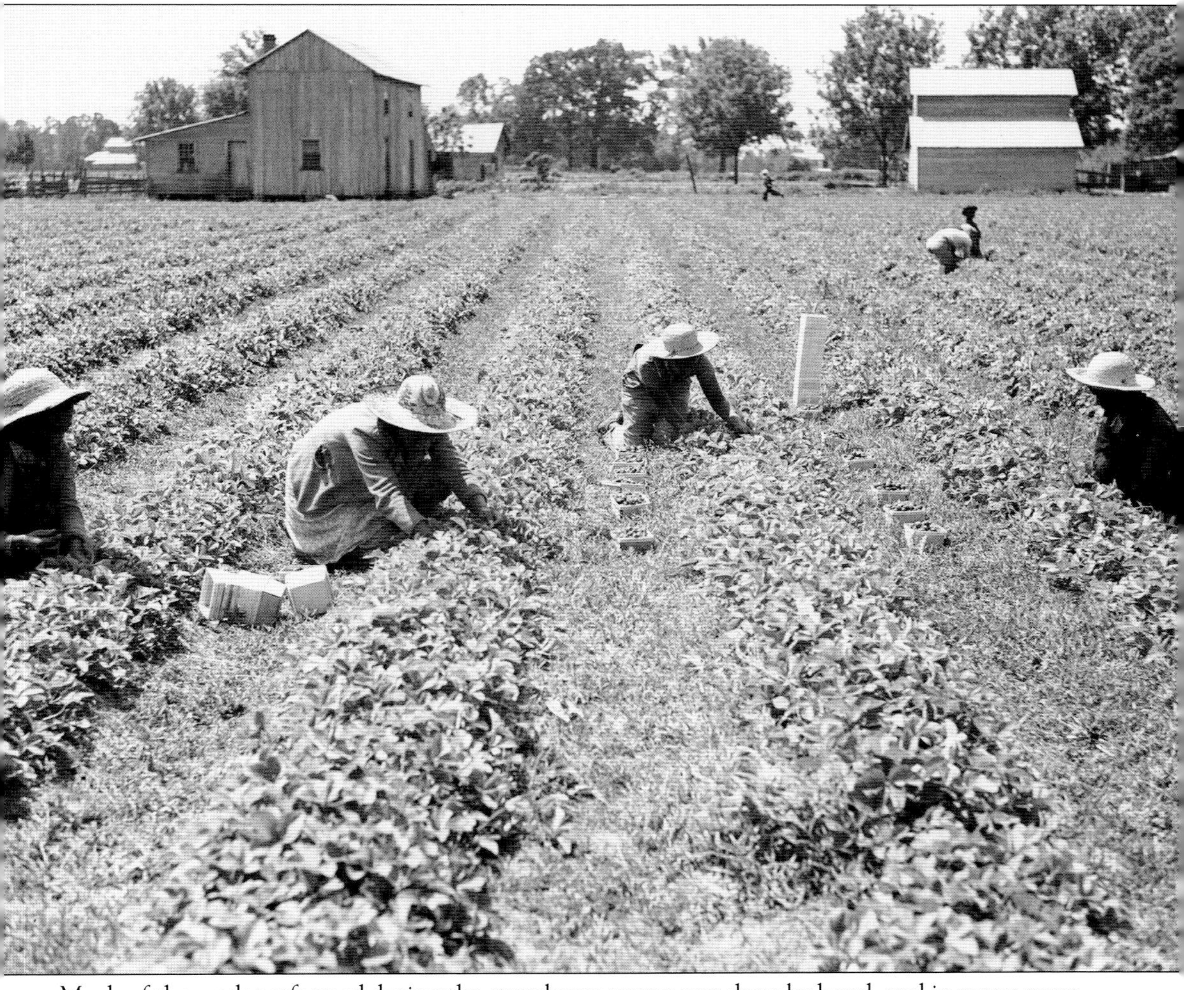

Much of the work performed during the strawberry season was done by hand, and in many cases still is today. Seen here, many of the workers wear wide-brim straw hats to shield them from the sun. (Courtesy of the State Archives of North Carolina.)

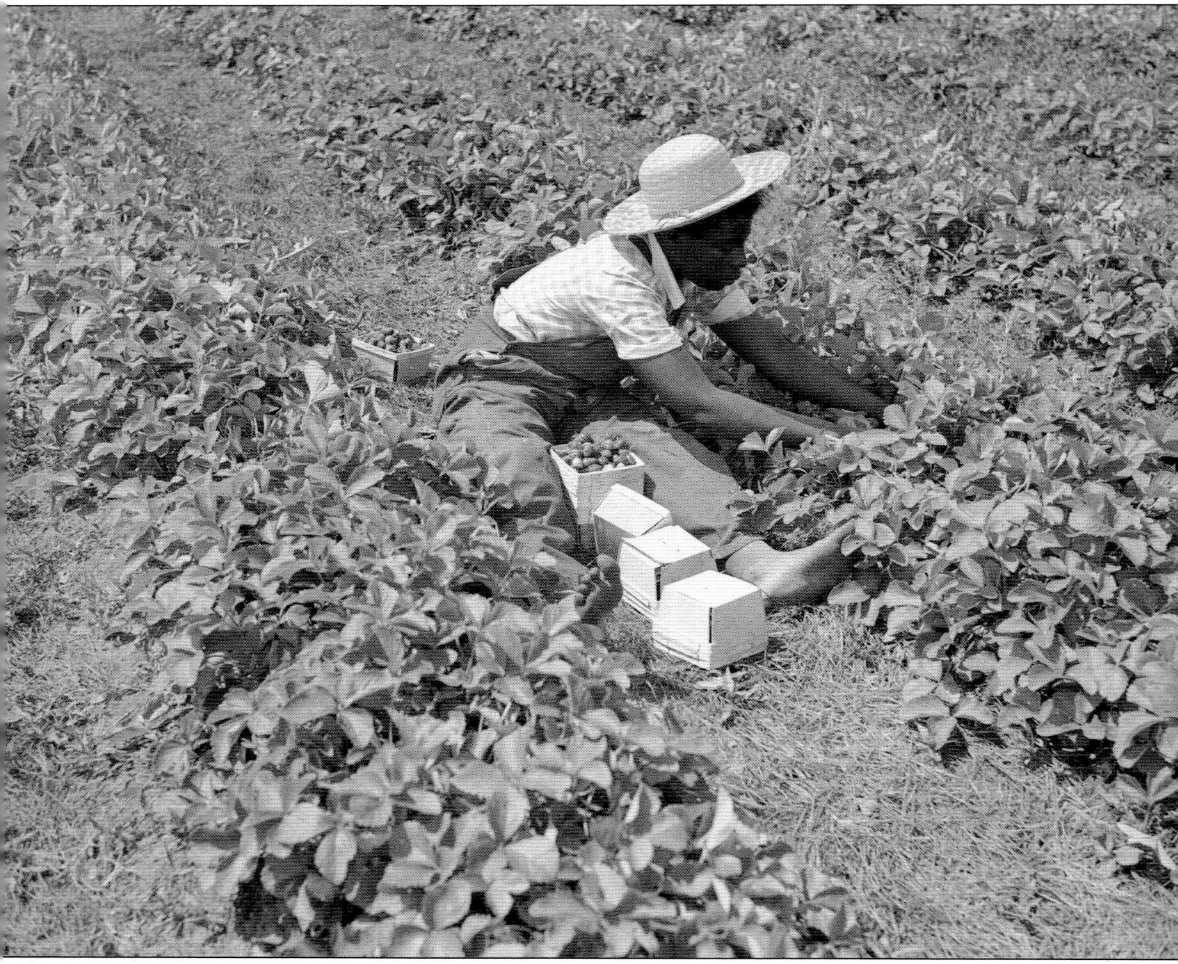

A barefoot teenager works to fill up cartons of strawberries during a harvest near Wallace. (Courtesy of the State Archives of North Carolina.)

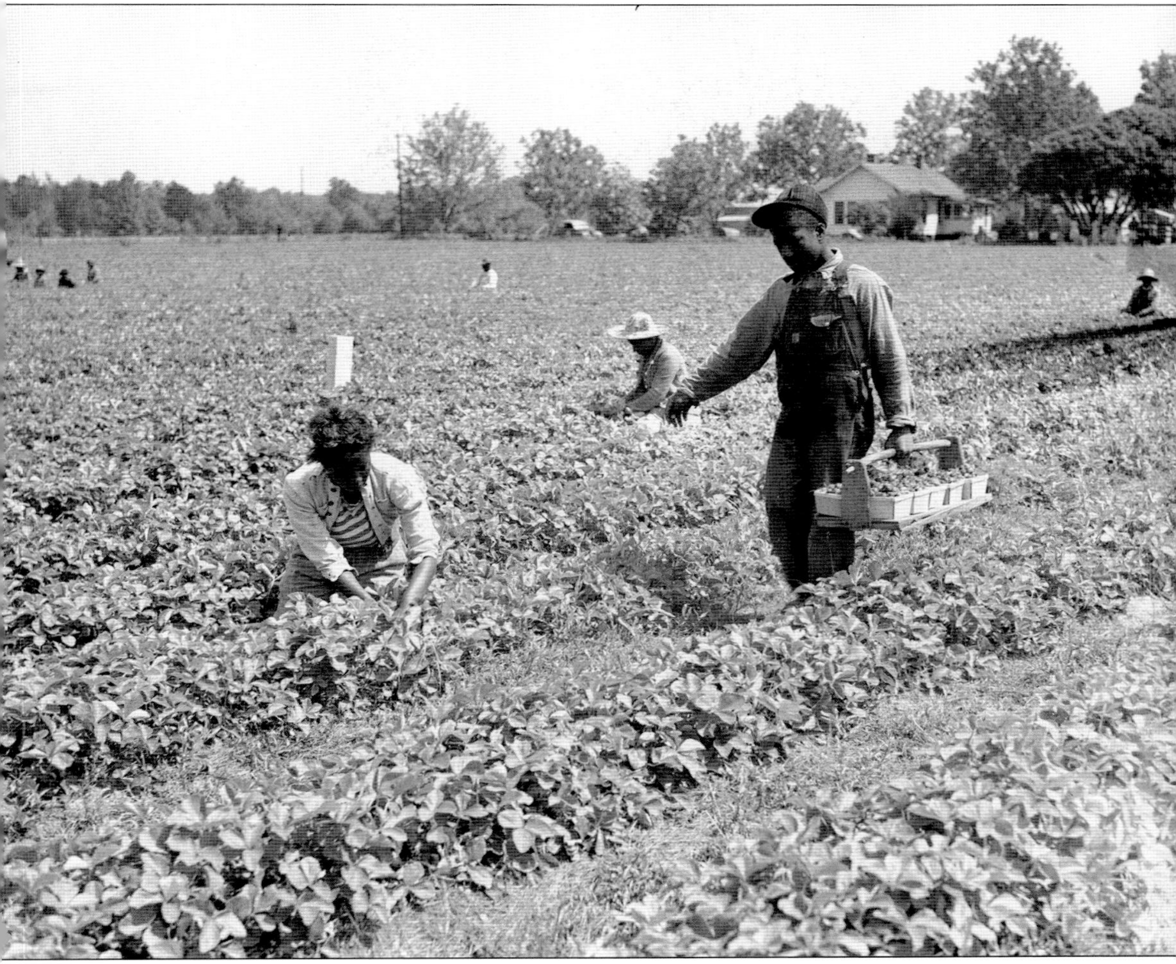

A farm hand uses a carrier to move full cartons of strawberries out of a field. The strawberries would then be sorted and taken to local produce markets to be sold. (Courtesy of the State Archives of North Carolina.)

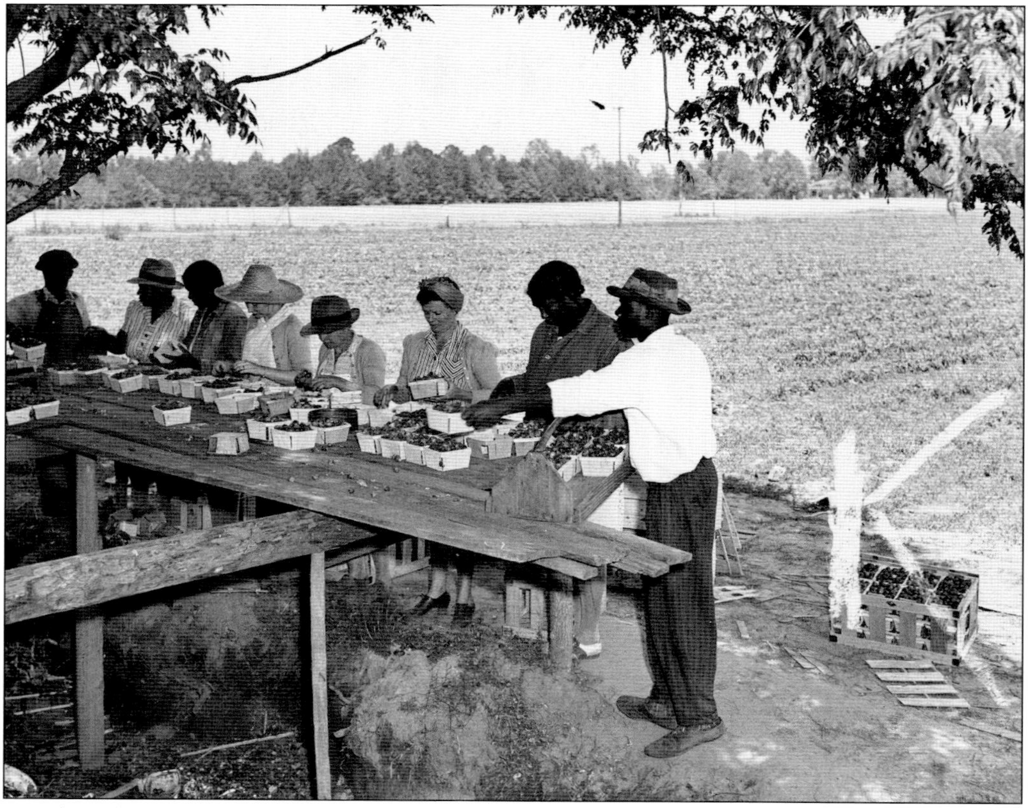

Locals gather under the shade of a tree to sort strawberries in 1944. (Courtesy of the State Archives of North Carolina.)

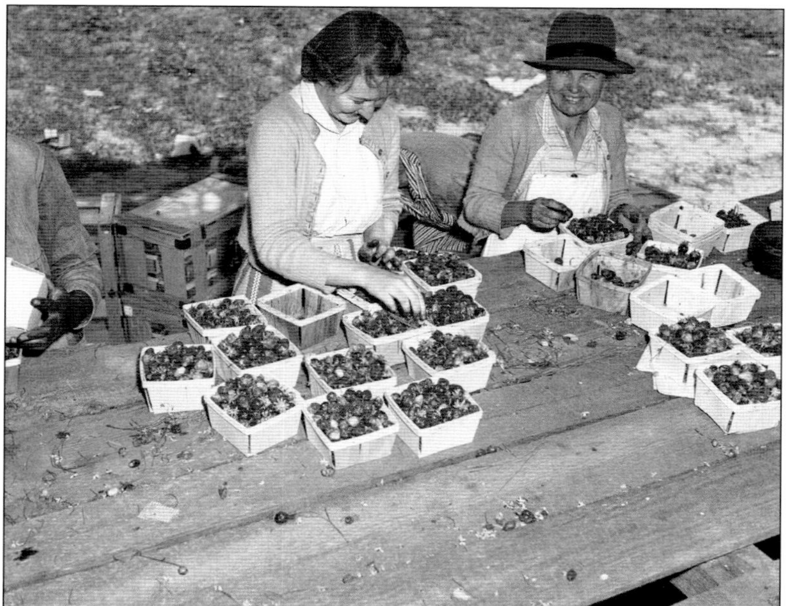

This 1944 photograph shows two women sharing a laugh while sorting strawberries near Wallace. (Courtesy of the State Archives of North Carolina.)

A man takes a closer look at the state of the produce being picked during the strawberry harvest just outside Wallace. (Courtesy of the State Archives of North Carolina.)

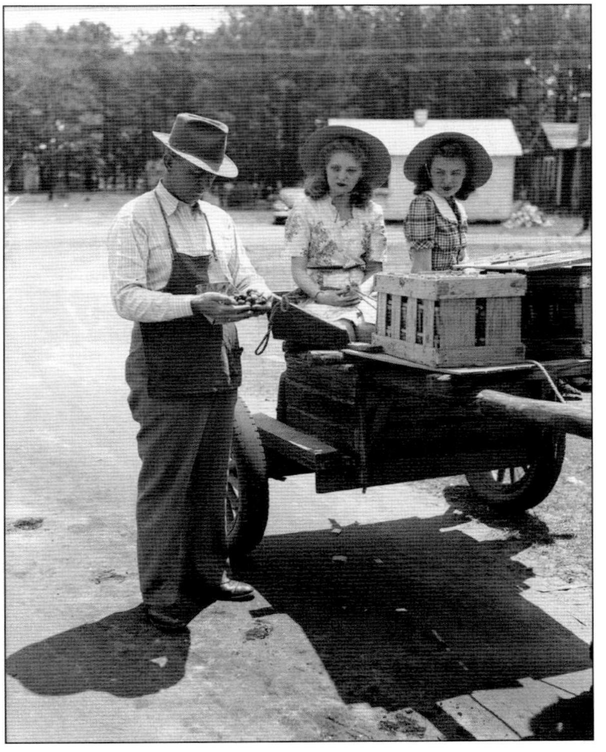

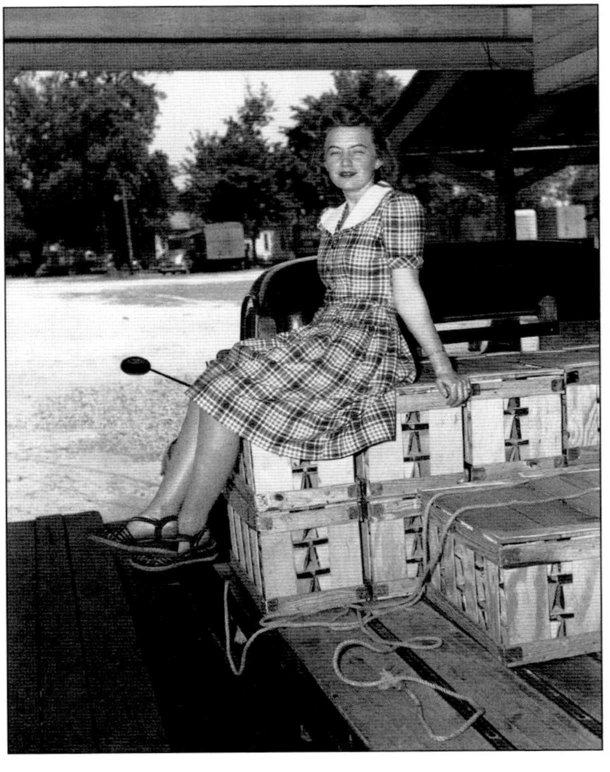

This young lady takes a rest on crates of strawberries under a produce shed prior to an auction. The railroad was essential to the success of Duplin County's strawberry industry. After harvesting the berries, farmers would transport them to the nearest rail town to be sold and shipped to northern markets. (Courtesy of the State Archives of North Carolina.)

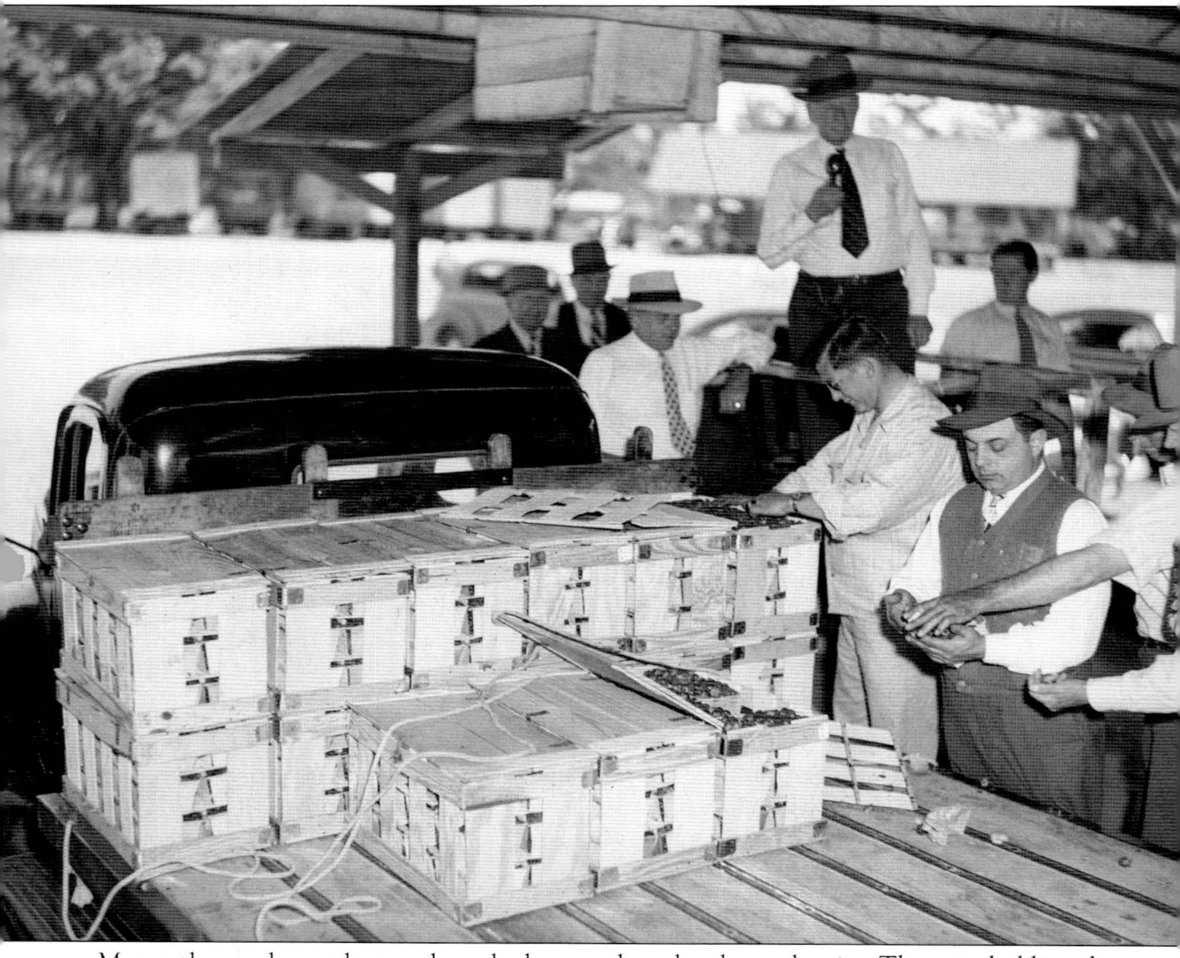

Men gather underneath a produce shed to purchase local strawberries. The man holding the microphone appears to be an auctioneer. This photograph was taken in 1944 in Wallace. (Courtesy of the State Archives of North Carolina.)

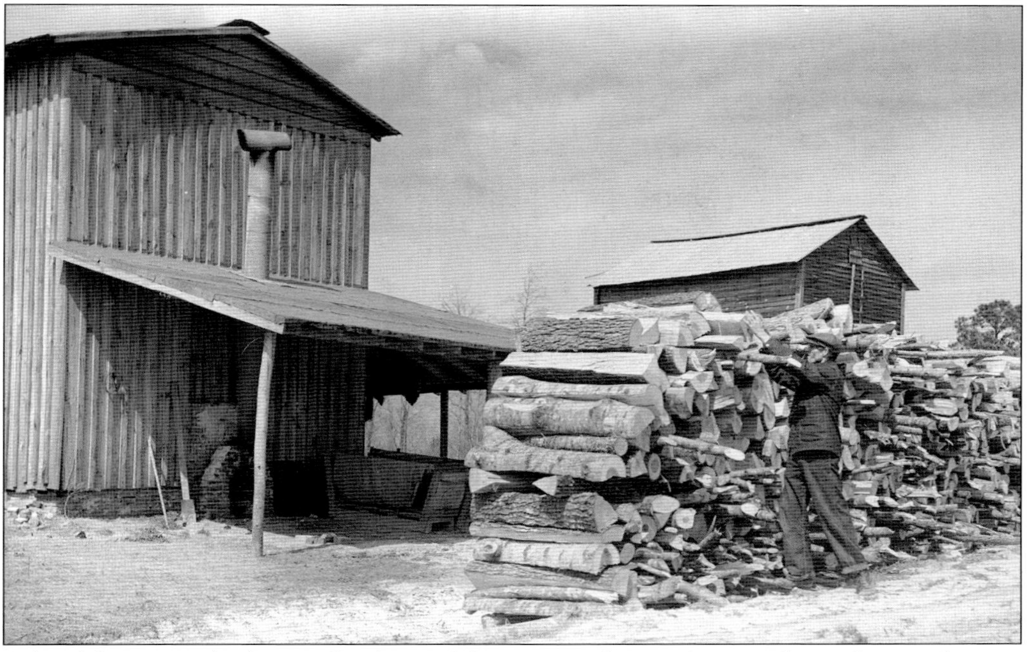

A local farmer stacks firewood to be used for curing tobacco. A somewhat tedious task, once hung in the barn, the tobacco leaves need to be heated at a consistent temperature. At times, this would require workers to spend the night at the tobacco barn to manage the fire. (Courtesy of the State Archives of North Carolina.)

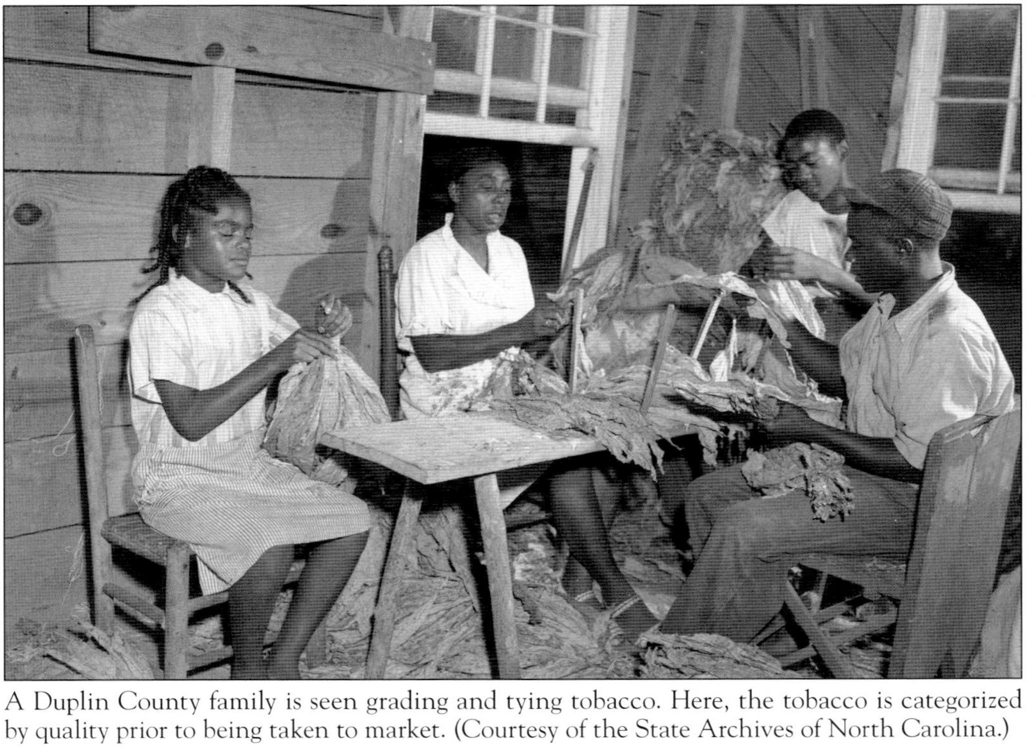

A Duplin County family is seen grading and tying tobacco. Here, the tobacco is categorized by quality prior to being taken to market. (Courtesy of the State Archives of North Carolina.)

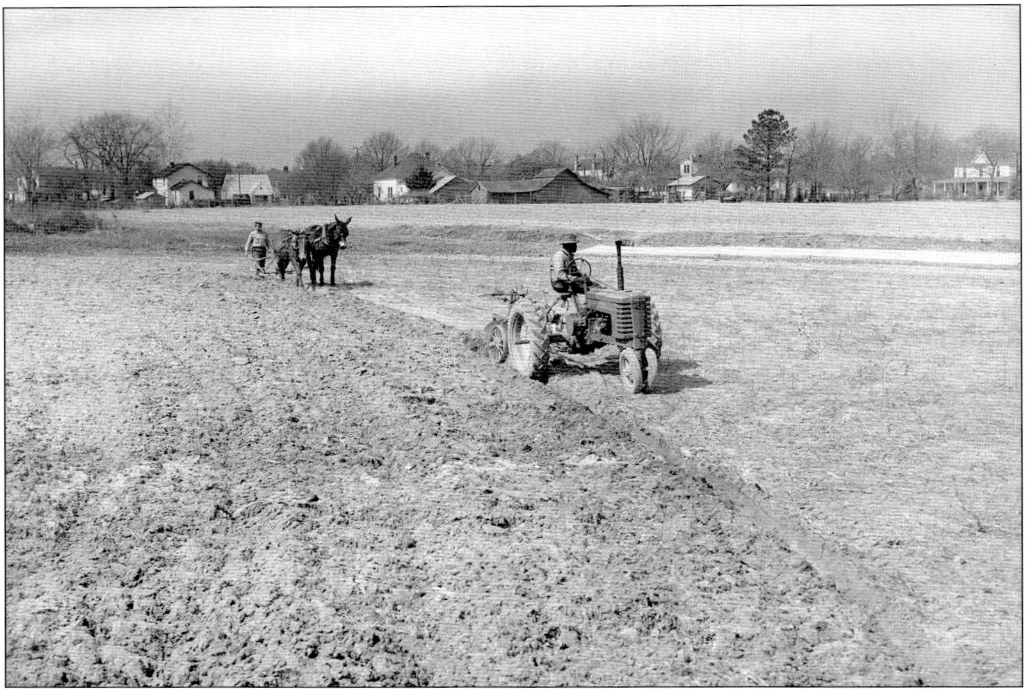

The future of agriculture meets the past as a tractor tills land near a mule-drawn plow on the farm of Lee Tucker outside Warsaw. (Courtesy of the State Archives of North Carolina.)

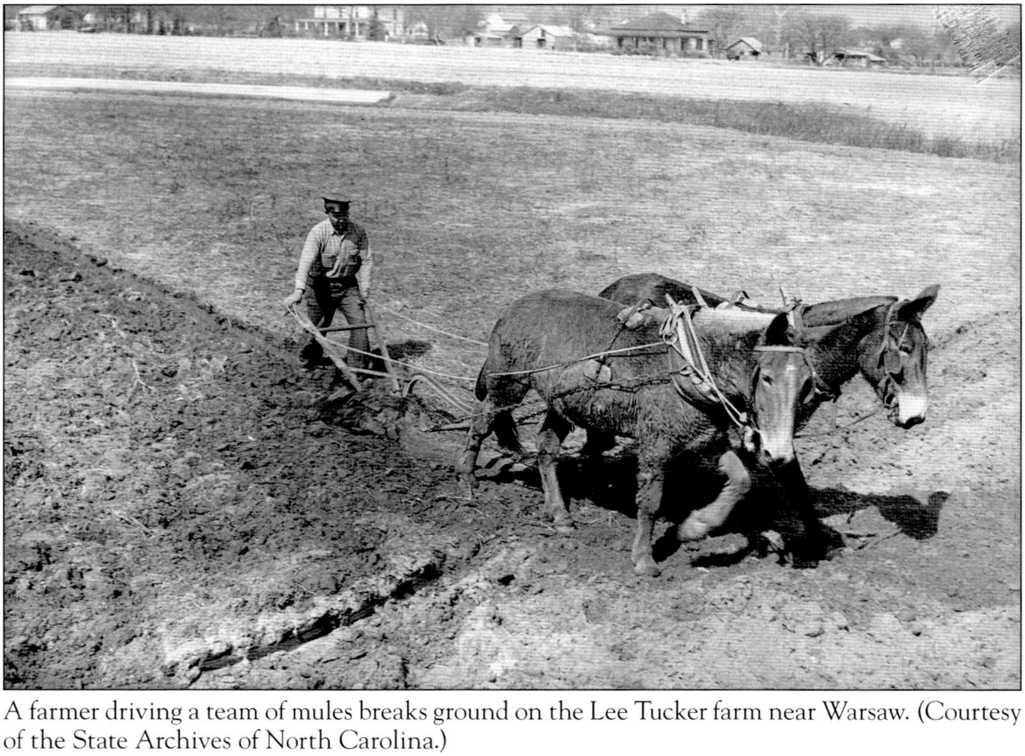

A farmer driving a team of mules breaks ground on the Lee Tucker farm near Warsaw. (Courtesy of the State Archives of North Carolina.)

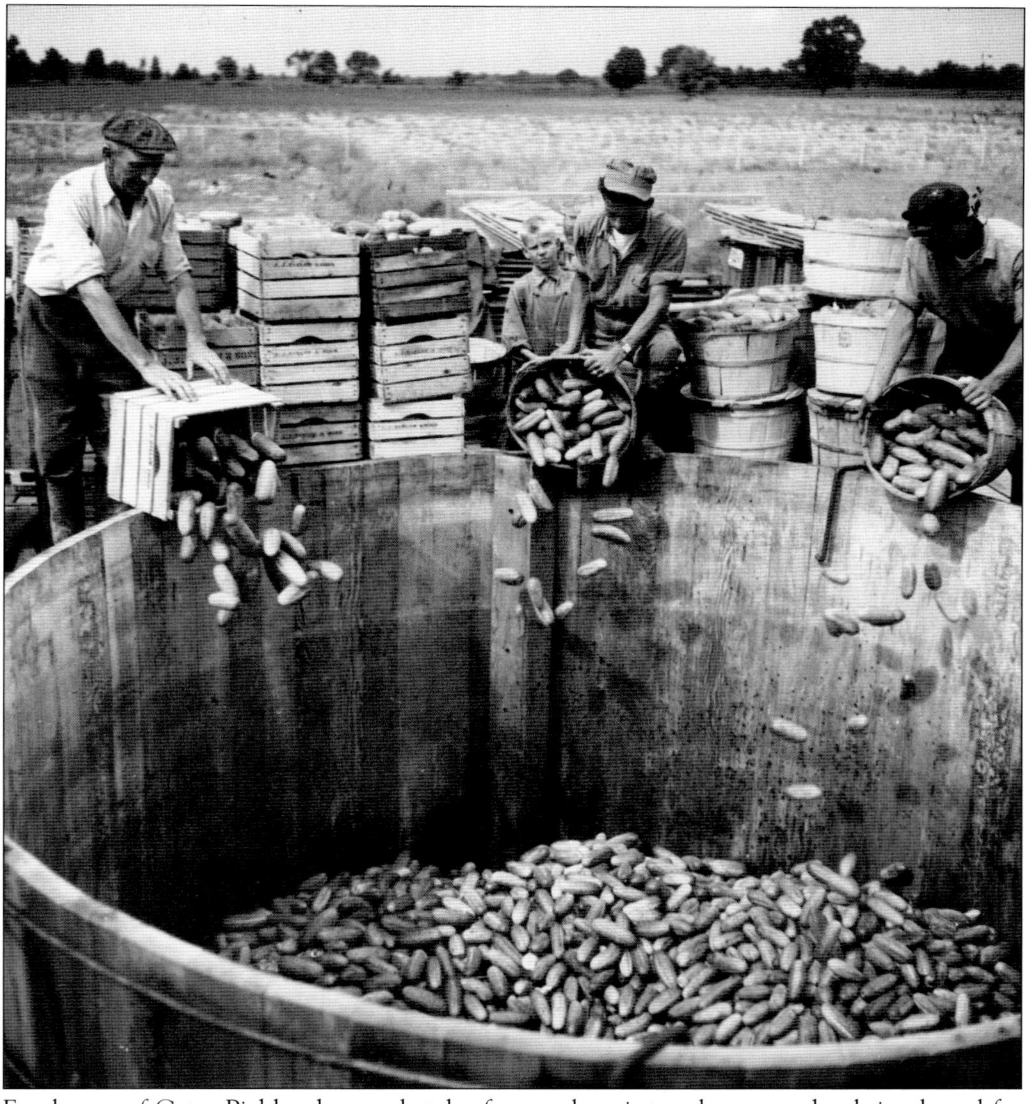

Employees of Cates Pickles dump a batch of cucumbers into a large wooden brine barrel for pickling during the 1940s. Charles F. Cates and Sons Inc. opened its Faison-based pickle plant in 1929. (Courtesy of the Faison Museum.)

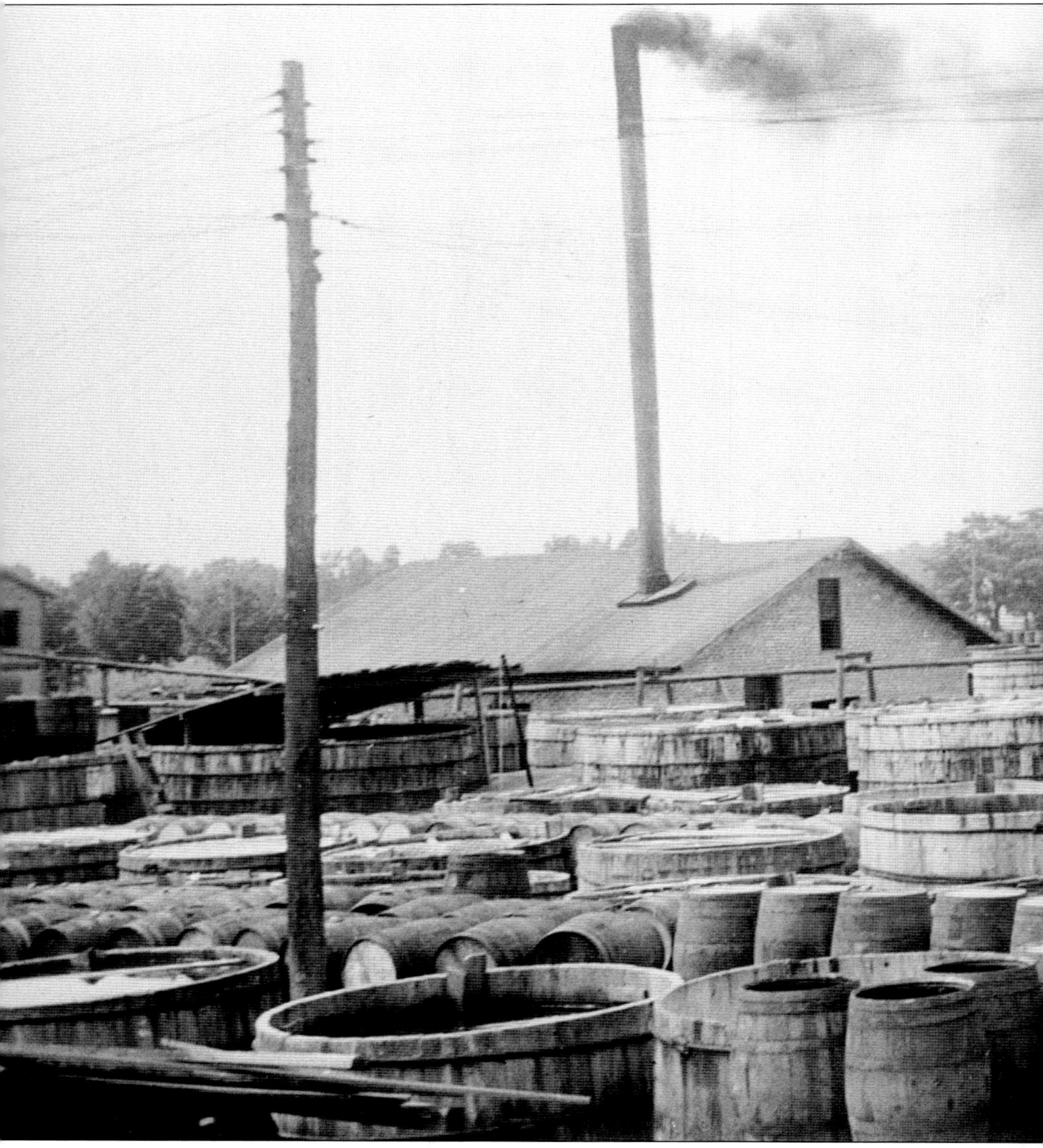

A stockpile of barrels is seen outside the Cates Pickles plant in Faison during the 1940s. Note

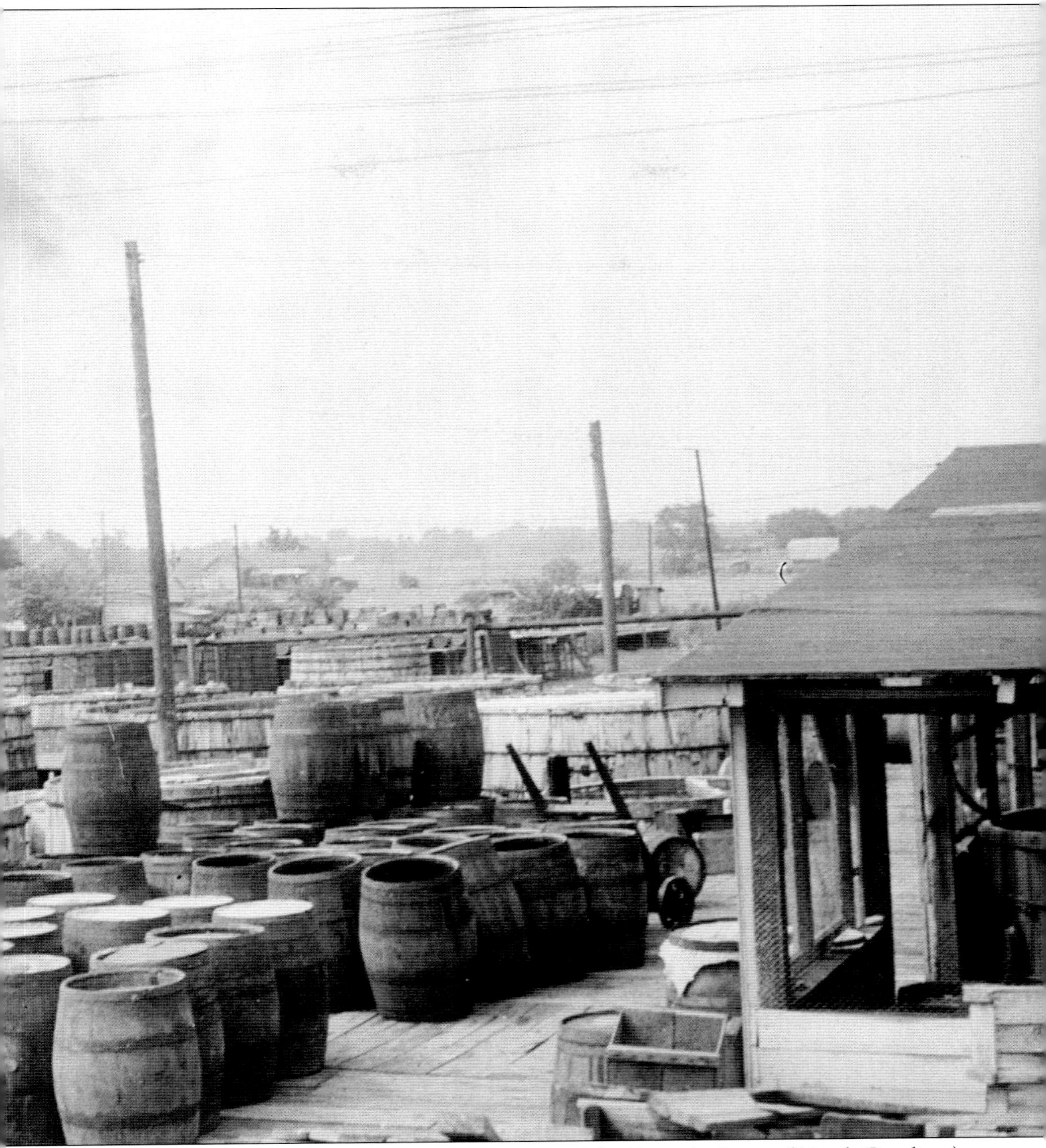

the large brining vats in the background. (Courtesy of the State Archives of North Carolina.)

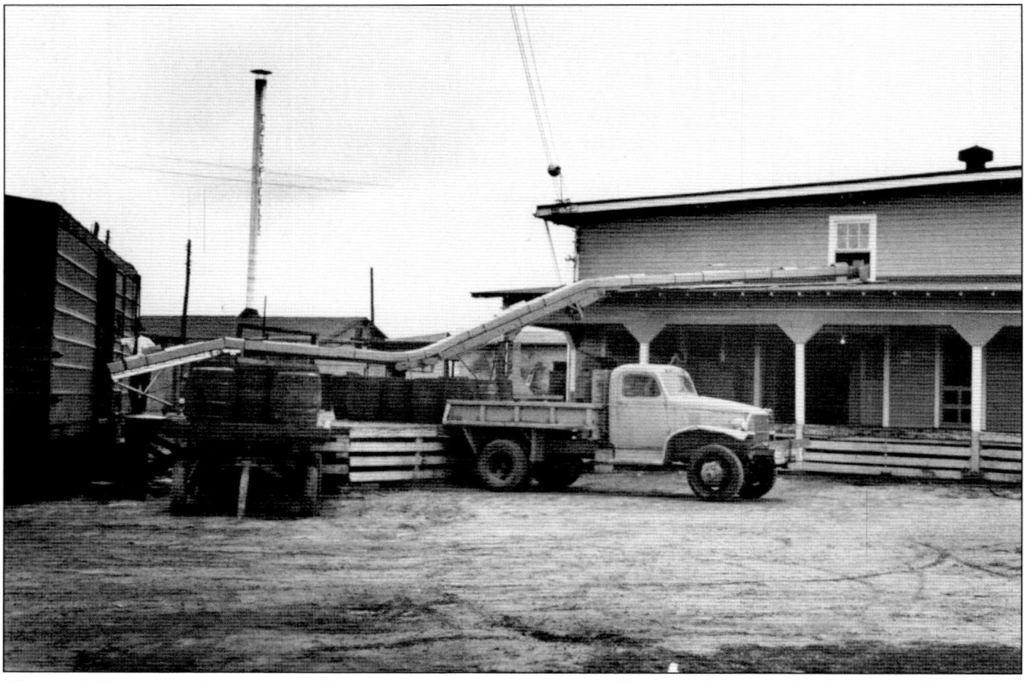

Cases of Cates products make their way down a conveyor belt into a boxcar for shipping. (Courtesy of the Faison Museum.)

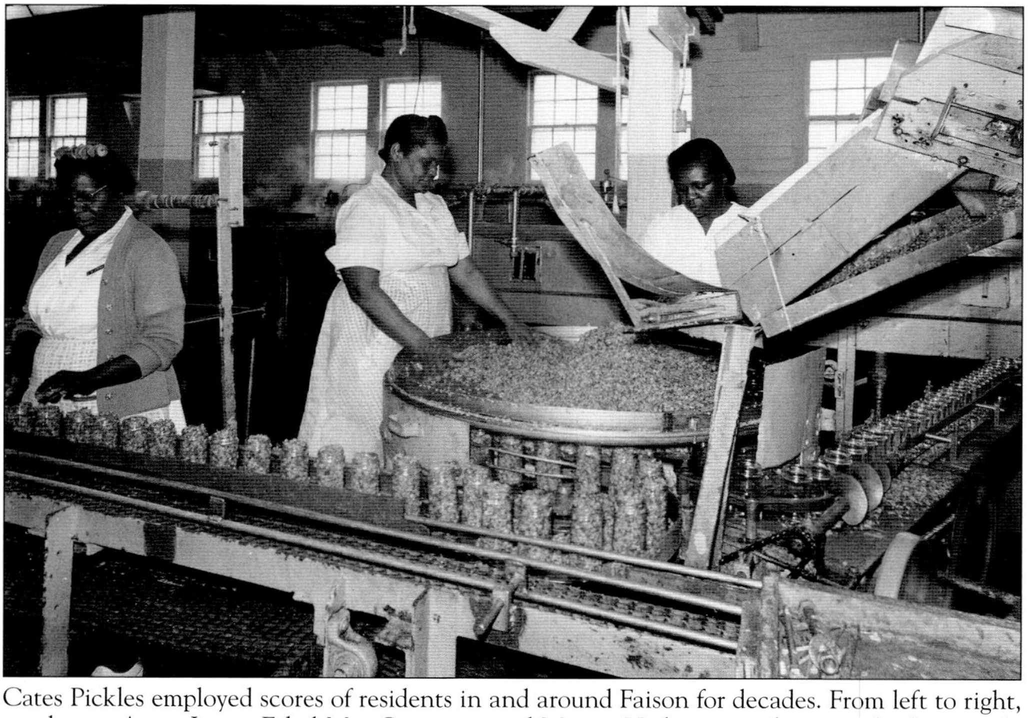

Cates Pickles employed scores of residents in and around Faison for decades. From left to right, employees Anna Jones, Ethel Mae Sampson, and Mamie Hicks are working on the line inside the Cates Pickles plant. (Courtesy of the Faison Museum.)

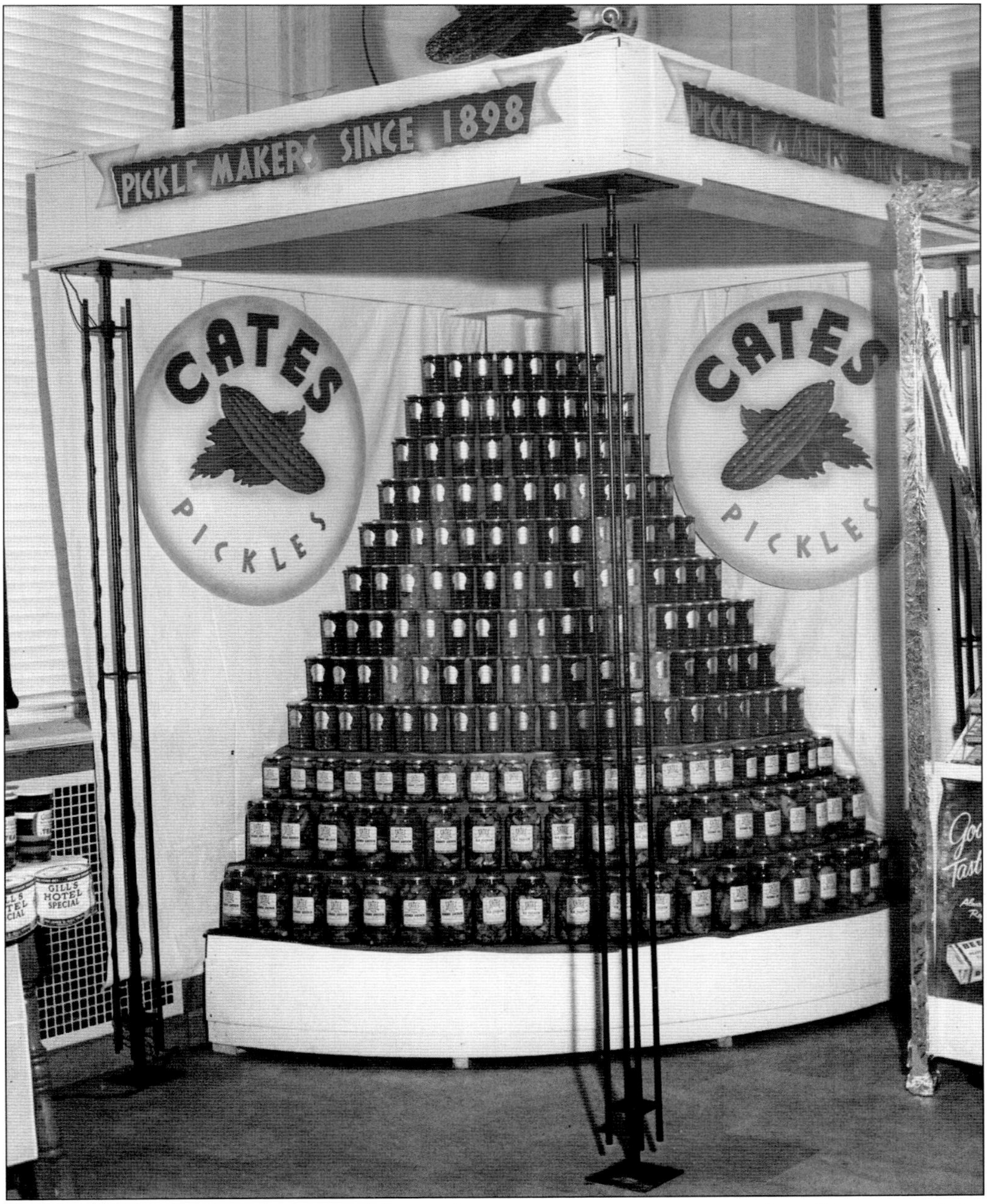

This elaborate display of Cates Pickles products was set up in a supermarket. (Courtesy of the Faison Museum.)

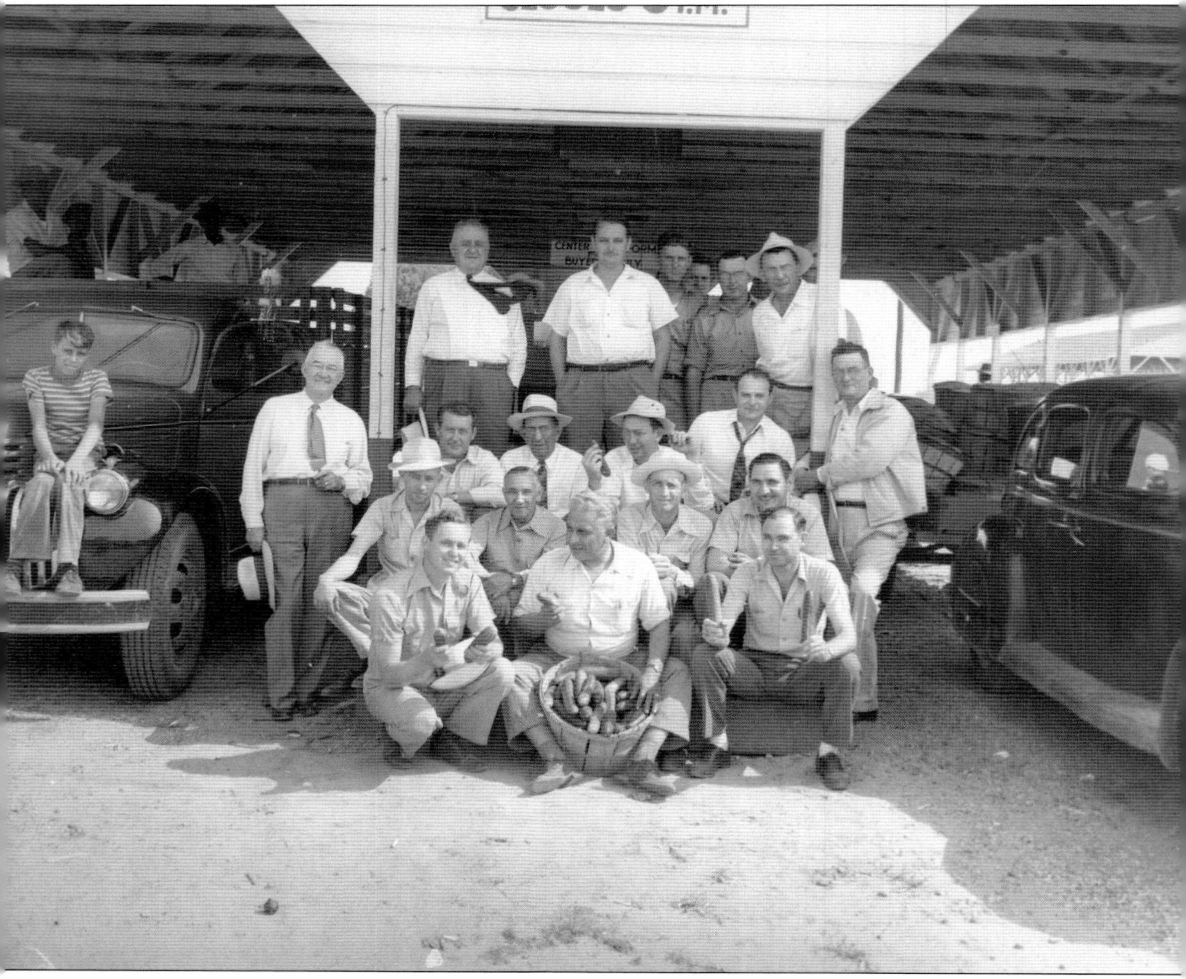

Locals pose with the community's cash crop at Faison's produce market in 1947. From left to right are (first row) unidentified, George Joseph, and Chester Ellis; (second row) Ralph Precythe, Ross Vacaro, and two unidentified; (third row) Buster Precythe (sitting on truck), Joe King (standing beside truck), two unidentified, Harold Precythe, Durwood Clifton, and Charles Lee (holding pole). The others are unidentified. (Courtesy of the Faison Museum.)

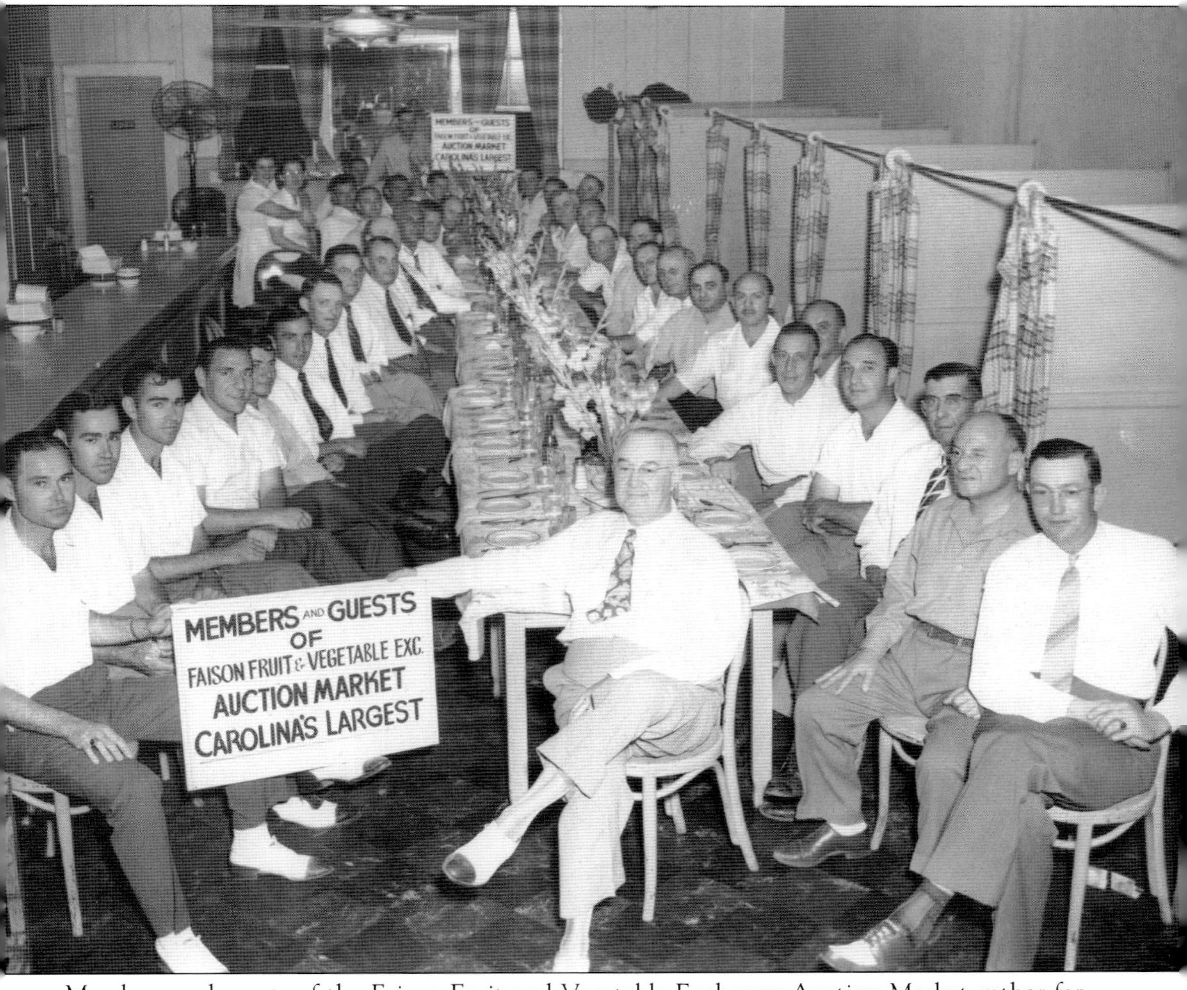

Members and guests of the Faison Fruit and Vegetable Exchange Auction Market gather for what appears to be a dinner event. The sign by the tables boasts that their market is "Carolina's Largest." (Courtesy of the Mount Olive Area Historical Society.)

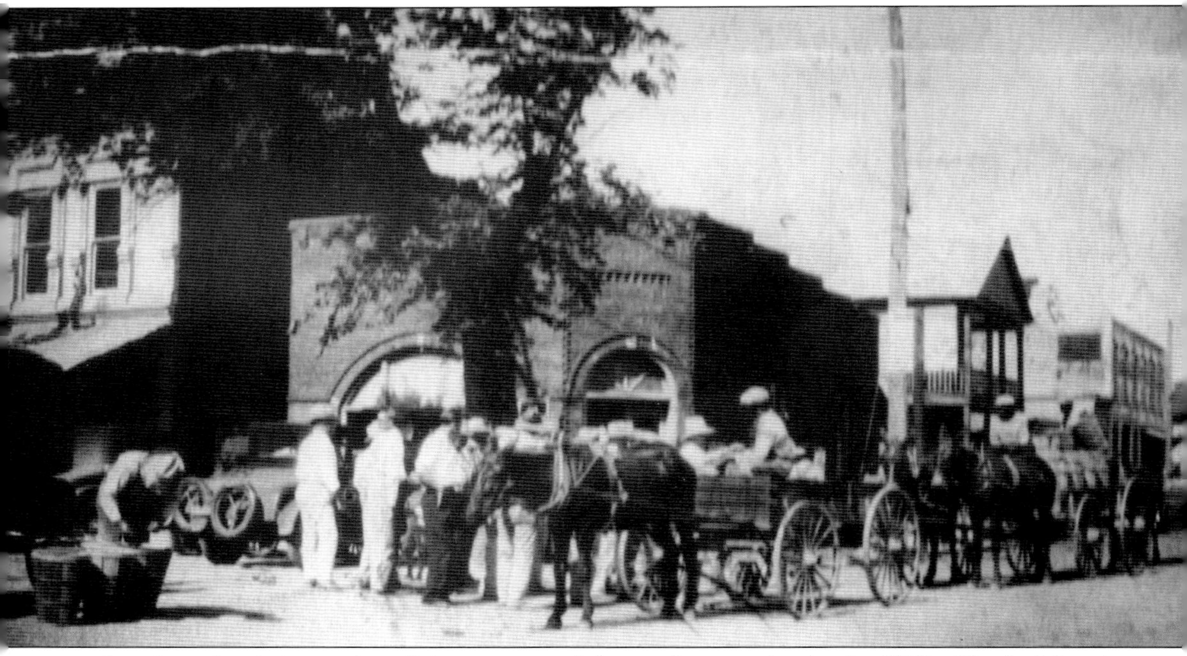

Locals make their way into Faison to attend the produce market in the 1930s. The building in the background was the Bank of Faison. (Courtesy of the Faison Museum.)

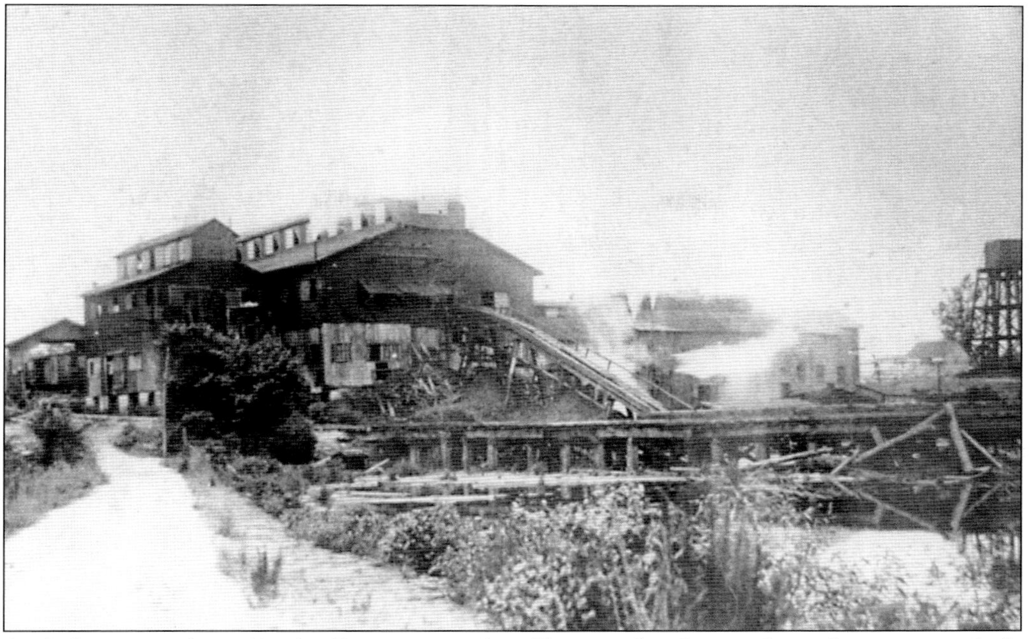

Aside from agriculture, Duplin County once played host to a bustling timber industry, particularly during the late 19th and early 20th centuries. Here is an early photograph of the Rowland Lumber Company in Bowdens. It was one of several timber companies that sprang up in Duplin County near the end of the 1800s. Others included the Hilton Lumber Company, Norfolk Lumber Company, and Enterprise Lumber Company. (Courtesy of Leon Sikes.)

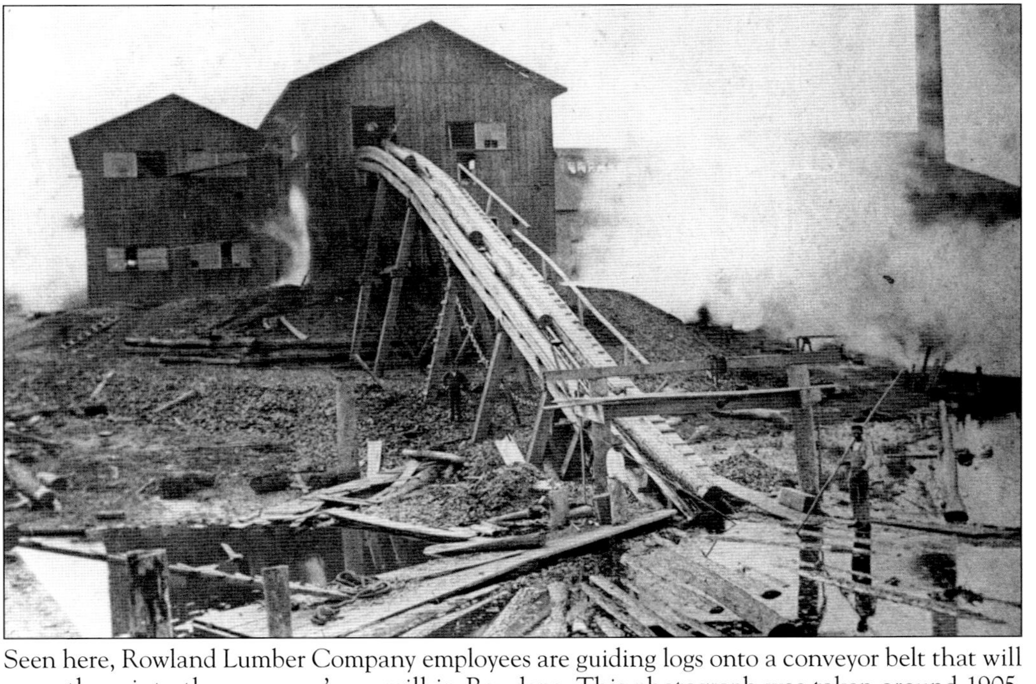

Seen here, Rowland Lumber Company employees are guiding logs onto a conveyor belt that will carry them into the company's sawmill in Bowdens. This photograph was taken around 1905. (Courtesy of Leon Sikes.)

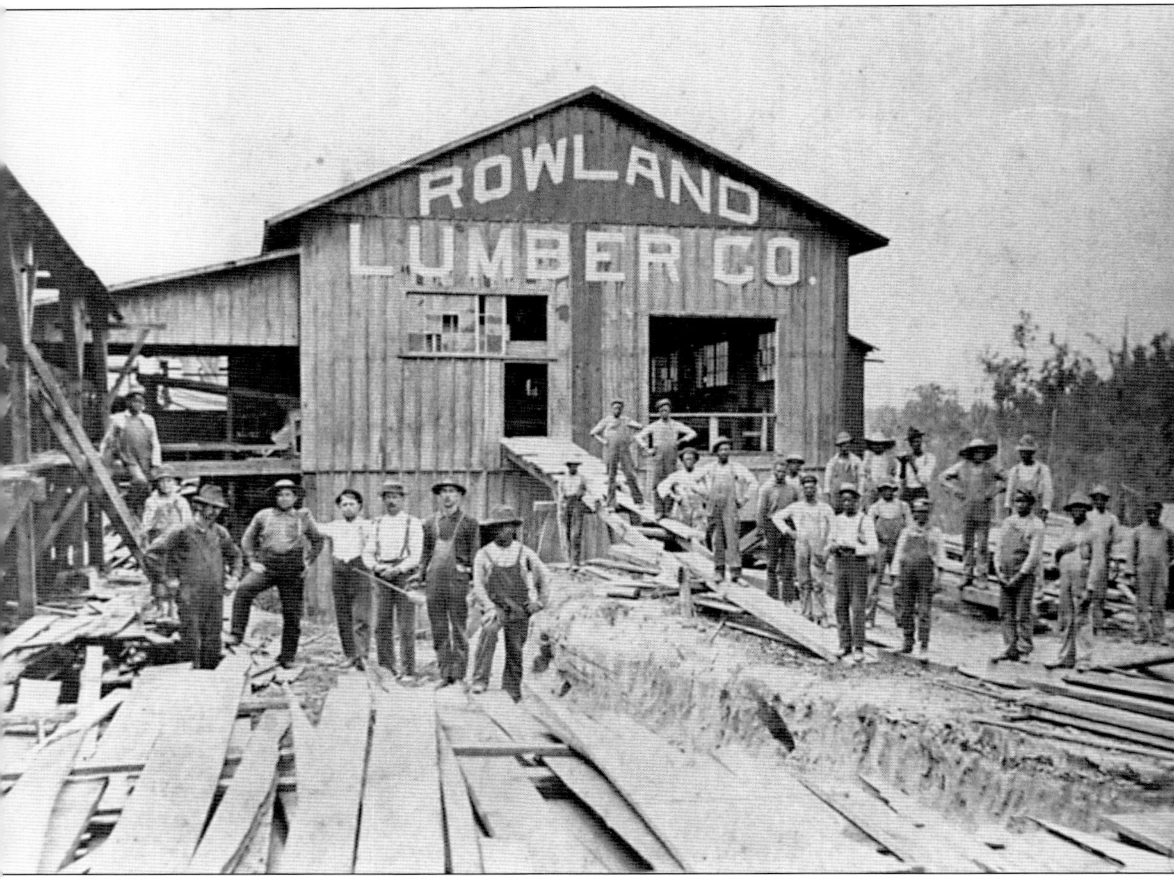

Workers pose for a photograph outside of the Rowland Lumber Company around 1905. The sixth man from the left is believed to be company foreman Daniel Barrs. (Courtesy of Leon Sikes.)

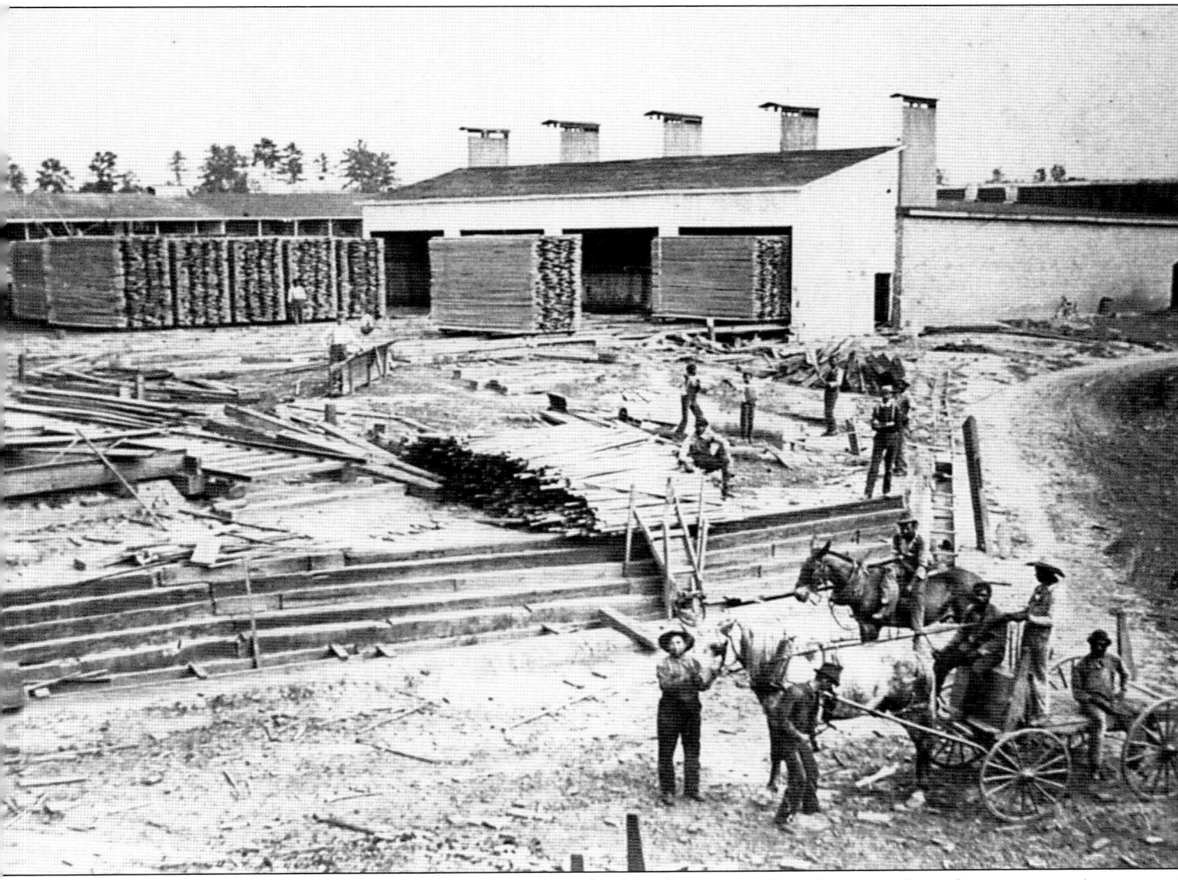

Rowland Lumber Company employees, along with their horses and mules, stand in the company's lumberyard around 1905. Note the large stacks of lumber in the background. (Courtesy of Leon Sikes.)

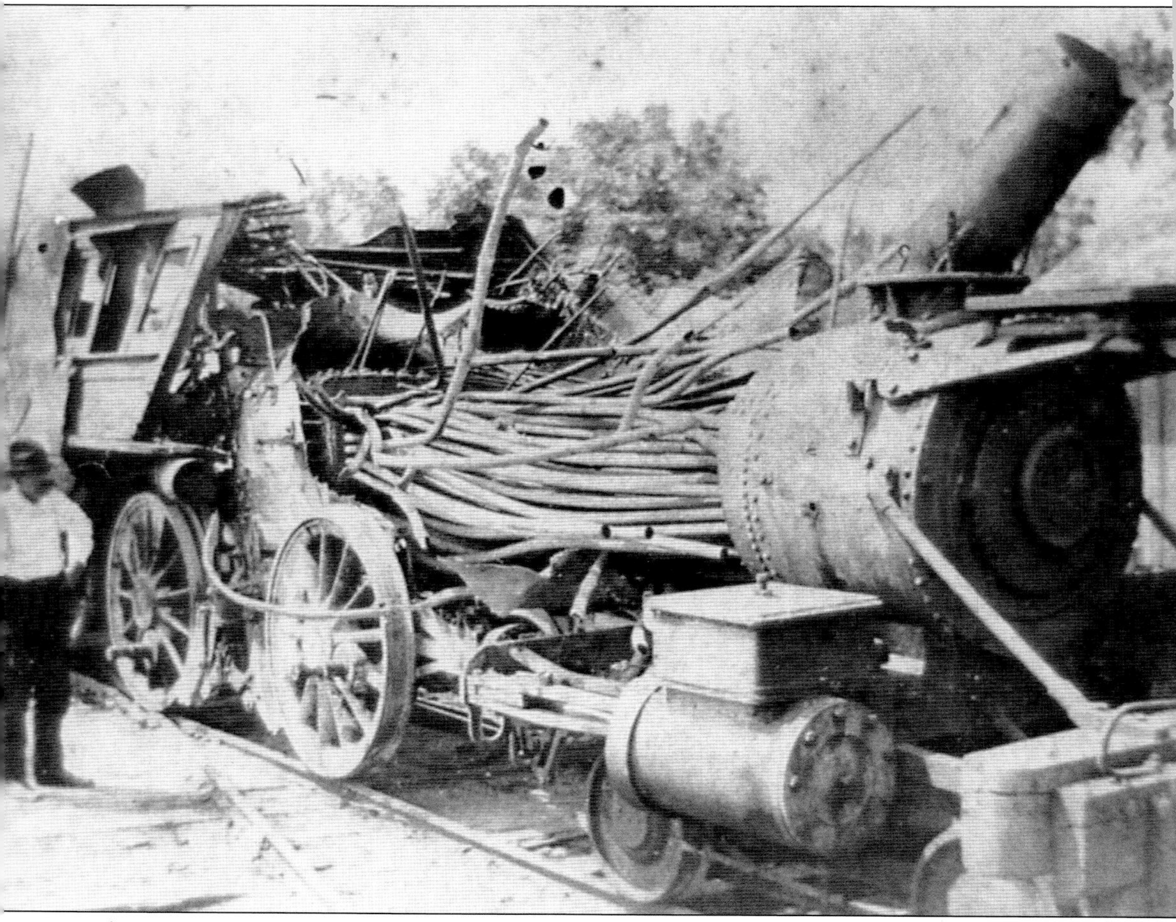

Like its produce industry, Duplin's timber industry depended on a network of rail lines for transportation. Low on water, this Rowland Timber Company train engine exploded in 1909. (Courtesy of Leon Sikes.)

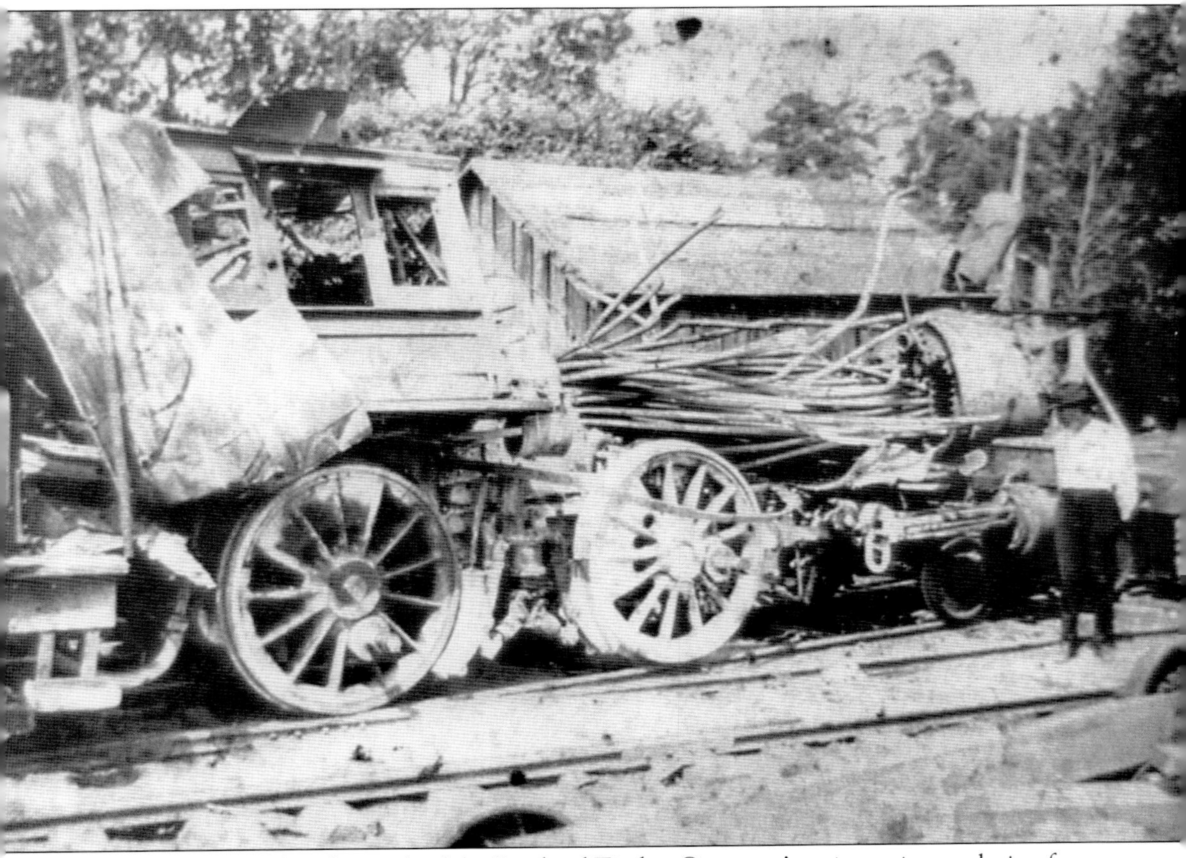

This image shows the aftermath of the Rowland Timber Company's train engine explosion from a different angle. (Courtesy of Leon Sikes.)

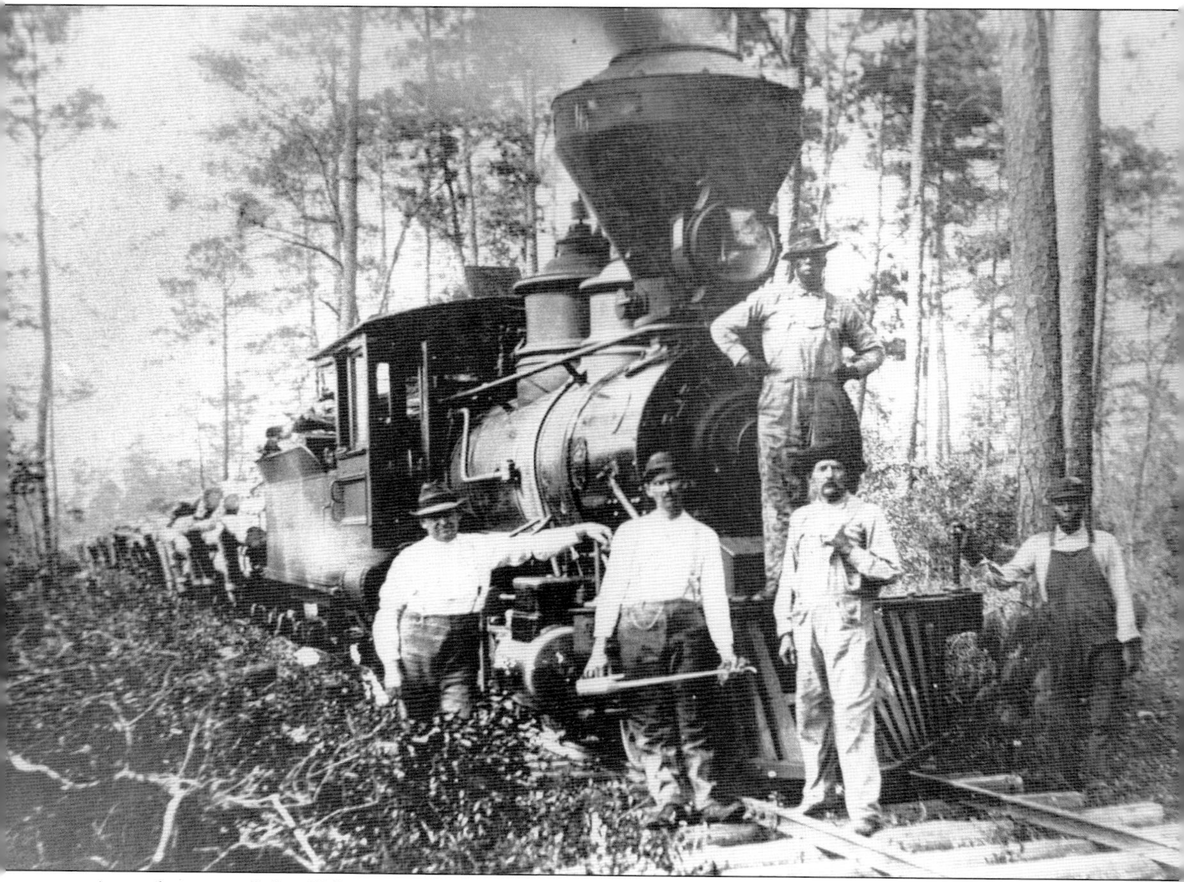

A work crew of the Hilton Lumber Company pauses for a photograph on its train engine near Wallace. The company had set up shop in the town during the early 1900s and based its commissary and machine shop there. (Courtesy of Leon Sikes.)

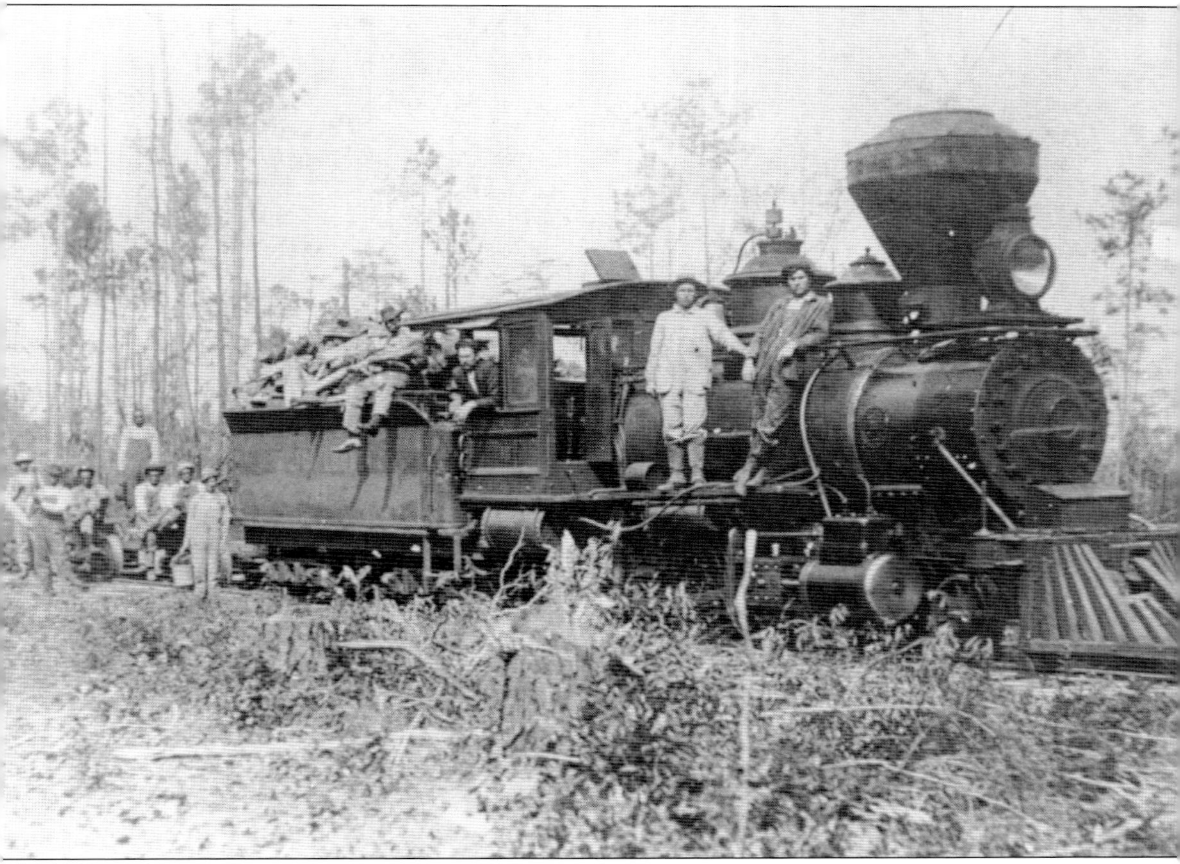

The Hilton Lumber Company laid a network of narrow-gauge rail lines between Chinquapin and Wallace to help transport timber out of Duplin County. Employees of the company are seen with its train outside Wallace. (Courtesy of Leon Sikes.)

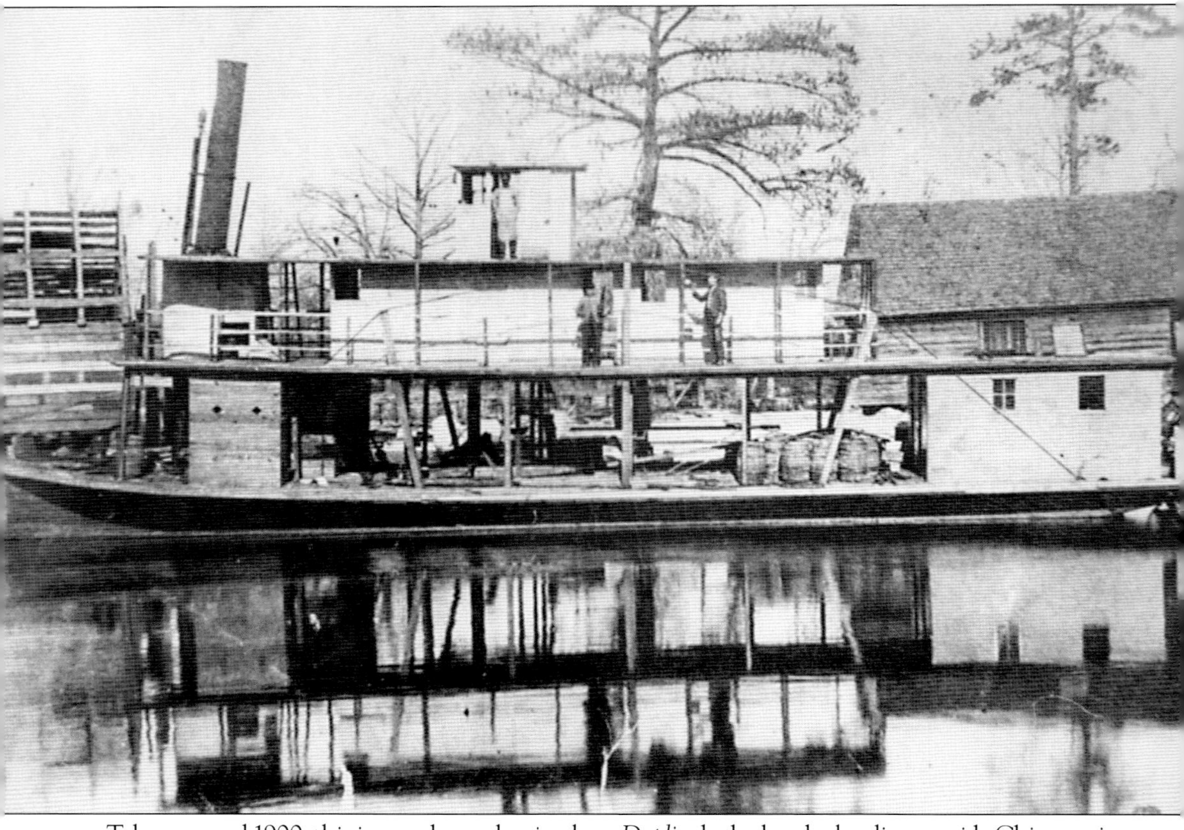

Taken around 1900, this image shows the riverboat *Duplin* docked at the landing outside Chinquapin. Operated by captain and pilot Jeff Stokes, the *Duplin* navigated the Northeast Cape Fear River between Chinquapin and Wilmington hauling freight and agricultural supplies. The increased use of trucks and railroad cars for transporting goods helped bring an end to riverboat transport in Duplin County. (Courtesy of Leon Sikes.)

Three

Friends and Neighbors

From the battlefields of Gettysburg to the grand expanse of outer space, history books often relate tales of heroic deeds performed by remarkable people.

History itself is made by individuals. It is composed of people from towns like Rose Hill, Kenansville, and Faison or communities like Greenevers and Beautancus. Through the years, Duplin County has been home to war heroes, astronauts, revolutionaries, riverboat pilots, and educators—people who have made their way into the pages of history.

Duplin County has also been home to another group of important residents who, despite not making it into the history books, played an important role. These people were teachers, mayors, shopkeepers, coaches, and grandparents. These seemingly ordinary figures from Duplin's past kept the region's crops growing and delivered the daily mail. They ran the corner store and built the old tobacco barn on the edge of the yard. Each one of these individuals—friends and neighbors—made an impact, and their influence on the county can still be felt in Duplin today.

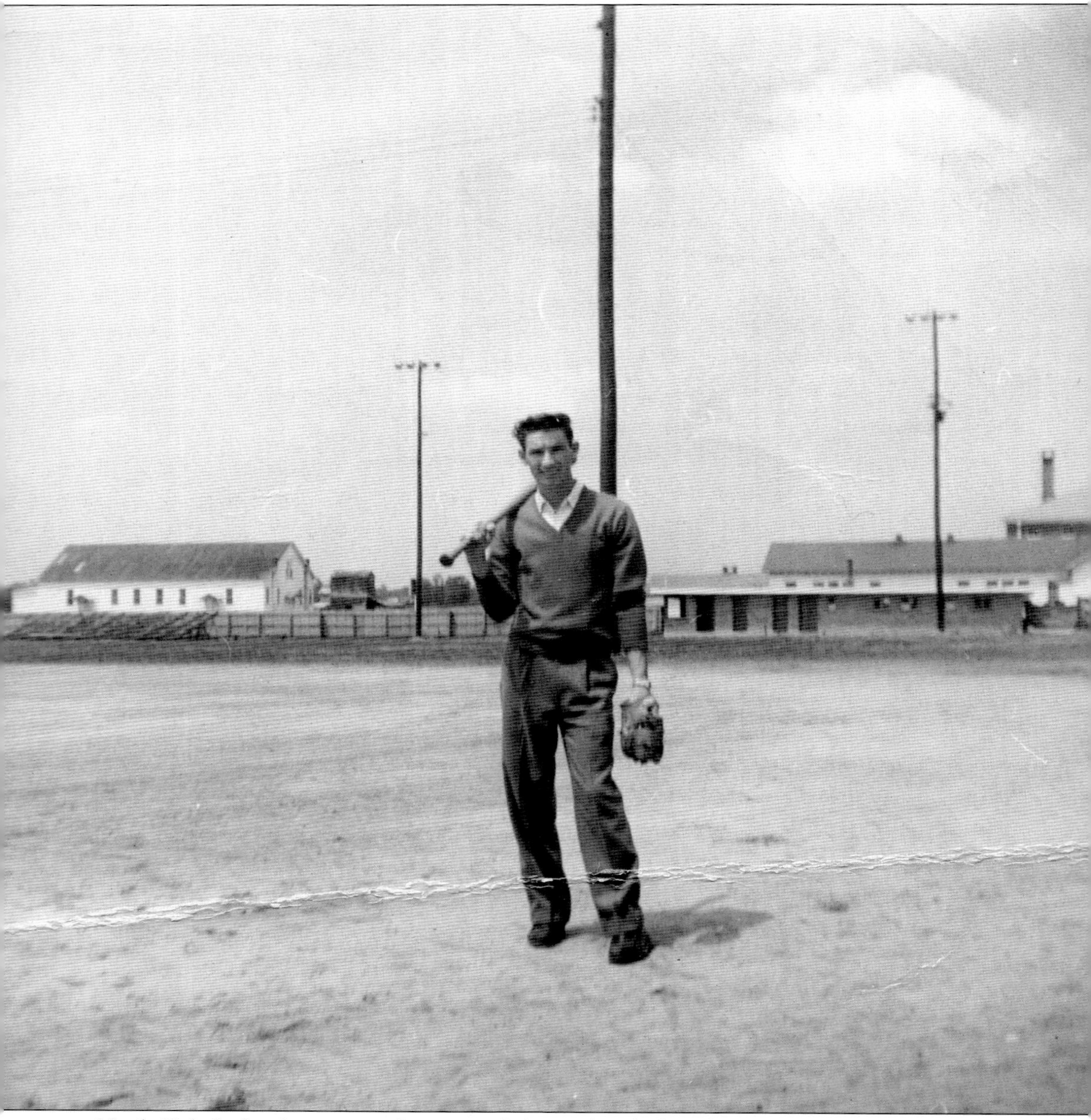

Noah Cole Jr. finishes up an afternoon of playing baseball at the school ball fields in Beulaville. The white structure on the left is the Beulaville School gymnasium. On the right, the ballpark's fieldhouse can be seen as well as the top of Beulaville School. (Courtesy of the Cole family.)

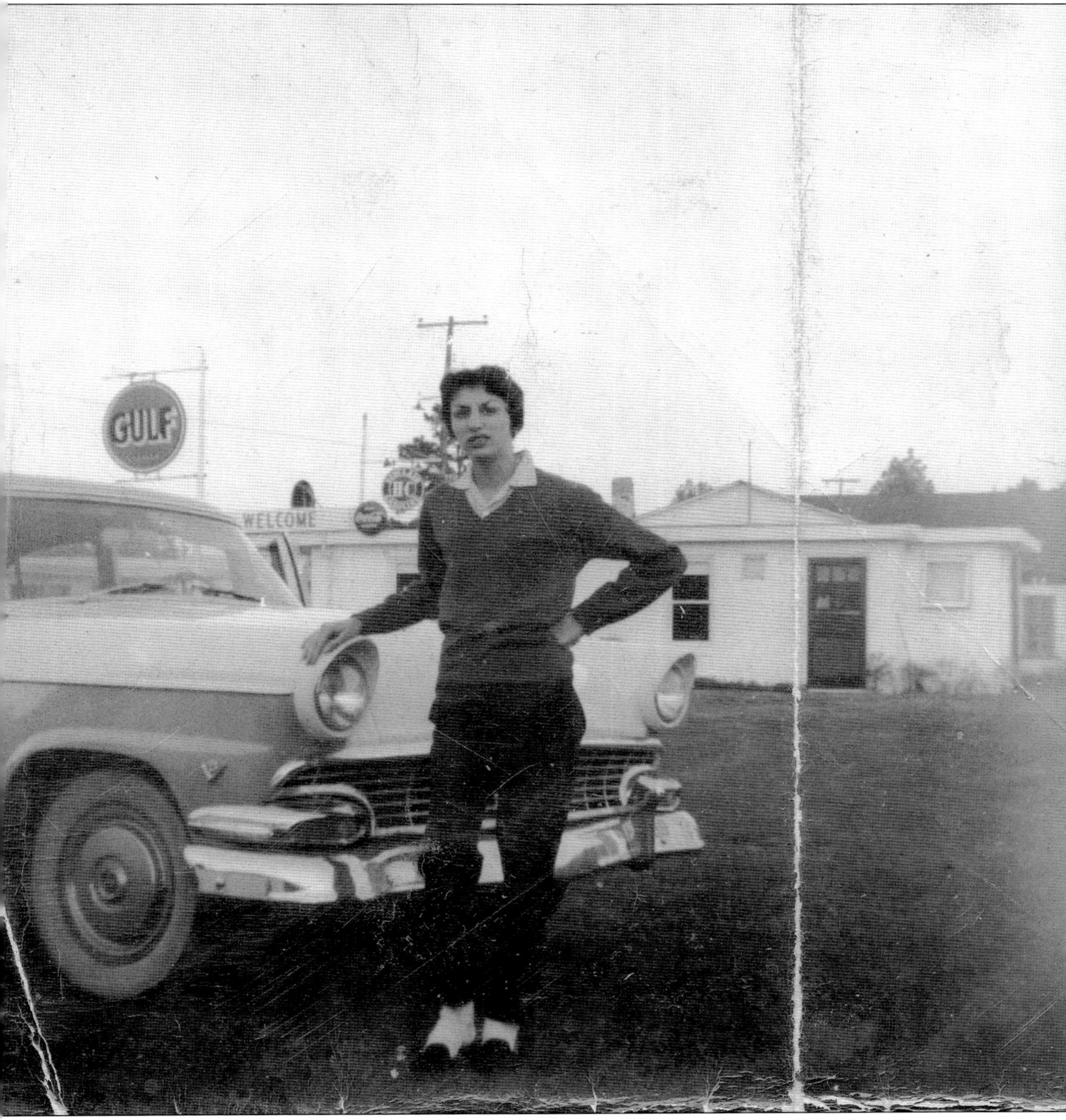

Patricia Williams stands outside a store owned by the Cole family on Beulaville's Main Street in 1957. The space is now occupied by the Country Smokehouse. Patricia married Noah Cole Jr. in 1957, and the couple remained married for 65 years. (Courtesy of the Cole family.)

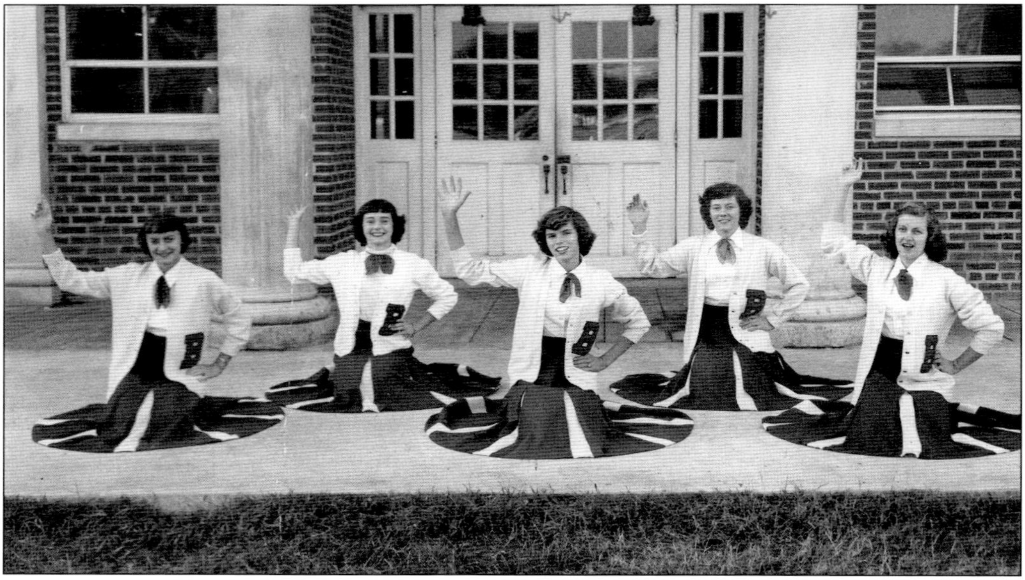

Beulaville School cheerleaders show off their uniforms in front of the school during the 1950s. From left to right are Katie Grey Miller, Veachie Rhodes, Susie Griffin, Raddie Faye Quinn, and Jessie Cottle. (Courtesy of the Bratcher family.)

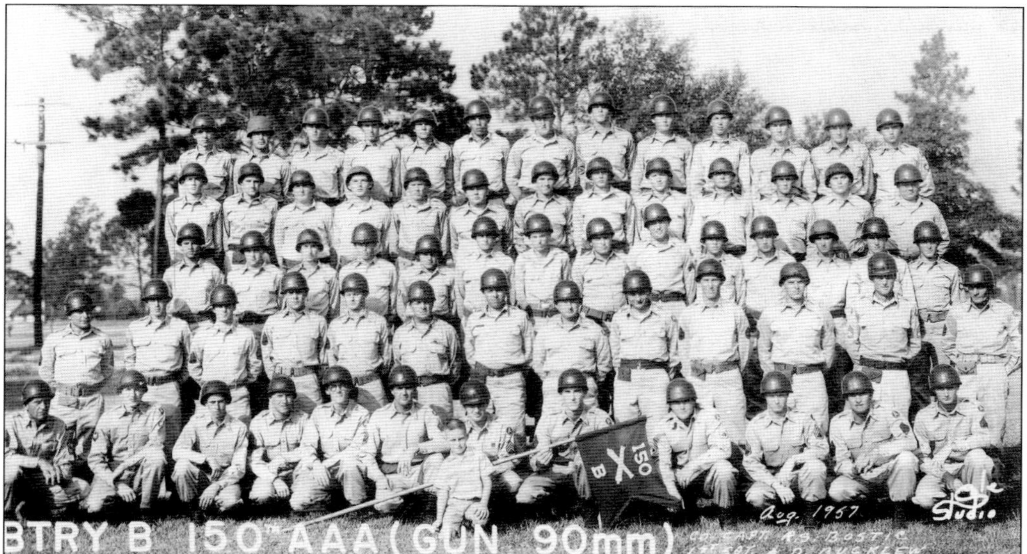

This photograph shows Beulaville's local National Guard unit, Battery B of the 150th Anti-Aircraft Artillery. The picture was taken in August 1957 and lists R.G. Bostic as the company captain and A.D. Bucklew as first sergeant. (Courtesy of the Bratcher family.)

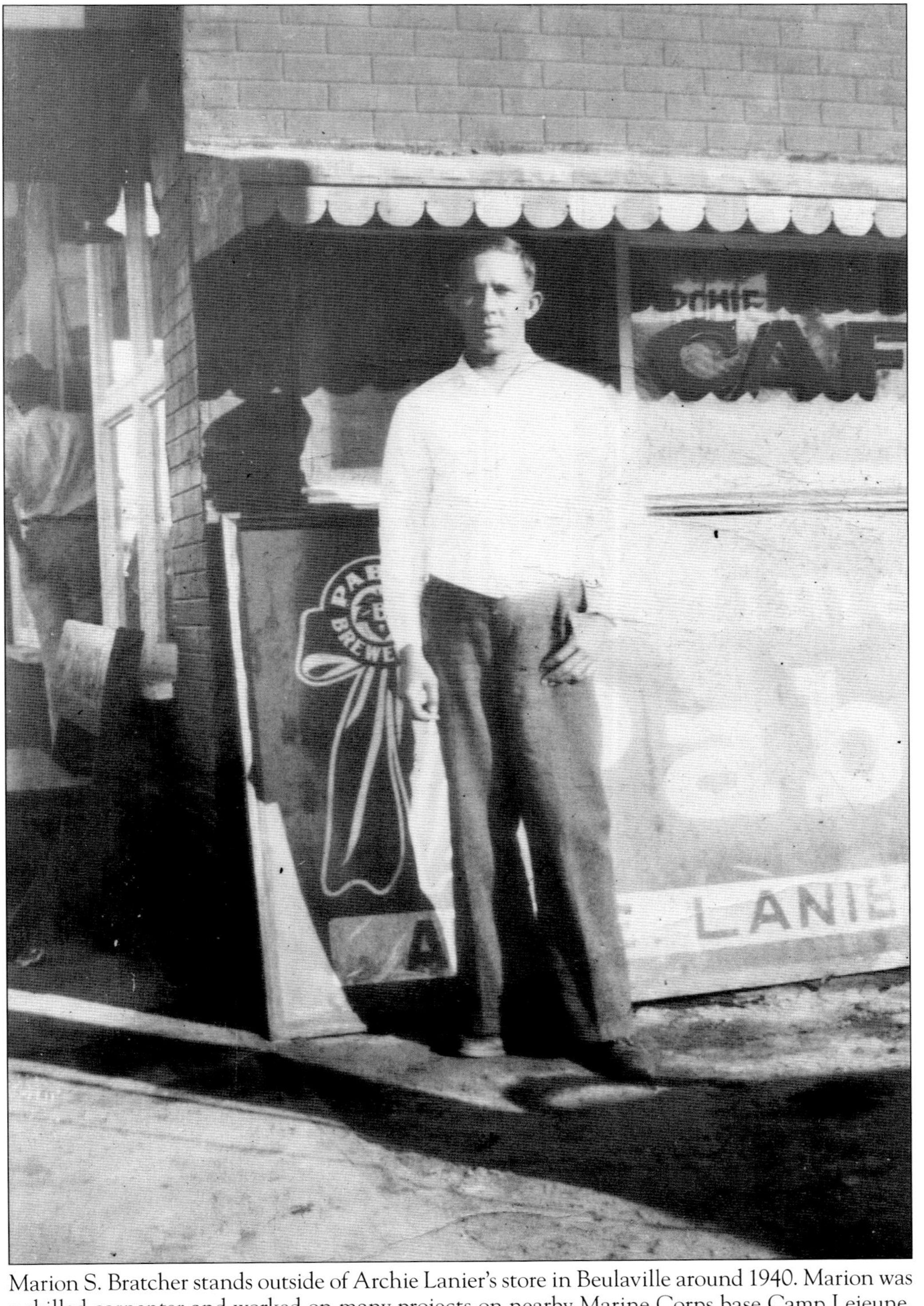

Marion S. Bratcher stands outside of Archie Lanier's store in Beulaville around 1940. Marion was a skilled carpenter and worked on many projects on nearby Marine Corps base Camp Lejeune. Bratcher married Louise Thigpen in 1929. (Courtesy of the Bratcher family.)

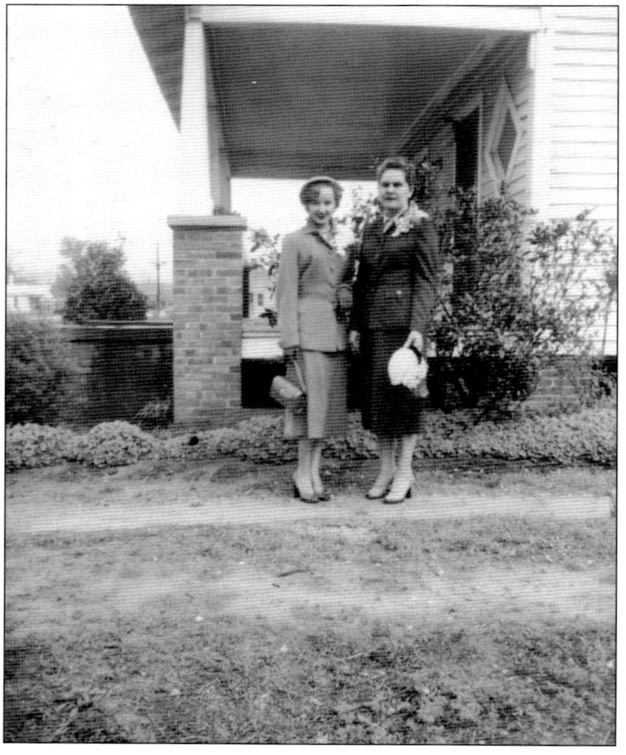

Louise Thigpen (right) and an unidentified woman (possibly Lucy Bell Thomas Whaley) stand in front of Thigpen's home along West Broad Street in Beulaville. The home was built in 1913 and still stands. (Courtesy of the Bratcher family.)

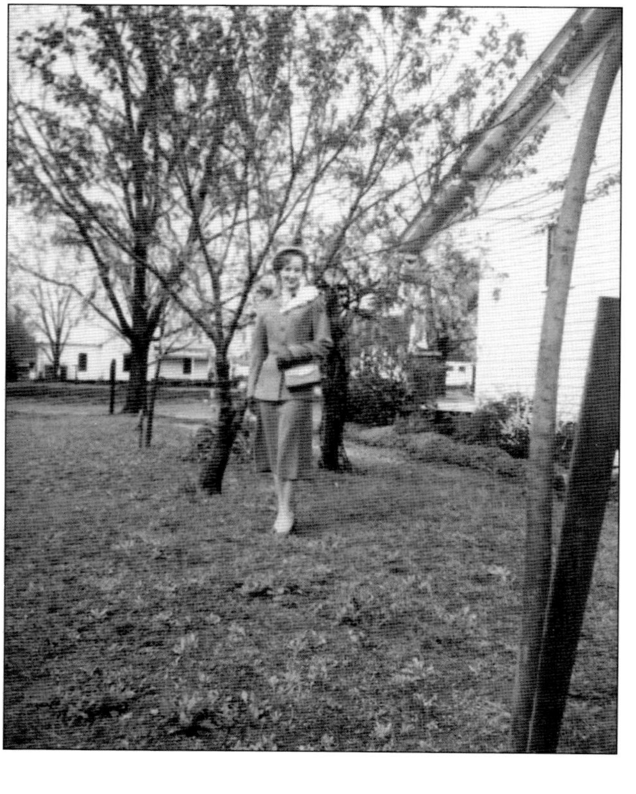

A woman, possibly Lucy Bell Thomas Whaley, stands in the side yard of Louisa Thigpen's home on West Broad Street in Beulaville. Many of the properties in the background have since been lost to development. (Courtesy of the Bratcher family.)

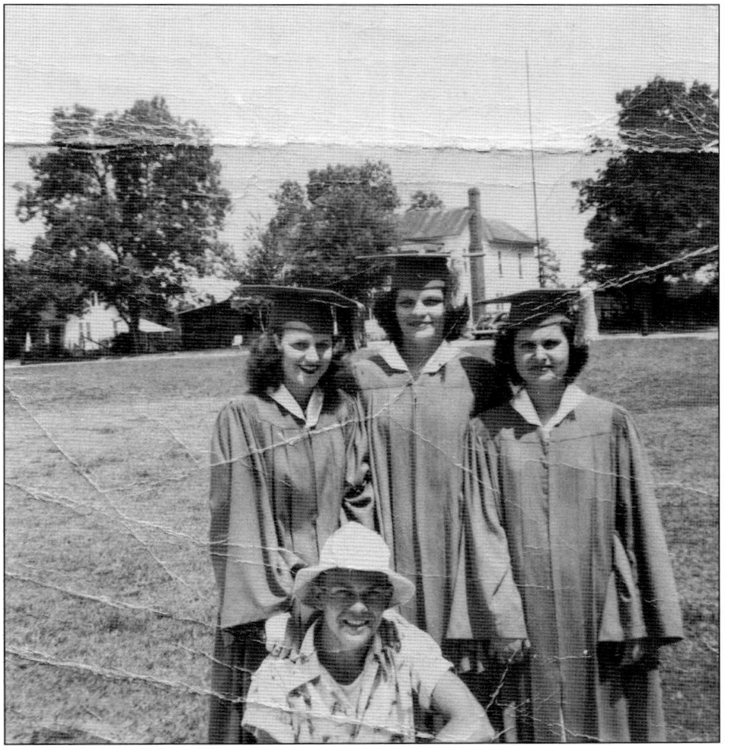

High school graduates show off their caps and gowns in Beulaville. Two of the graduates are believed to be Collie Thigpen and Pansy Edwards. (Courtesy of the Bratcher family.)

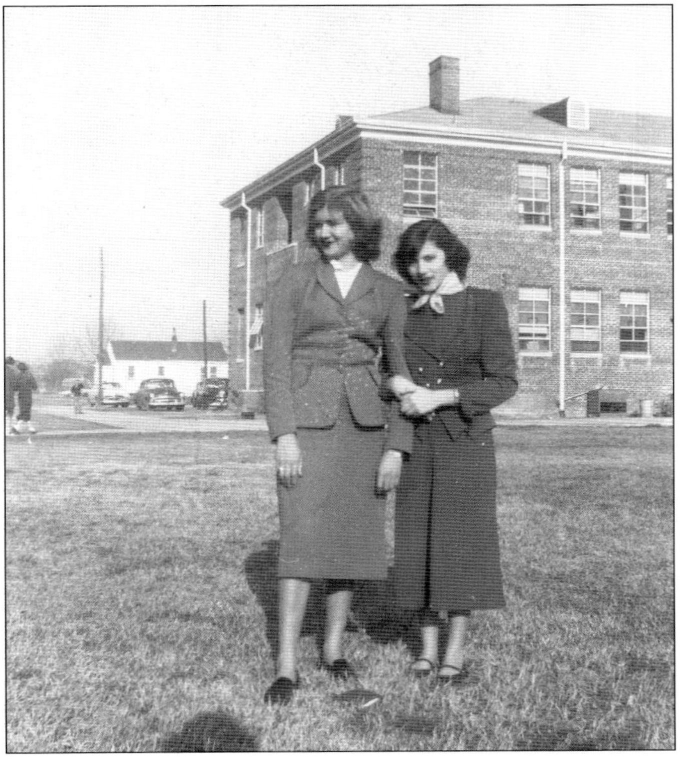

Geraldine Thompson (left) and Mary Williams pause for a photograph outside the Beulaville School during the 1950s. Beulaville School's original classroom building burned in 1945, but in 1947, two new buildings were erected in its place. (Courtesy of the Cole family.)

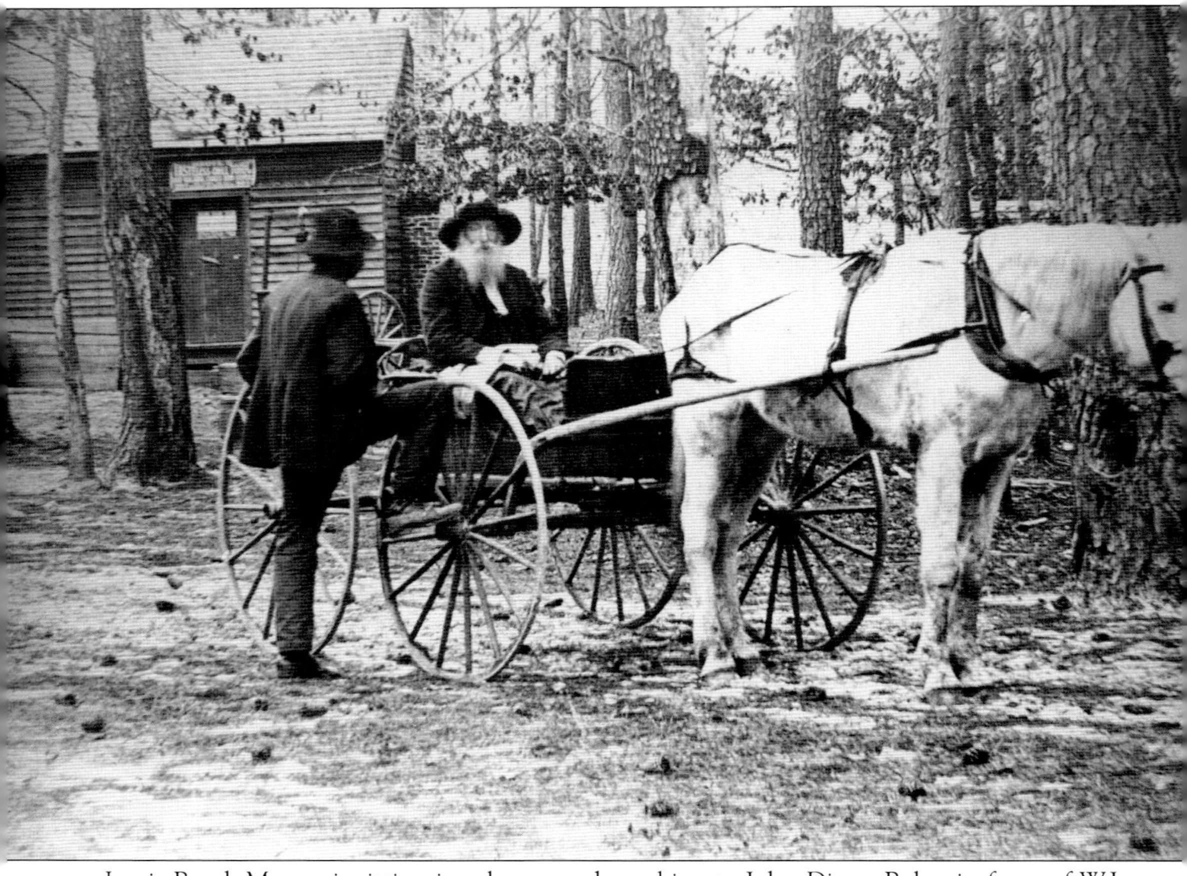

Louis Brock Mercer is sitting in a buggy and speaking to John Dixon Baker in front of W.J. Kennedy's store. During the early 1900s, Mercer served as the postmaster for the community of Cabin near Sarecta. (Courtesy of Leon Sikes.)

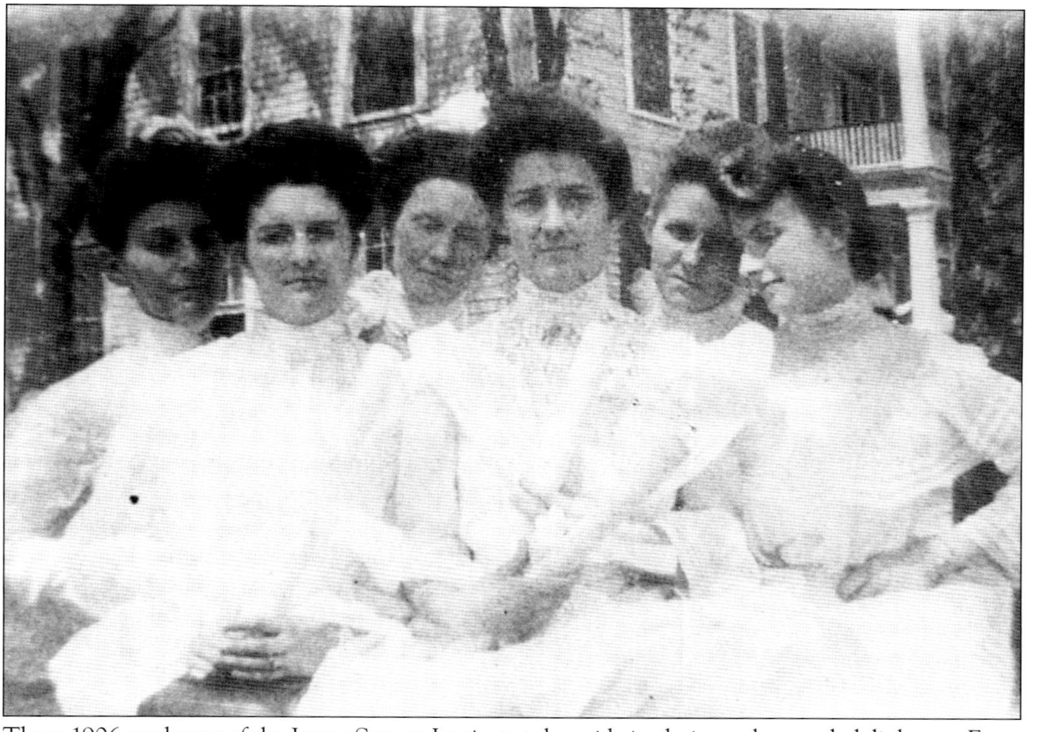

These 1906 graduates of the James Sprunt Institute take pride in their newly awarded diplomas. From left to right are Mary D. Carr, Carrie Newton, unidentified, Betty A. Southerland, unidentified, and Louise Pridgen. (Courtesy of Leon Sikes.)

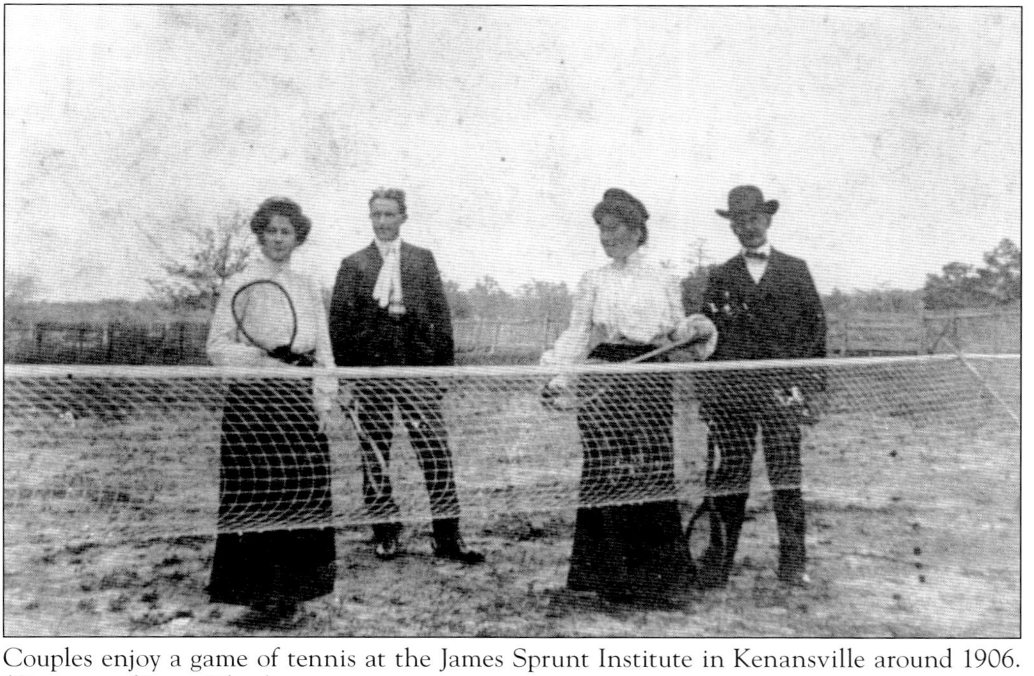

Couples enjoy a game of tennis at the James Sprunt Institute in Kenansville around 1906. (Courtesy of Leon Sikes.)

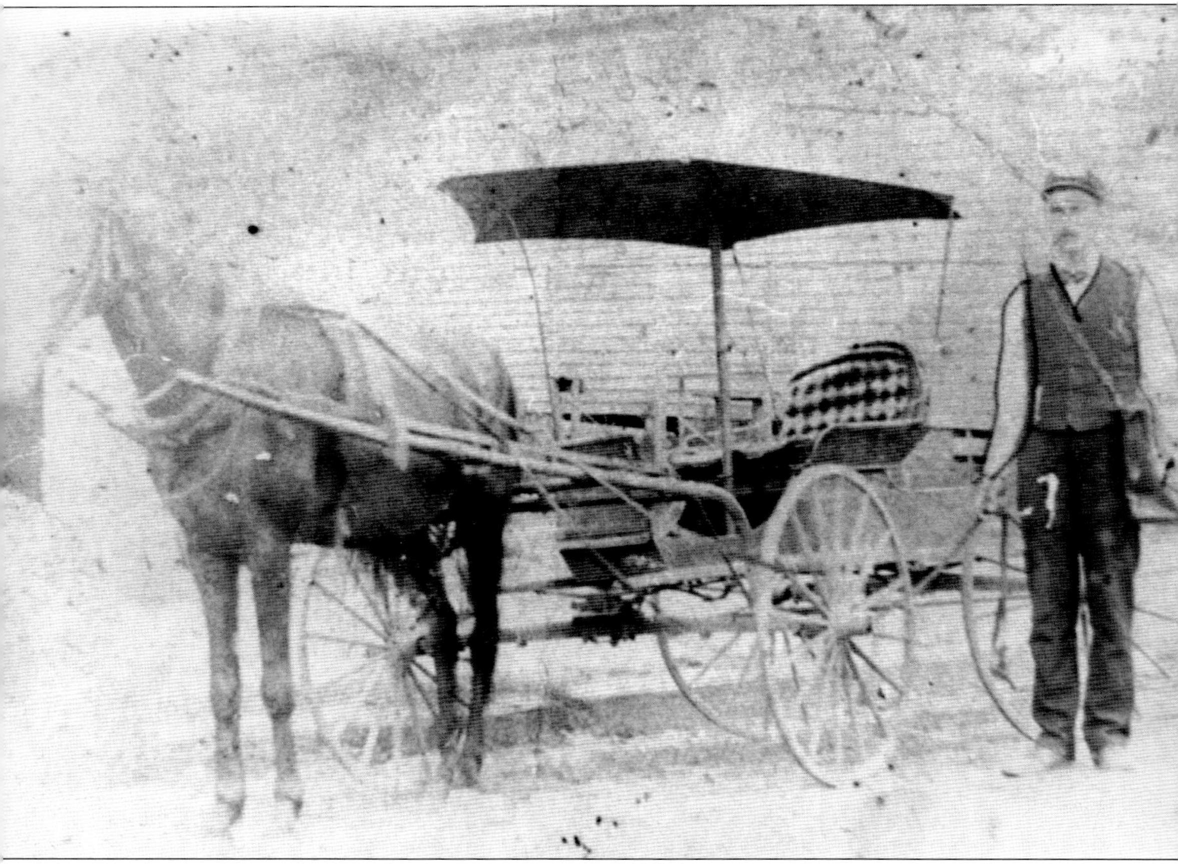

James Bryan, the first Rural Free Delivery mail carrier in Kenansville, is seen standing beside his mail wagon around 1901. (Courtesy of Leon Sikes.)

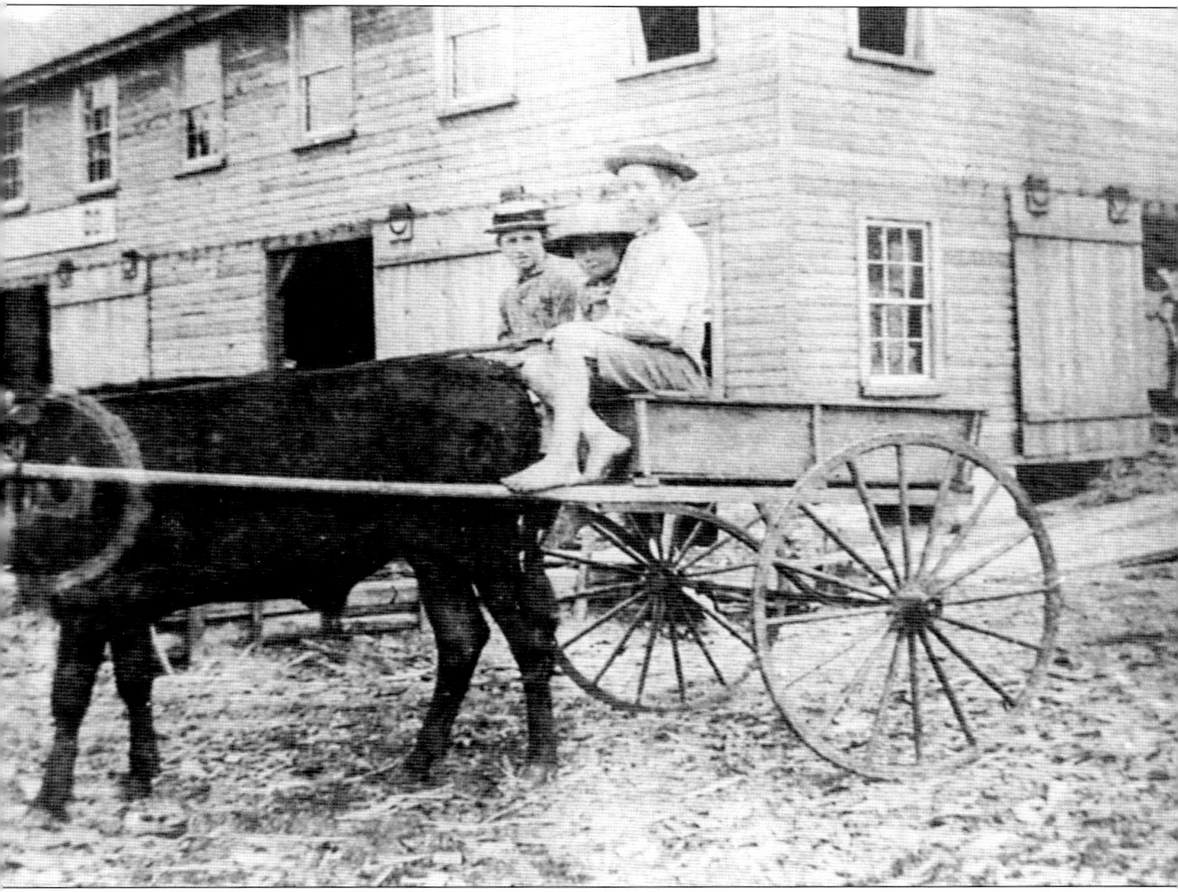

Kids ride in an ox-drawn cart outside the flower bulb warehouse of John F. Croom Sr. in Magnolia around 1912. From left to right are John Croom Jr., unidentified, and Polk Swinson. Croom was a local nurseryman known in the region for growing plant bulbs such as tuberoses and caladiums. Aside from his plant bulb venture, Croom and his brother produced crates such as the ones used to transport strawberries. (Courtesy of Leon Sikes.)

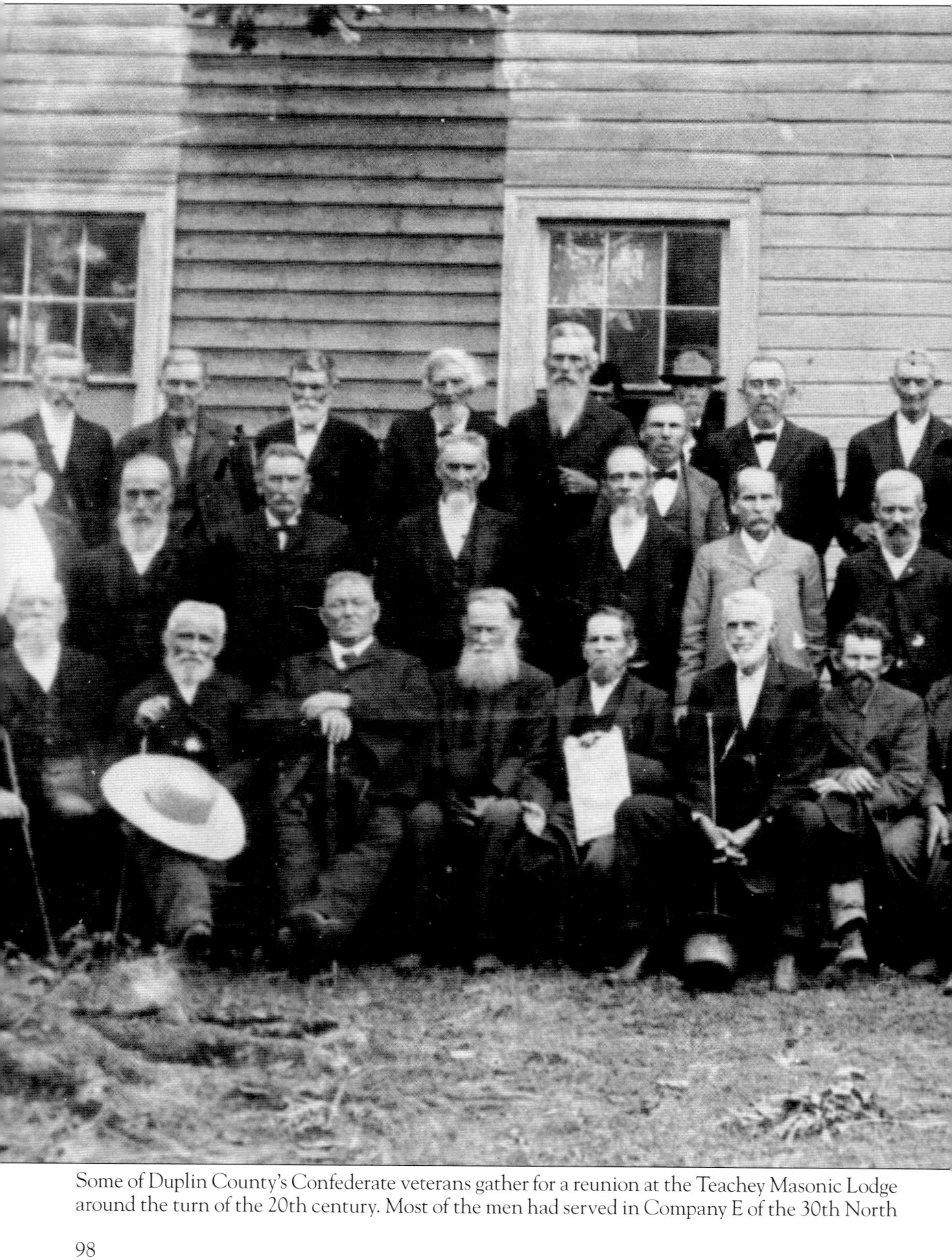

Some of Duplin County's Confederate veterans gather for a reunion at the Teachey Masonic Lodge around the turn of the 20th century. Most of the men had served in Company E of the 30th North

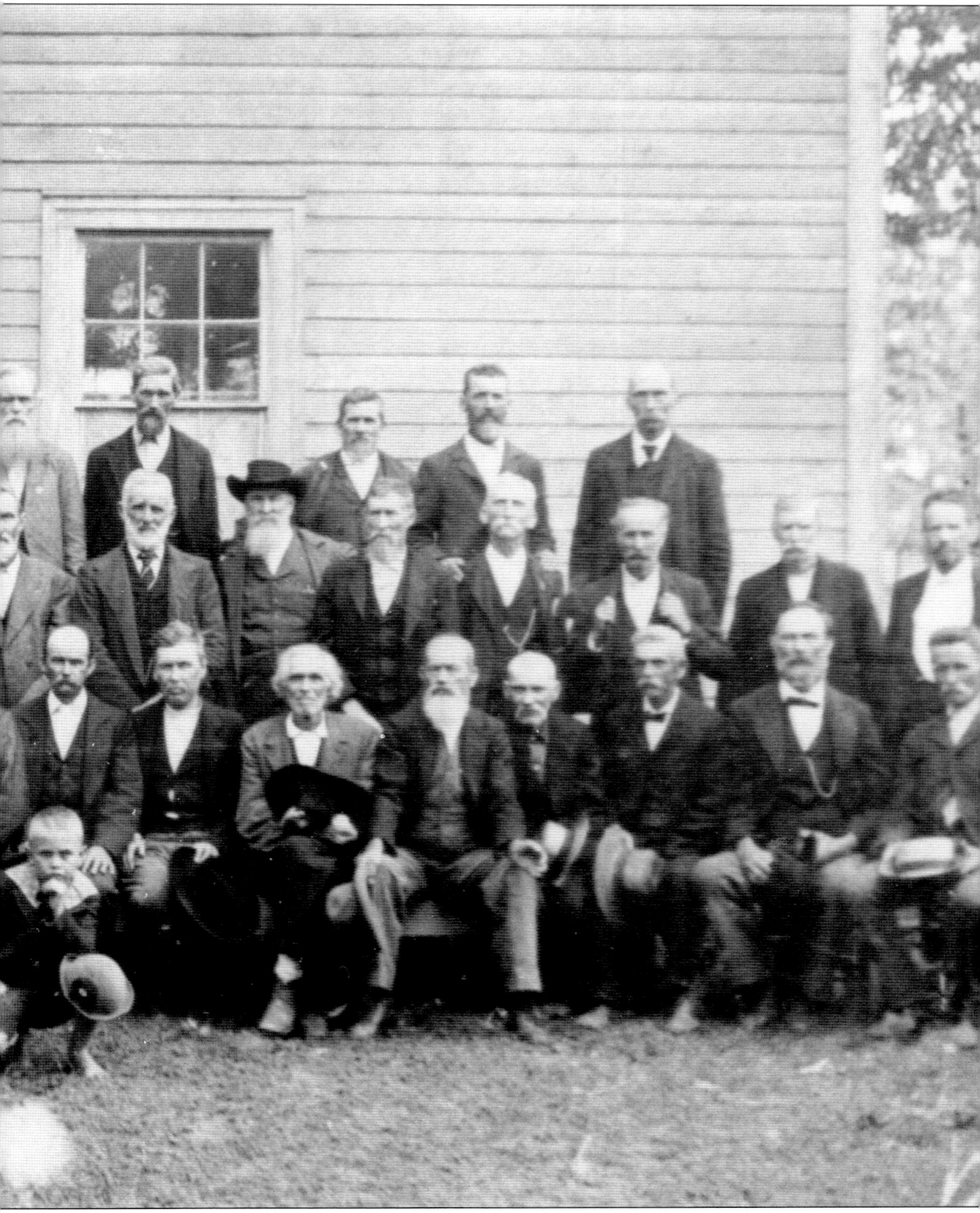

Carolina Infantry, nicknamed "The Duplin Turpentine Boys." The 30th North Carolina saw action in battles such as Seven Pines, Chancellorsville, and Gettysburg. (Courtesy of Leon Sikes.)

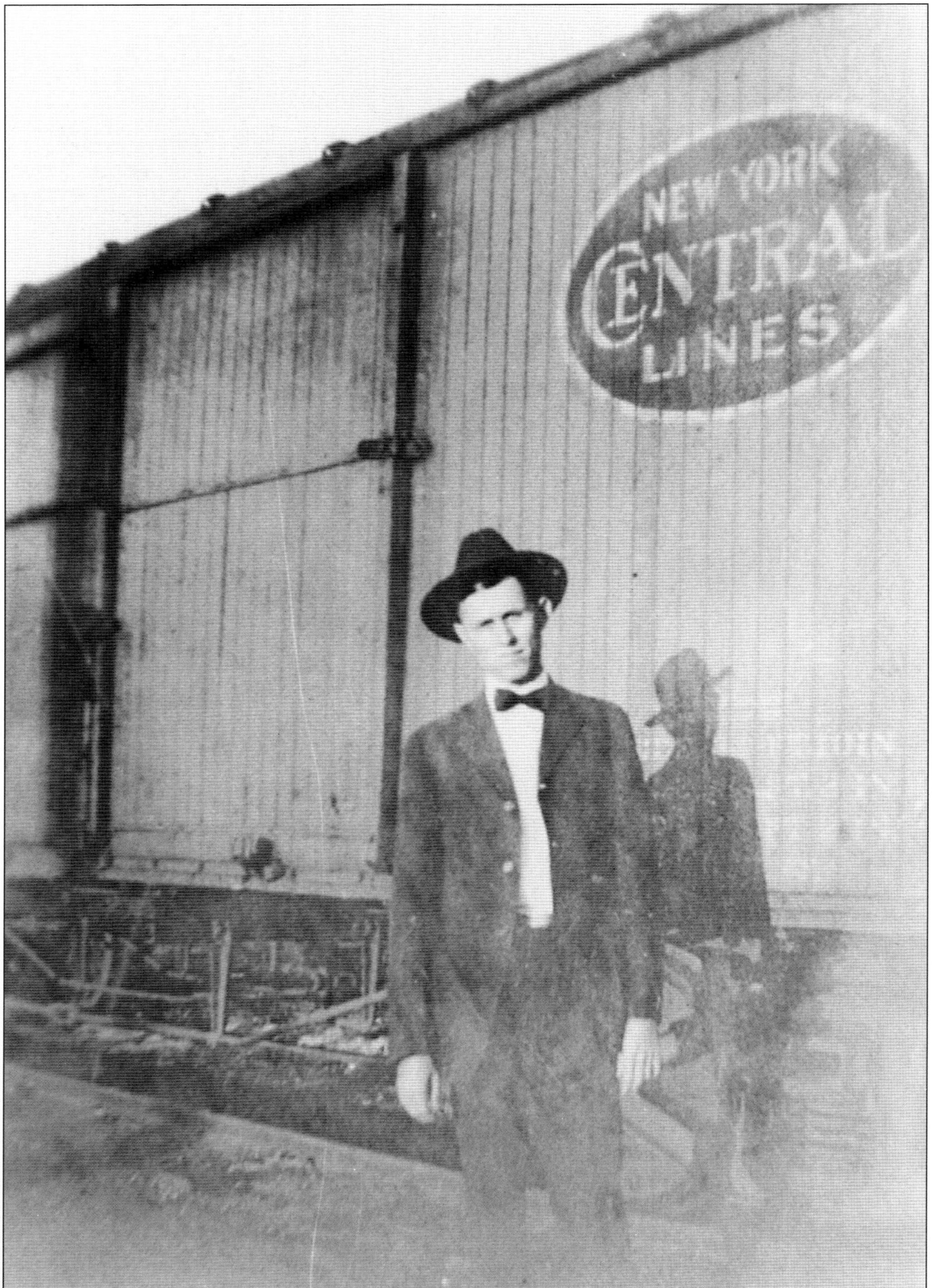

J.F. "Happy" Waters once served as the town clerk of Warsaw. Here he is seen standing in front of one of the many railroad freight cars that once rolled through town. (Courtesy of Leon Sikes.)

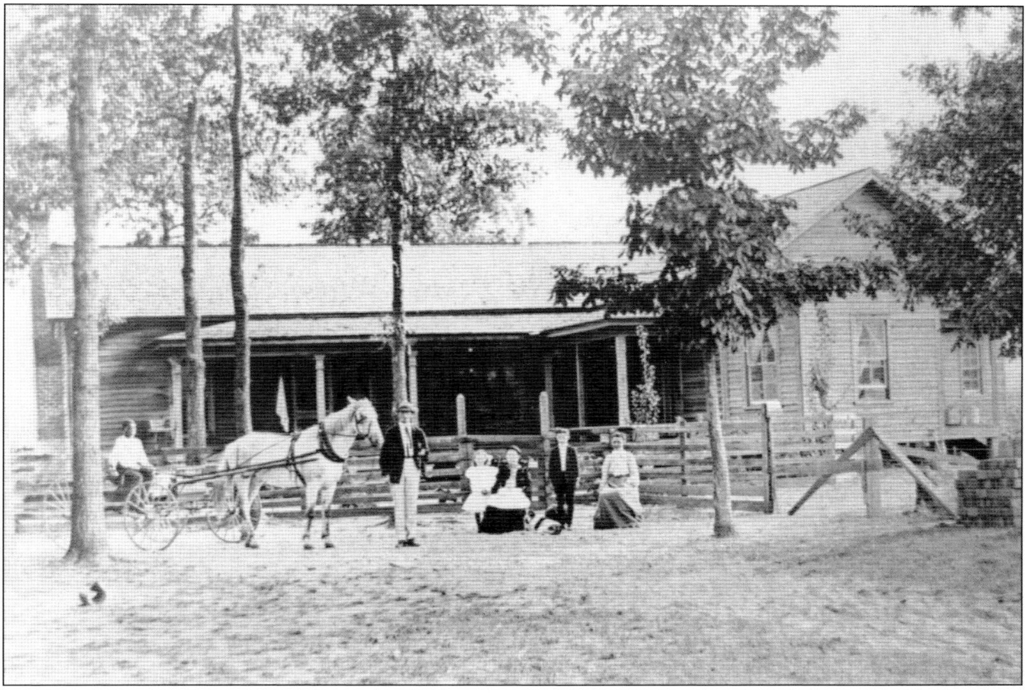

A Duplin County family poses for a photograph outside the Westbrook home in the community of Leon around 1900. (Courtesy of Leon Sikes.)

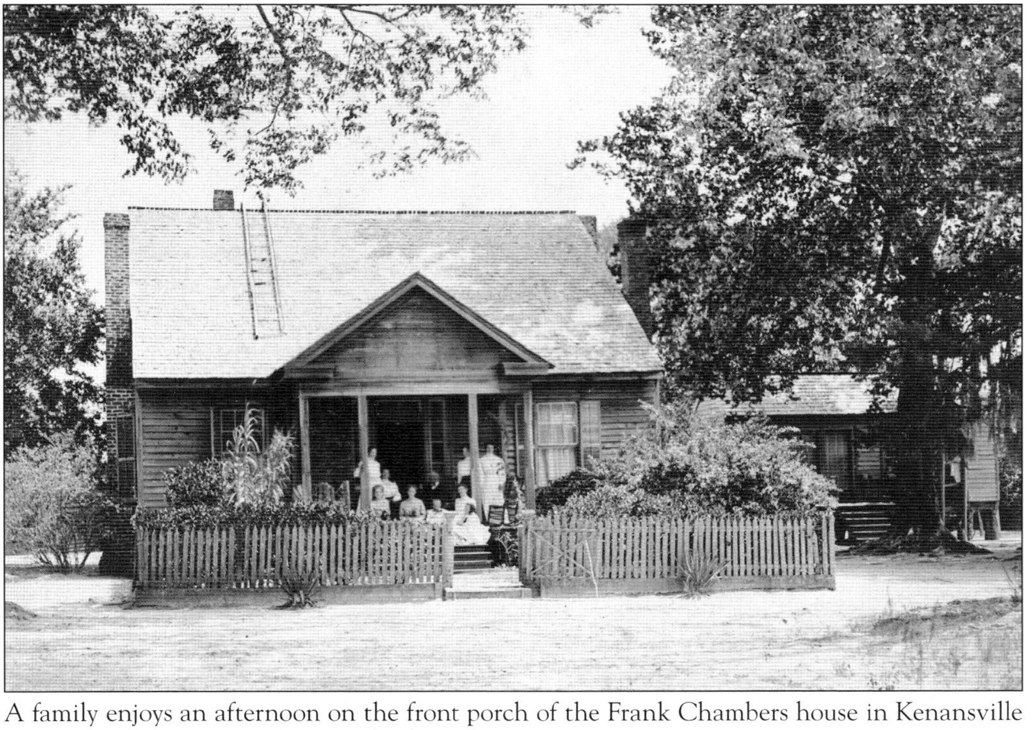

A family enjoys an afternoon on the front porch of the Frank Chambers house in Kenansville around 1910. (Courtesy of Leon Sikes.)

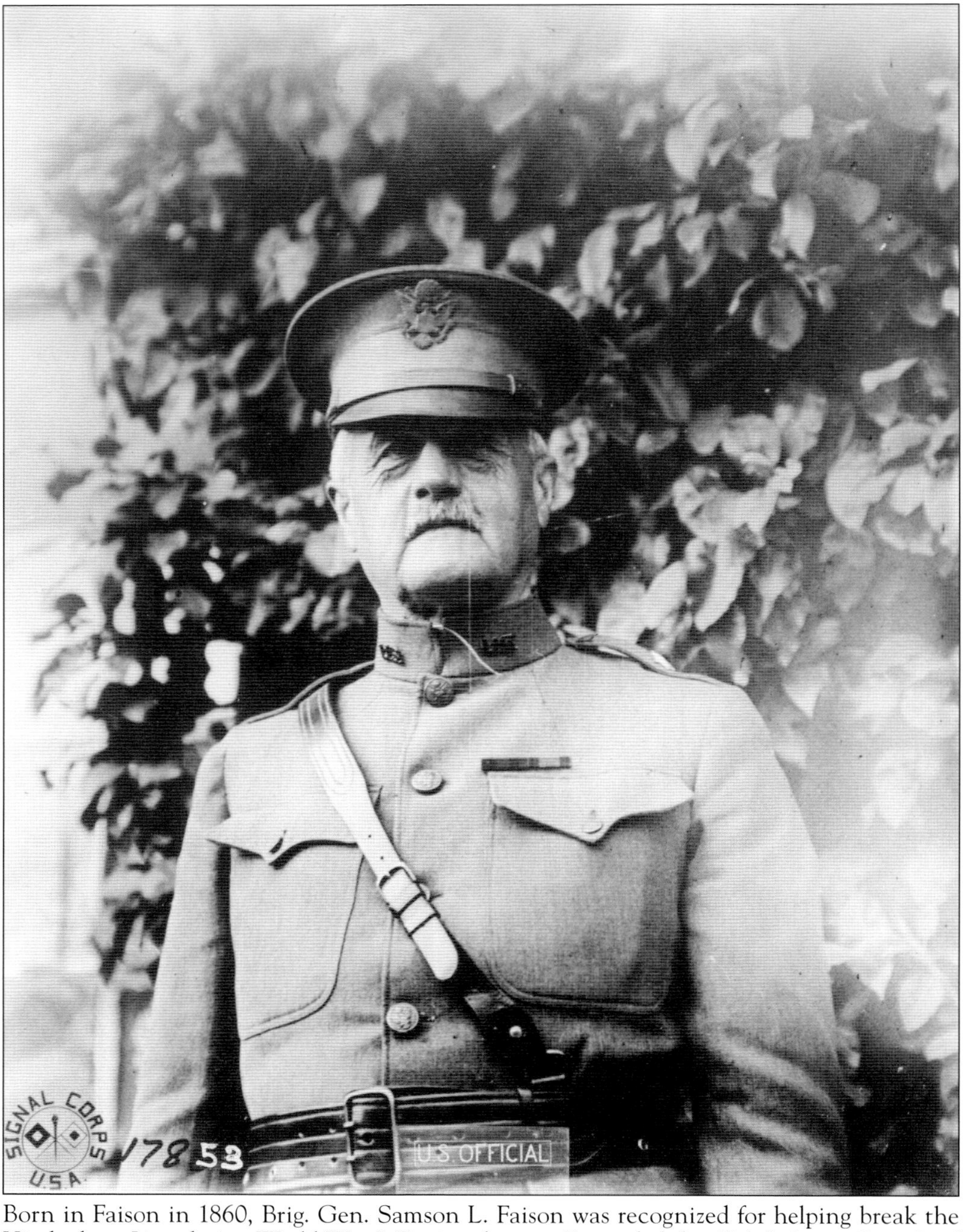

Born in Faison in 1860, Brig. Gen. Samson L. Faison was recognized for helping break the Hindenburg Line during World War I. During the war, Faison led the 60th Infantry Brigade of the 30th Infantry Division, also known as "Old Hickory." The 30th Infantry Division served in both Belgium and France, where it helped penetrate Germany's heavily fortified Hindenburg Line on September 29, 1918, thus helping bring an end to the Great War. Faison is interred in Arlington National Cemetery. (Courtesy of the State Archives of North Carolina.)

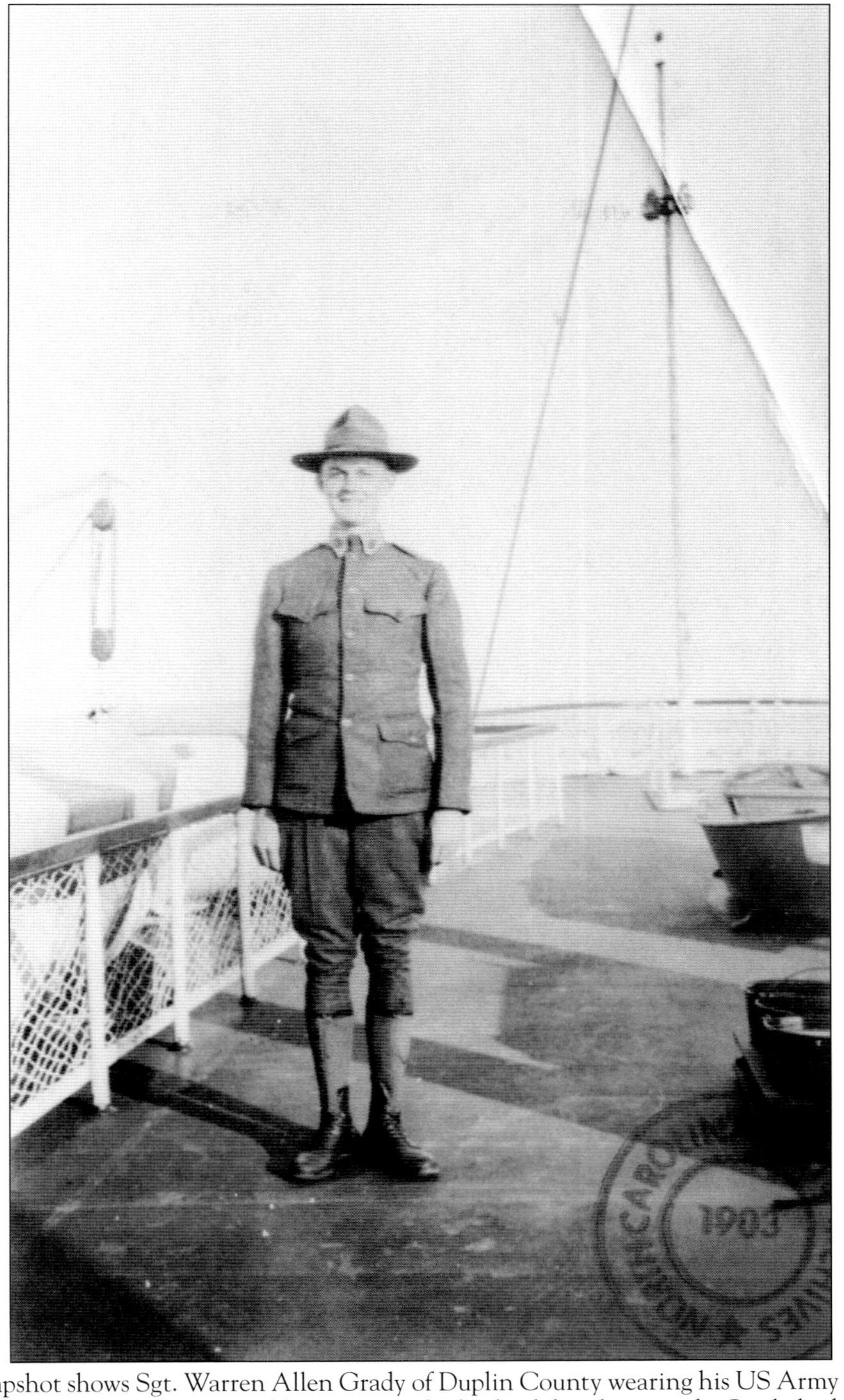

This snapshot shows Sgt. Warren Allen Grady of Duplin County wearing his US Army uniform on the deck of a ship during World War I. On the back of the photograph, Grady had jokingly written "Director general of the Air Service. Maybe not much of a Soldier in appearance but a hell of a military man. Also a winner with the ladies. That's me all over." Grady served in the 76th Aero Squadron, US Army Air Service. (Courtesy of the State Archives of North Carolina.)

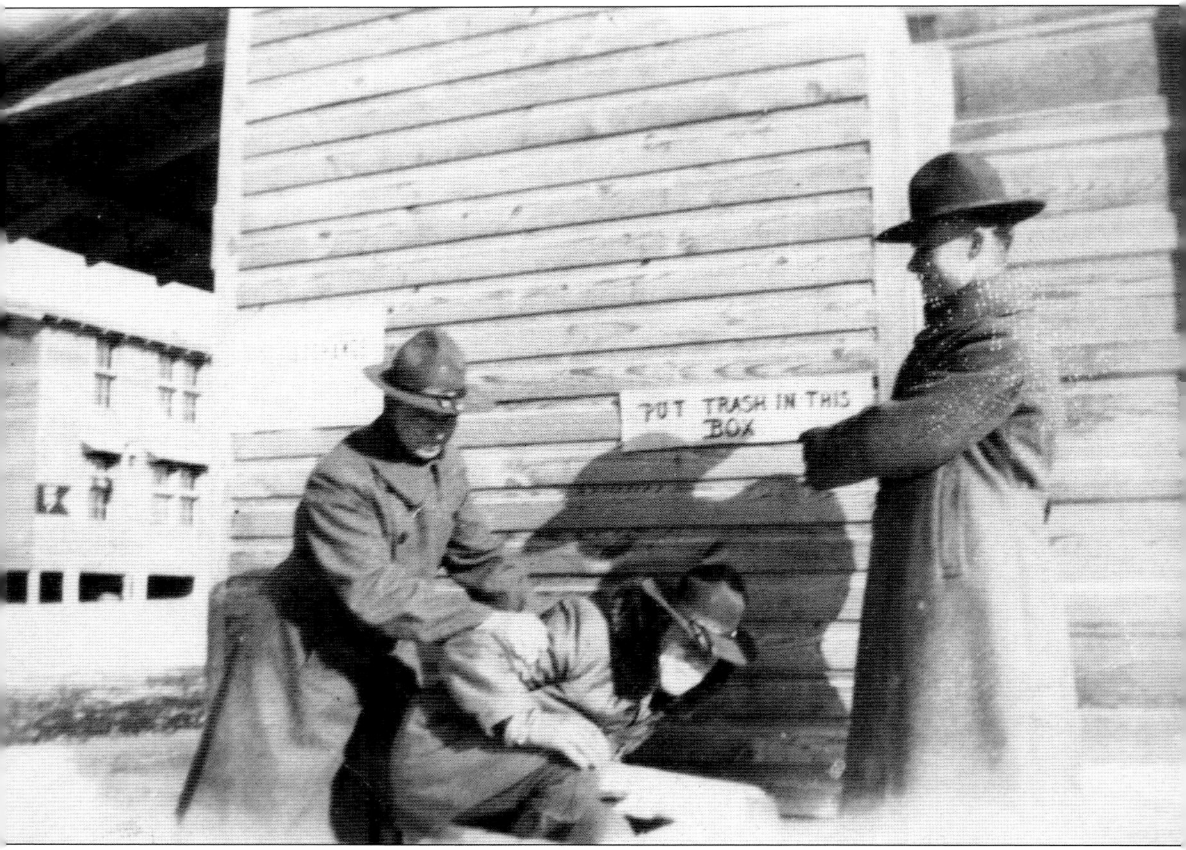

Second Lt. John D. Grady of Duplin (left) goofs around outside the post exchange of a military camp with two other Army officers. Grady is helping one of the men get inside a bin; the sign above it reads "Put Trash in this Box." Grady served in Battery F, 316th Field Artillery, 81st Division during World War I. (Courtesy of the State Archives of North Carolina.)

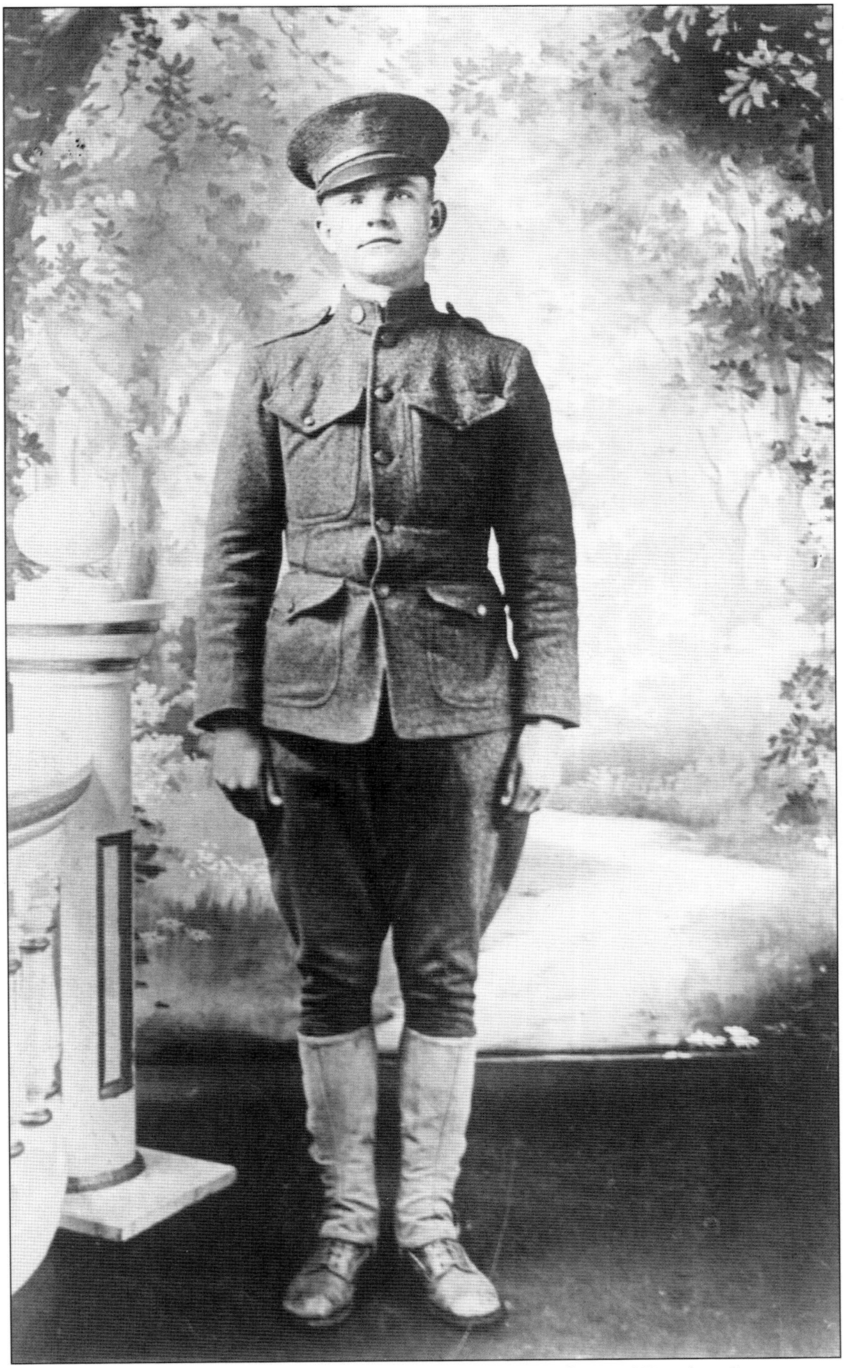

This postcard shows a studio portrait of Cpl. William S. Gardner of Duplin County wearing his US Army uniform in front of a hand-painted backdrop. While overseas, Gardner served with Company G, 16th Infantry Regiment, 1st Infantry Division. He died in France on July 29, 1918, and was eventually buried in the Knowles Family Cemetery in Rose Hill. (Courtesy of the State Archives of North Carolina.)

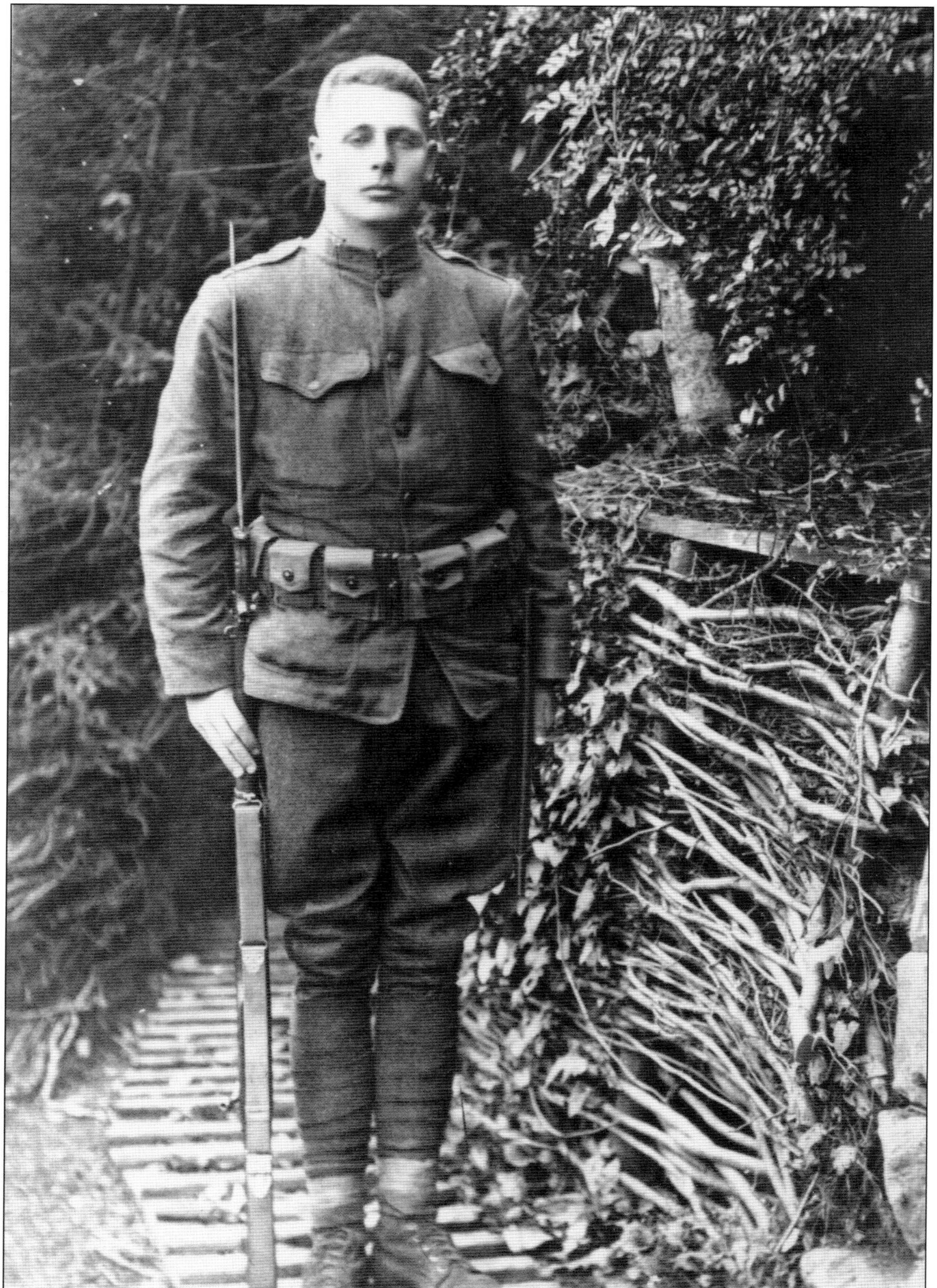

Joseph F. Williams stands in a trench during World War I during his time as a private in the US Army. He was the son of Eck Williams, and his grandfather Dr. Daniel Allen Williams served in the Confederate army with the 61st North Carolina during the Civil War. Private Williams survived the war and is buried in Teachey. (Courtesy of the Cole family.)

Allen Williams is seen sporting an Army uniform during his time in the service. Williams would become a prominent resident in Duplin County, particularly in Wallace, where he managed the local Piggly Wiggly. Throughout his life, he was heavily involved in civic affairs, most notably local athletics and recreation. Both a gymnasium and ball field in Wallace were named in his honor. In 1999, Williams was awarded the Order of the Longleaf Pine, one of North Carolina's most prestigious awards. (Courtesy of the Cole family.)

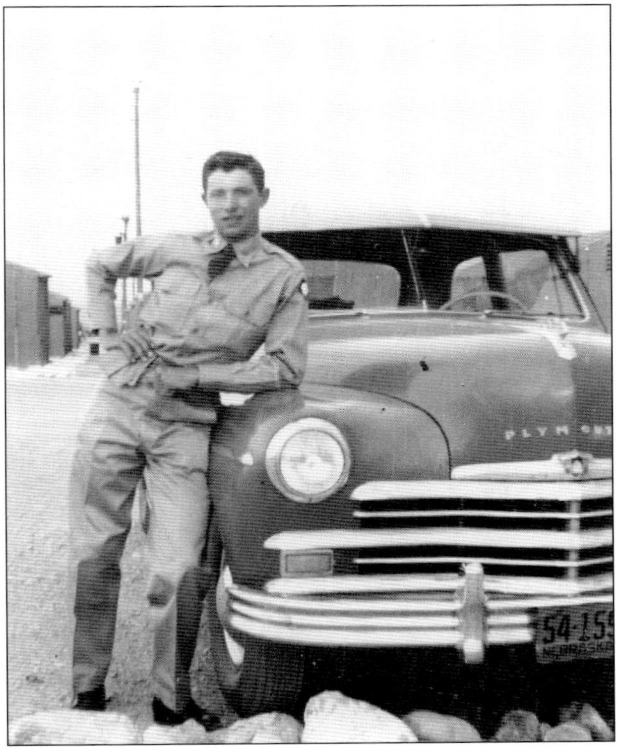

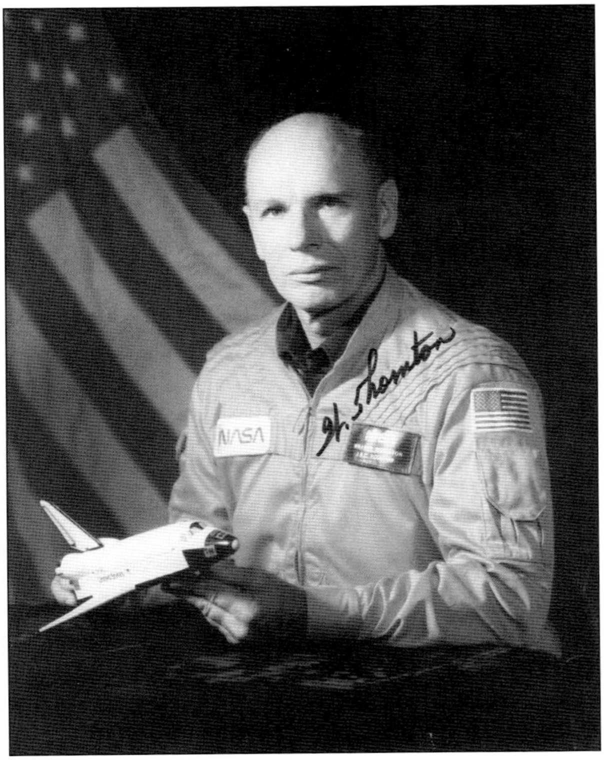

A native of Faison, Dr. William E. Thornton earned his bachelor's and medical degrees from UNC Chapel Hill prior to entering the US Air Force. In 1967, Thorton was selected to serve as a scientist-astronaut by NASA. He flew on the space shuttle *Challenger* twice, logging a total of 313 hours in space. (Courtesy of the Faison Museum.)

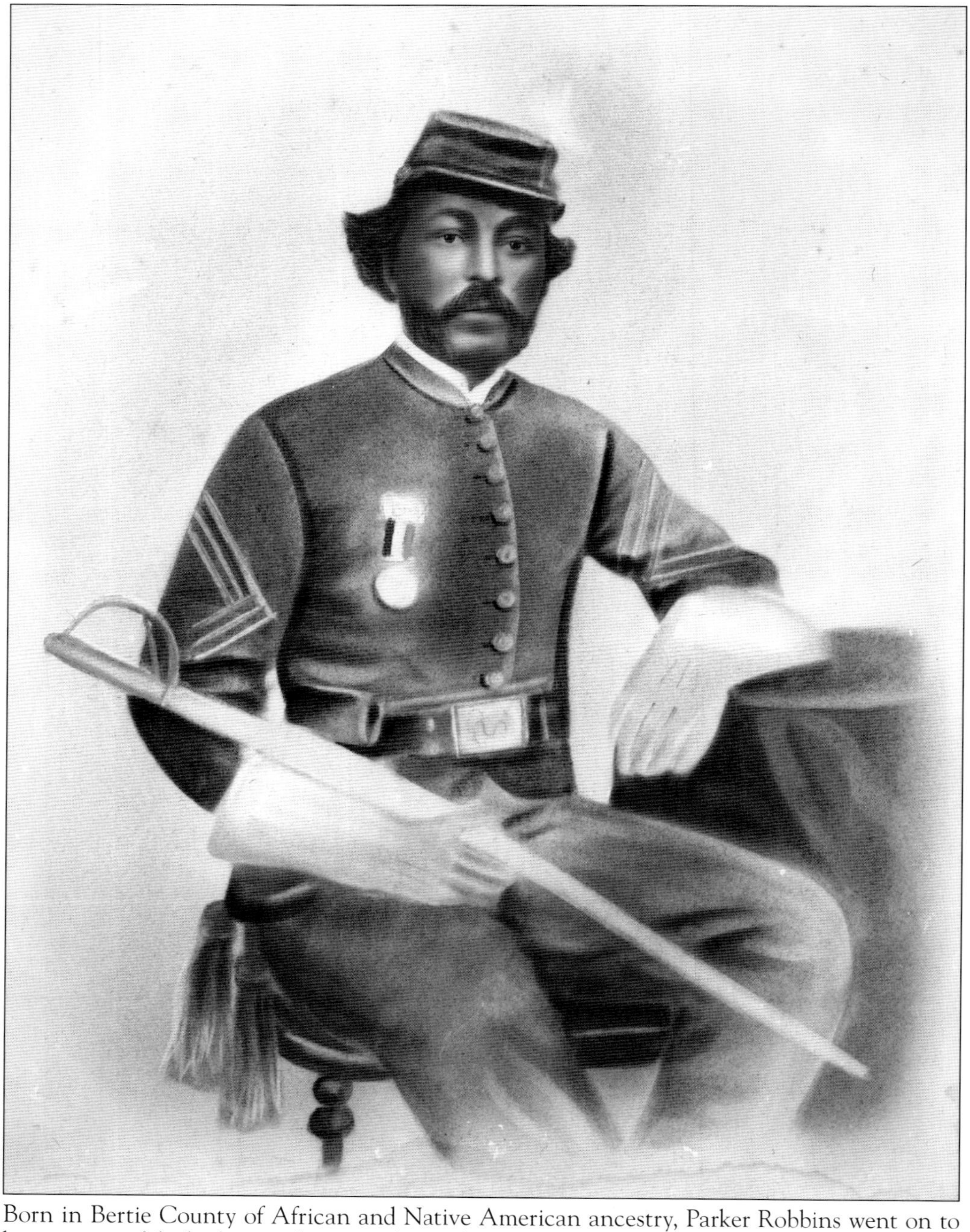

Born in Bertie County of African and Native American ancestry, Parker Robbins went on to become one of the highest-ranking North Carolinians to serve in the US Colored Troops. Robbins enlisted in the 2nd US Colored Cavalry during the Civil War and attained the rank of sergeant major. Following the war, he was elected a delegate to the 1868 Constitutional Convention and served two terms as a state representative. After his stint in politics, Robbins moved to Duplin County, where he ran a sawmill and cotton gin and operated a steamboat along the Northeast Cape Fear River. Robbins is buried in a family cemetery in Magnolia. (Courtesy of the State Archives of North Carolina.)

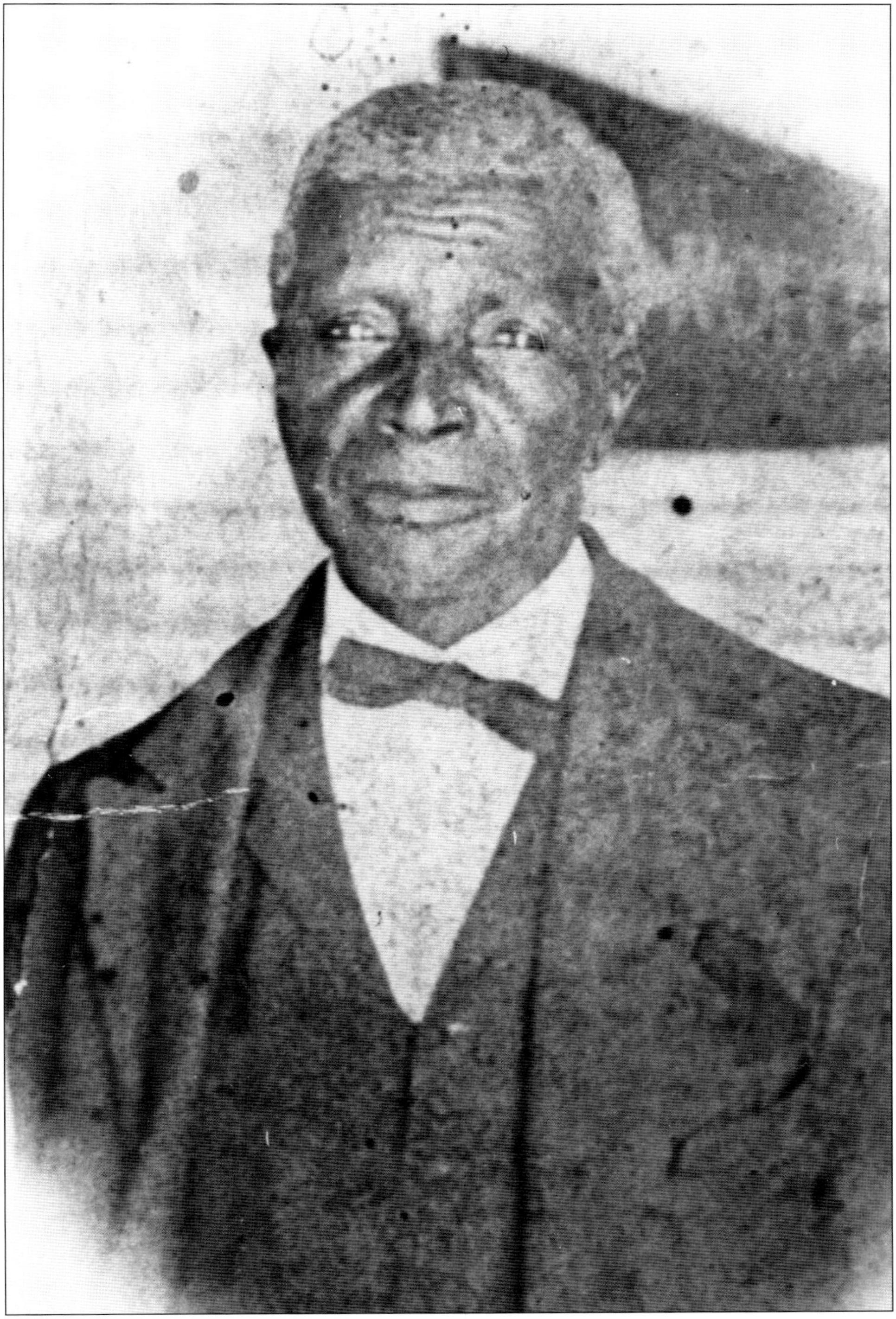

Though born into slavery, Rev. Isaac Powers eventually became a prosperous land owner in Duplin County, acquiring more than 200 acres of land that he farmed. During his life, he served as a circuit minister and become involved in the Republican Party. (Courtesy of Leon Sikes.)

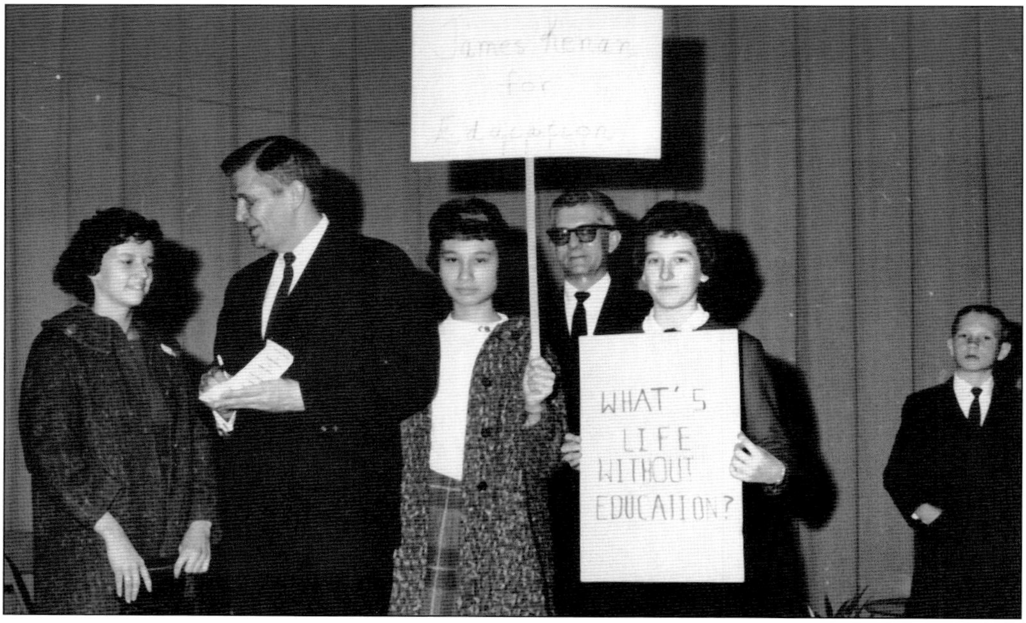

Gov. Terry Sanford (second from left) meets with Duplin County residents in Kenansville during his 1962 education tour. The young woman at center holds a sign reading "James Kenan for Education." (Courtesy of the State Archives of North Carolina.)

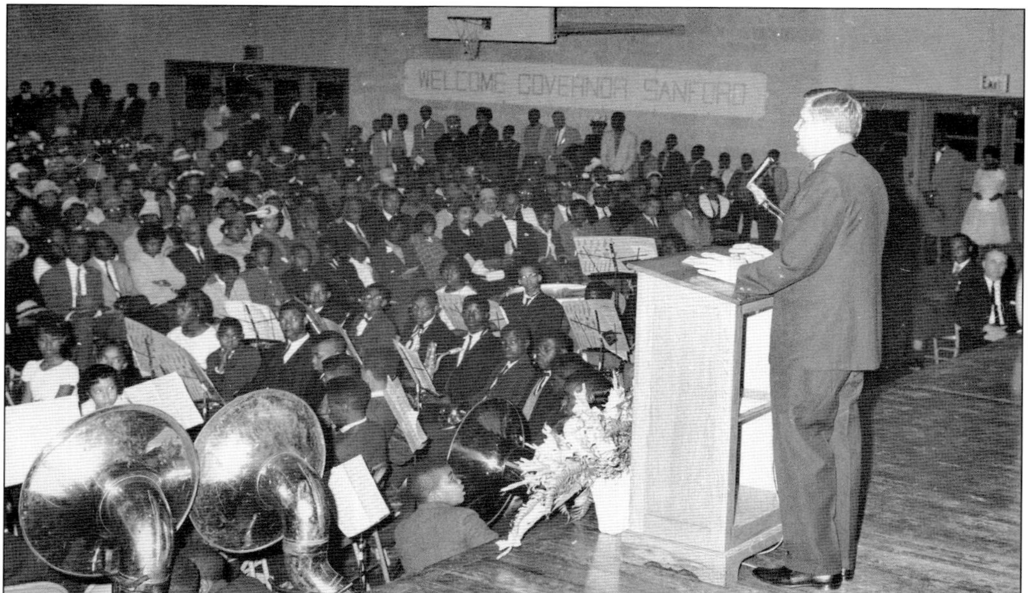

Governor Sanford addresses a crowd at the E.E. Smith School during his 1962 education tour. The school takes its name from African American educator Ezekiel Ezra Smith, who was born in the Duplin County community of Beautancus in 1852. Smith presided as president of the State Colored Normal School (now Fayetteville State University) for 40 years and served as minister to the Republic of Liberia. There is currently an E.E. Smith High School in Fayetteville, North Carolina. (Courtesy of the State Archives of North Carolina.)

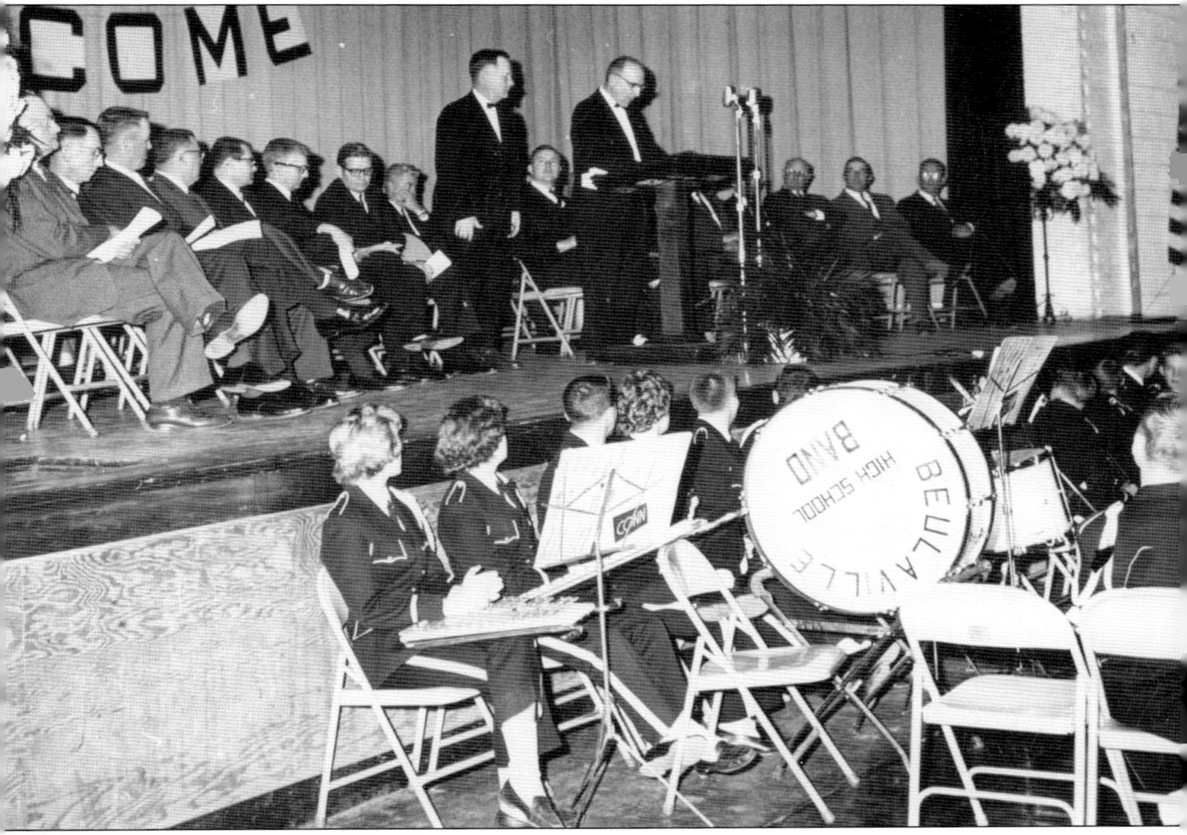

The Beulaville School band performs during Governor Sanford's 1962 visit. (Courtesy of the State Archives of North Carolina.)

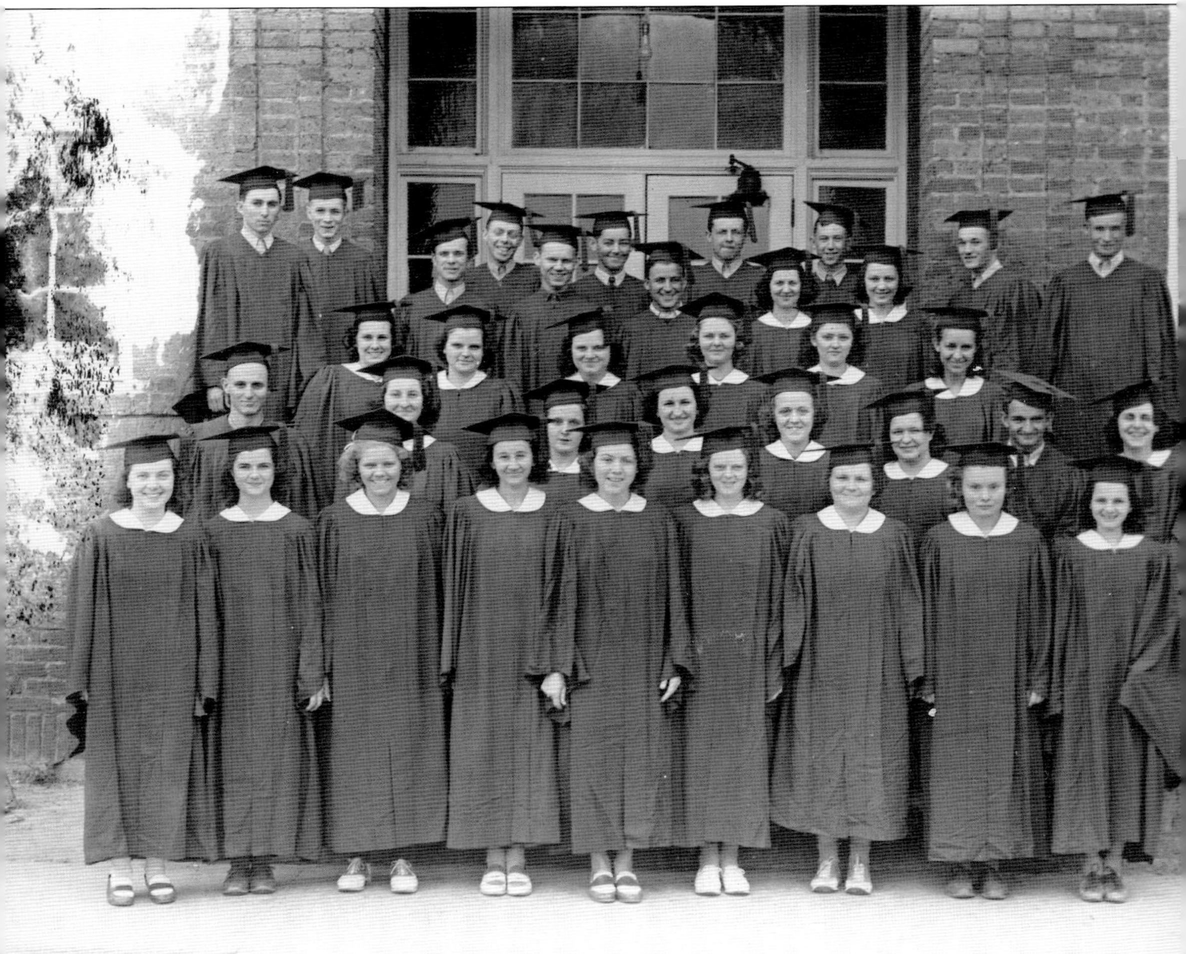

This photograph shows the 1941 graduating class of Calypso High School. (Courtesy of the Mount Olive Historical Society.)

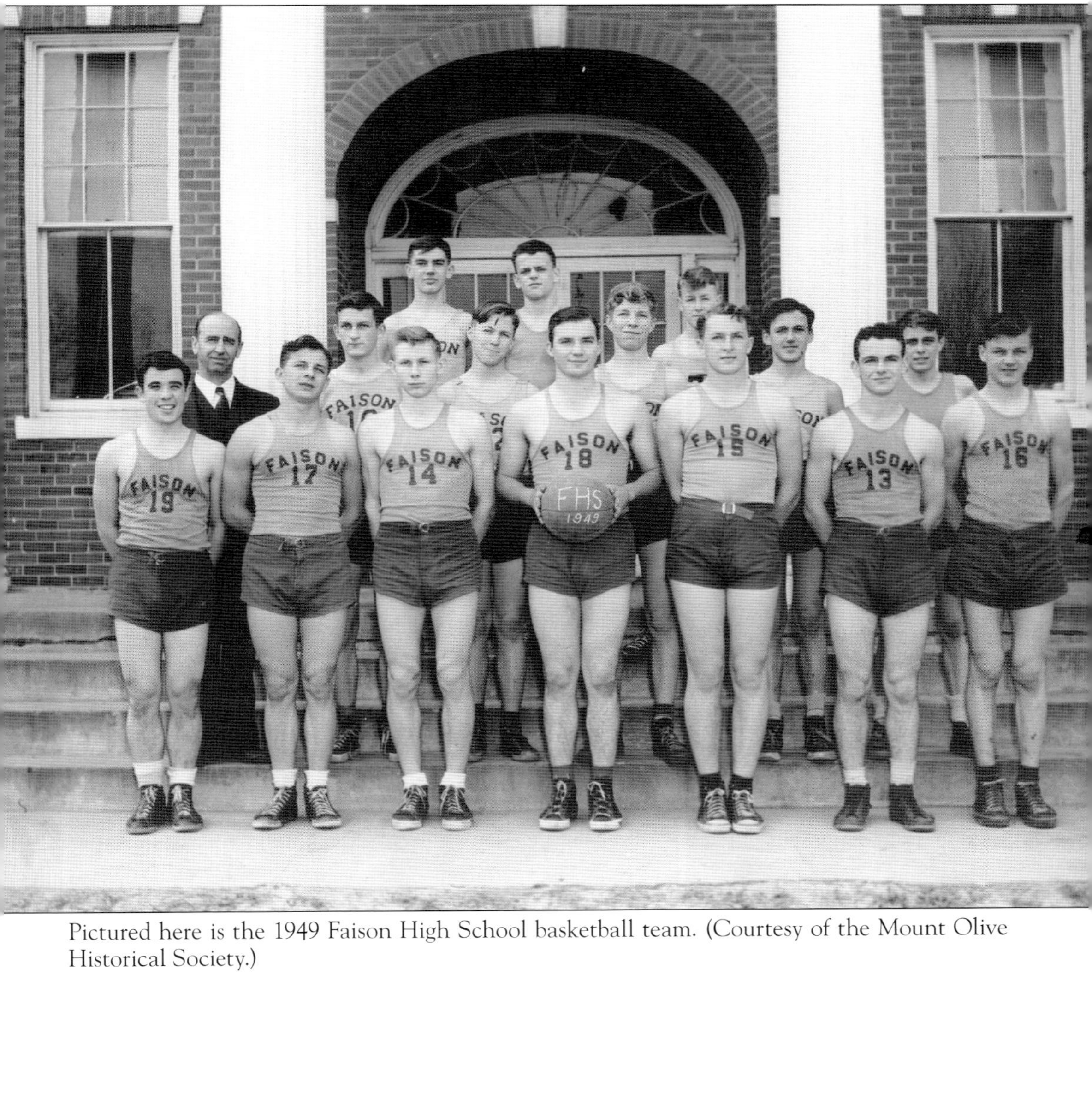

Pictured here is the 1949 Faison High School basketball team. (Courtesy of the Mount Olive Historical Society.)

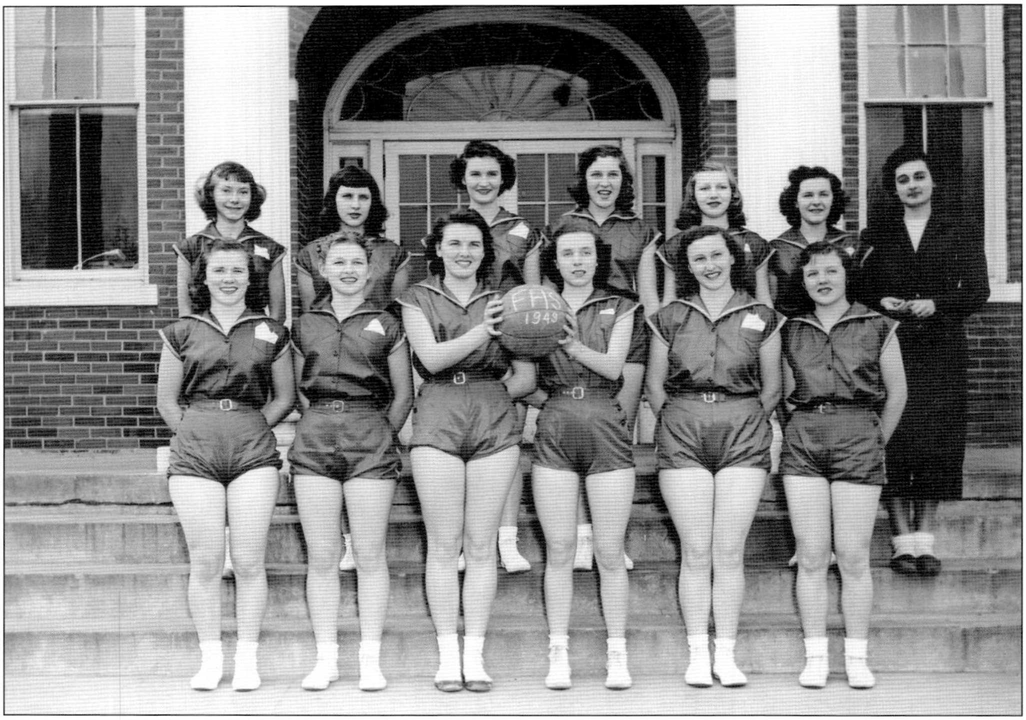

Members of the 1949 Faison High School women's basketball team pose on the front steps of the school. (Courtesy of the Mount Olive Historical Society.)

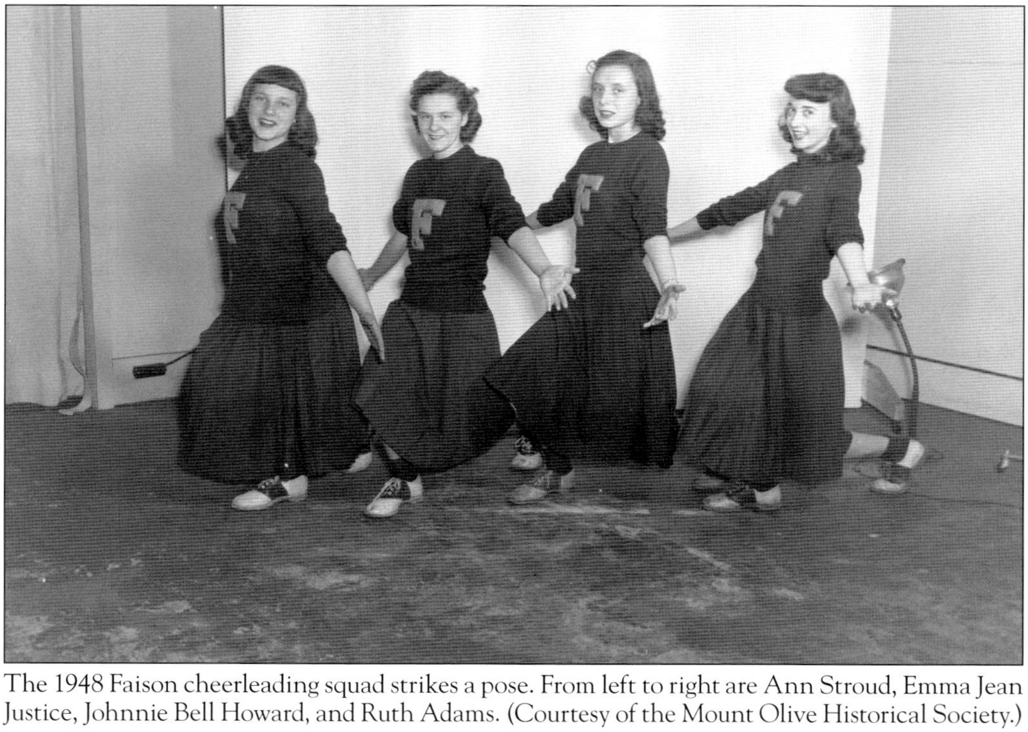

The 1948 Faison cheerleading squad strikes a pose. From left to right are Ann Stroud, Emma Jean Justice, Johnnie Bell Howard, and Ruth Adams. (Courtesy of the Mount Olive Historical Society.)

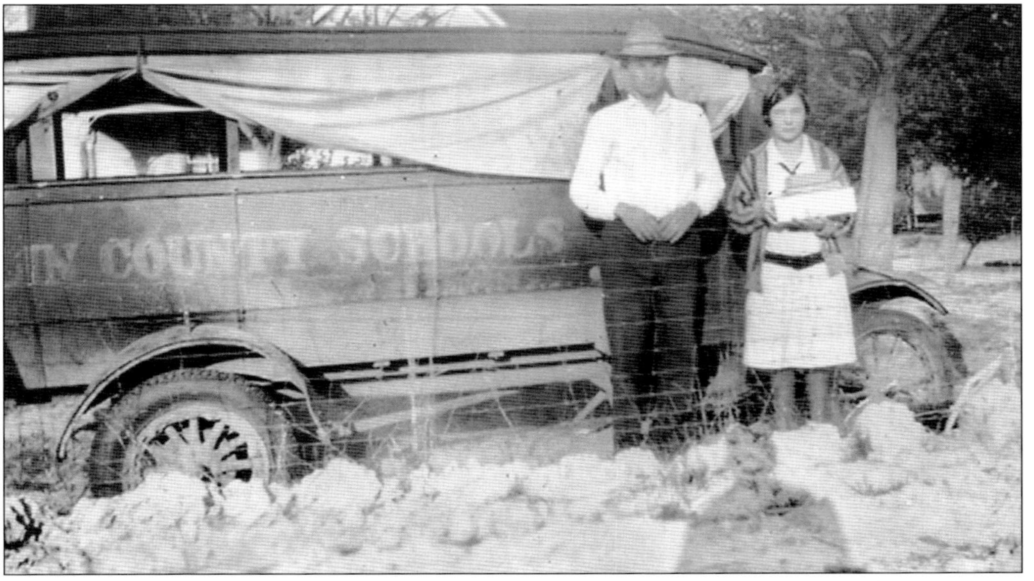

Raymond Mercer and Pearl Stroud stand beside an early Duplin County school bus in 1926. (Courtesy of Leon Sikes.)

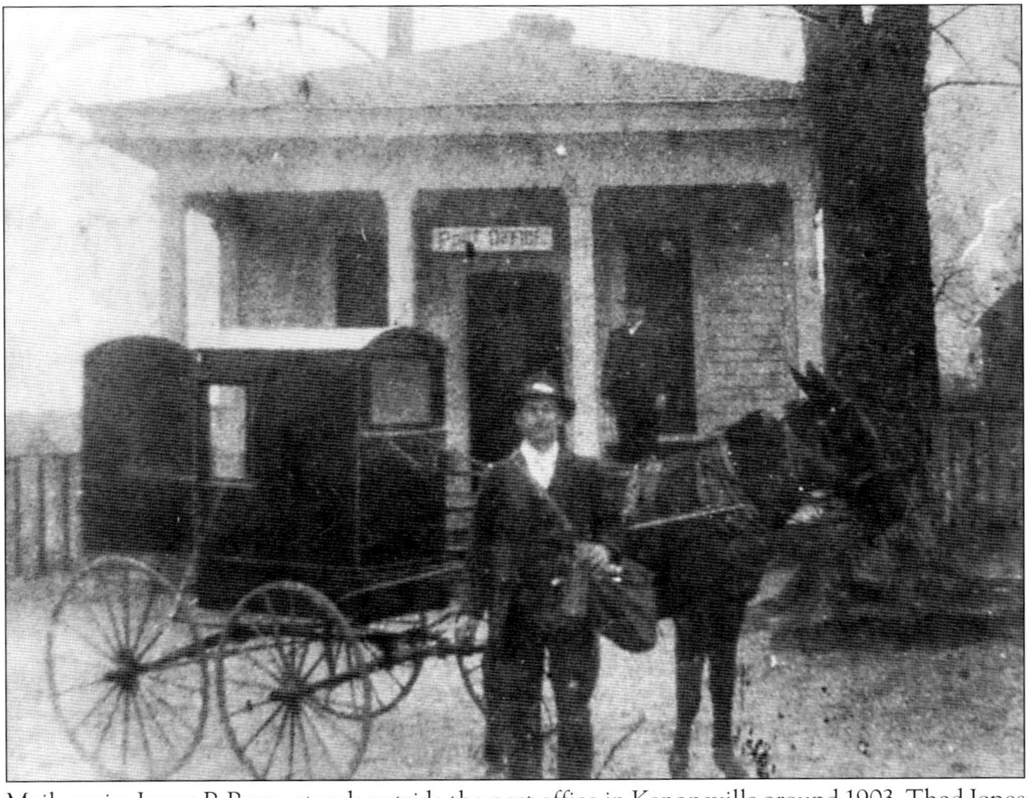

Mail carrier James P. Bryan stands outside the post office in Kenansville around 1903. Thad Jones is on the porch in the background. (Courtesy of Leon Sikes.)

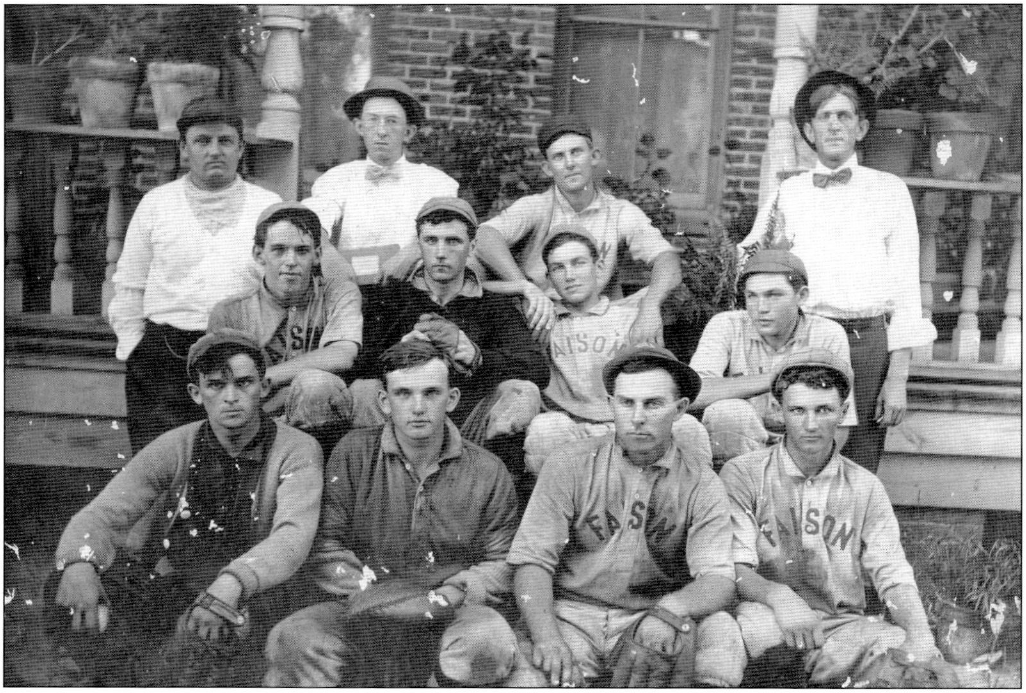

Members of the Faison Academy baseball team make time for a photograph around 1910. From left to right are (first row) Norwood Whitman, Faison Witherington, Ross Ireland, and Roland Williams; (second row) George Trust, John Shine, Marshall Williams, and Robert Witherington. The third player from the left in the third row is Henry Faison. The rest are unidentified. (Courtesy of the Faison Museum.)

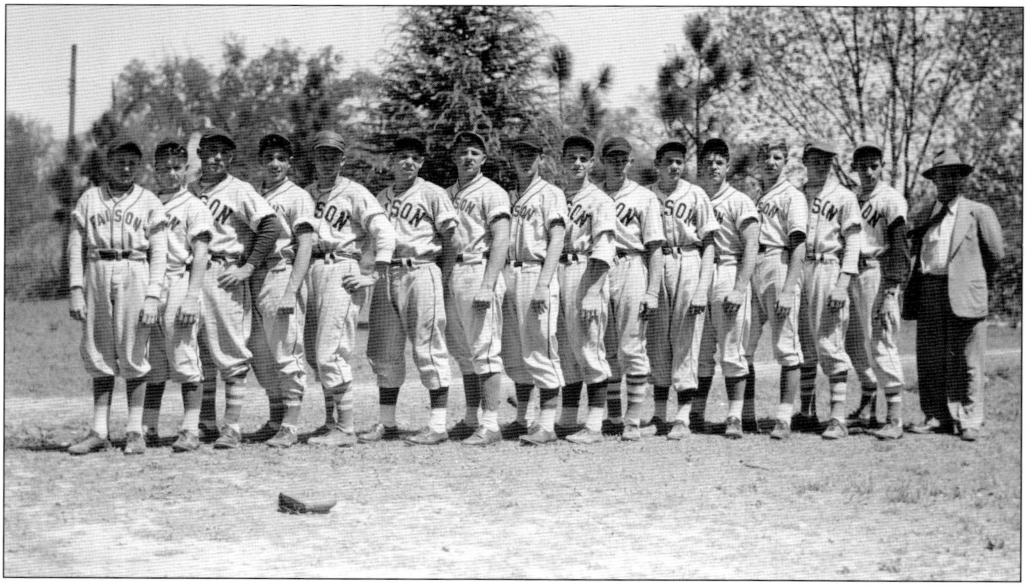

Members of the Faison High School baseball team line up. The exact date is unknown, but the photograph is thought to have been taken during the late 1940s or early 1950s. (Courtesy of the Mount Olive Area Historical Society.)

Laura "Tena" Griffin Williams holds her grandson Curtis D. Cole on her hip outside her home in Potters Hill. Tena was married to farmer Andrew Pickett Williams. (Courtesy of the Cole family.)

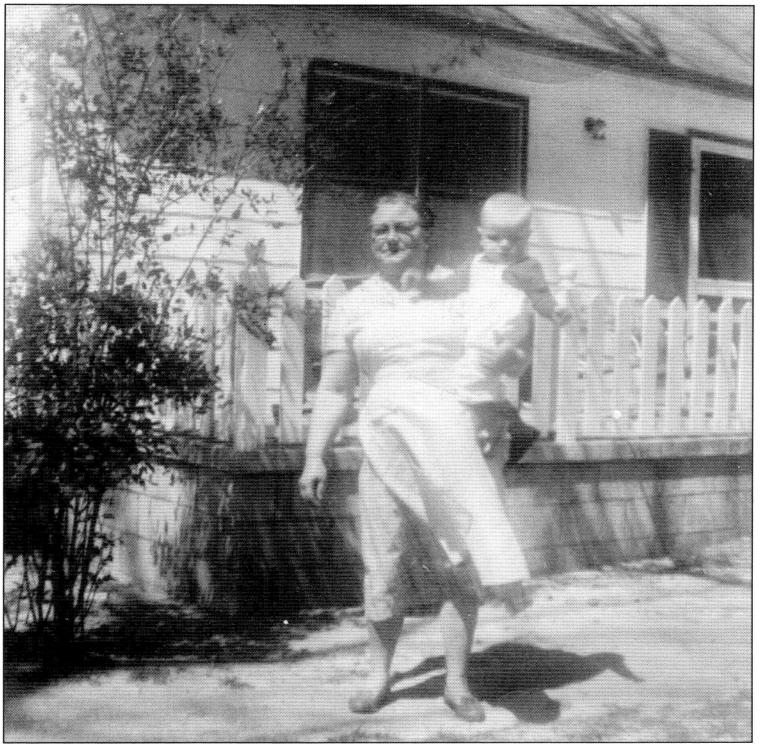

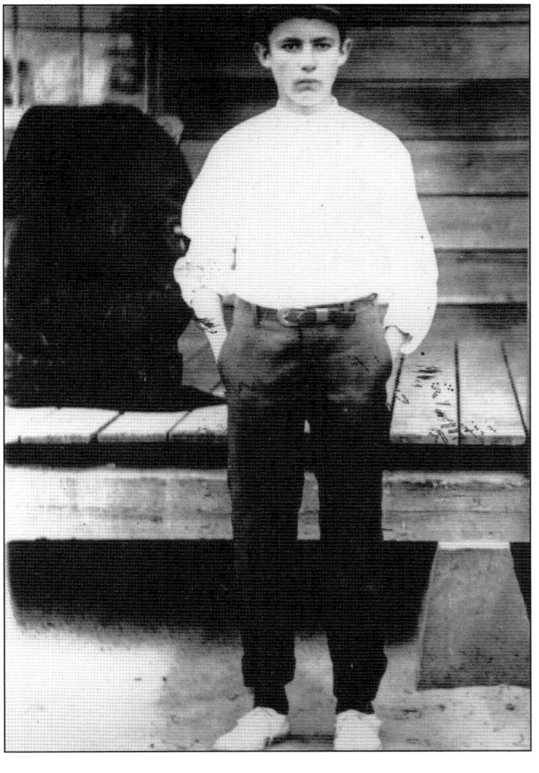

This photograph shows a young Andrew Pickett Williams. Williams was born in 1899 and eventually married Laura "Tena" Griffin. Together, the couple raised 14 children while farming in Potters Hill. (Courtesy of the Cole family.)

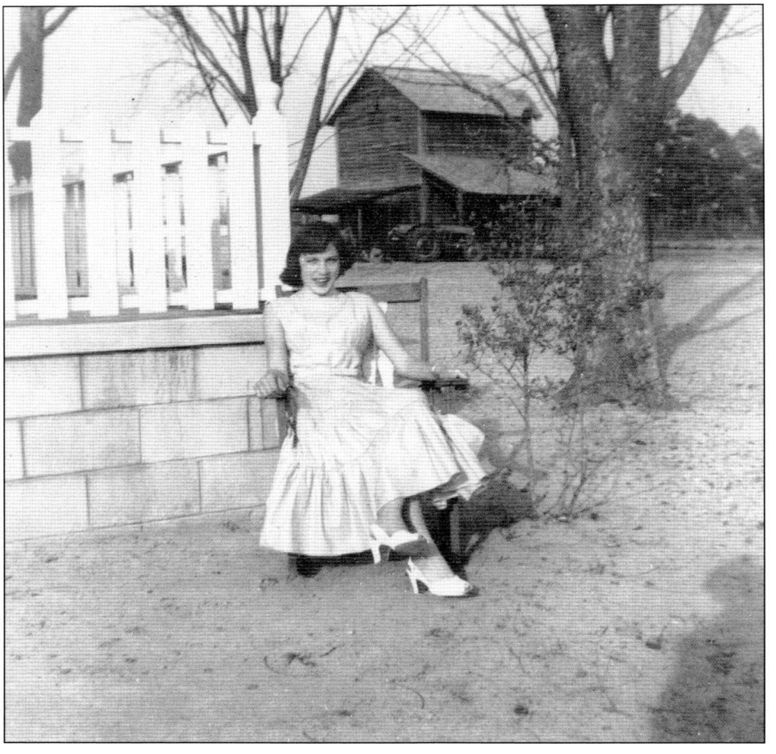

In this 1955 photograph, Mary Williams shows off her dress outside her family's home in Potters Hill. Mary had a twin sister named Martha. Like many in Duplin County, the Williamses were a family of farmers; note the tobacco barn and tractor in the background. (Courtesy of the Cole family.)

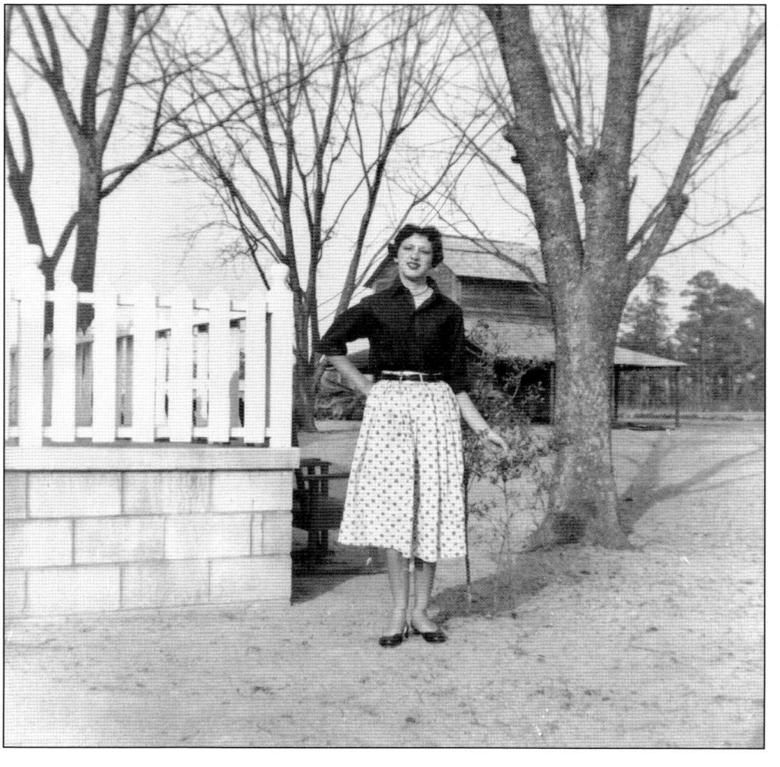

Patricia Williams poses outside her family's home during the 1950s. Patricia and her husband, Noah Cole Jr., would eventually move into the house, which still stands in Potters Hill. (Courtesy of the Cole family.)

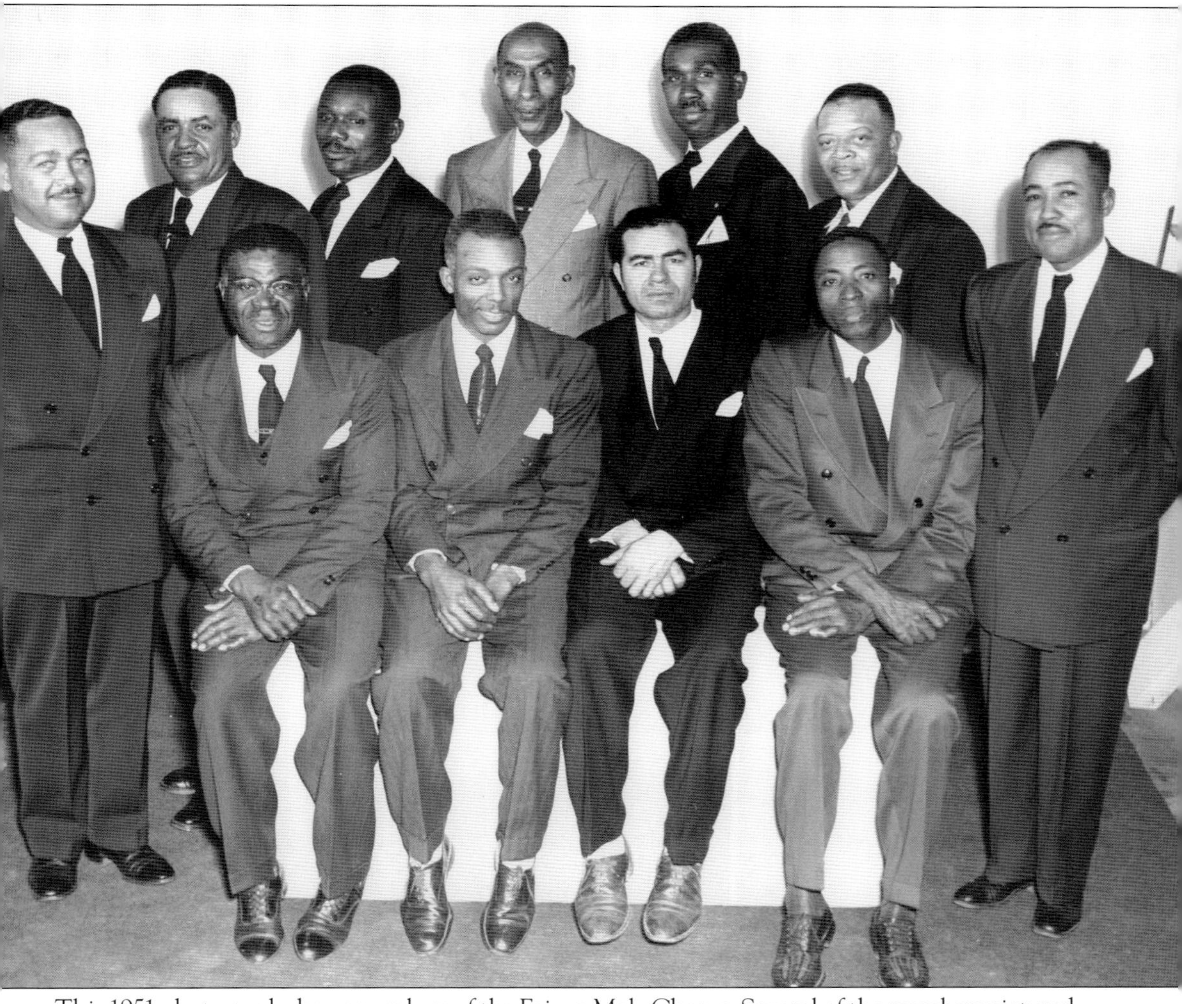

This 1951 photograph shows members of the Faison Male Chorus. Several of the members pictured here have been identified by members of the community. From left to right in the first row are Randall Faison, Theodre Lee, Joe Sampson, and Charlie Thompson. Standing in the second row are ? Chalmers, Levie Brewington, Newt Barksdale, and Jesse Adams. The rest of the chorus members have yet to be identified. (Courtesy of the Mount Olive Historical Society.)

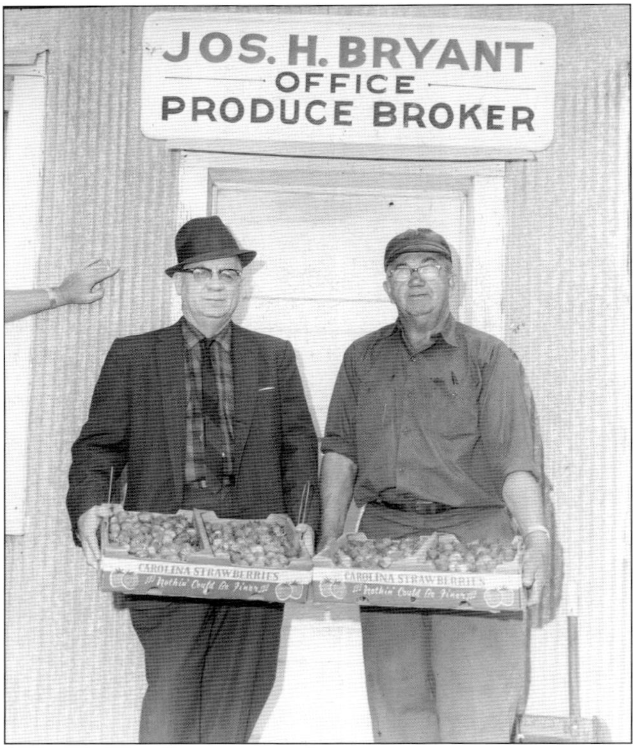

Local produce broker Joseph Bryant (left) poses with a crate of strawberries alongside produce buyer Emil Jones around 1950. Bryant's office was located in Wallace. (Courtesy of Leon Sikes.)

Duplin County girls strike a pose while participating in the 1937 Wallace Strawberry Festival motorcade. In the days prior to their departure, the *Wallace Enterprise* announced that the "goodwill emissaries from the Strawberry Capital" were going to advertise the festival, and that their "red and white satin costumes presented a colorful sight." The motorcade was to visit "56 towns and cities" in the weeks leading up to the Strawberry Festival. (Courtesy of the State Archives of North Carolina.)

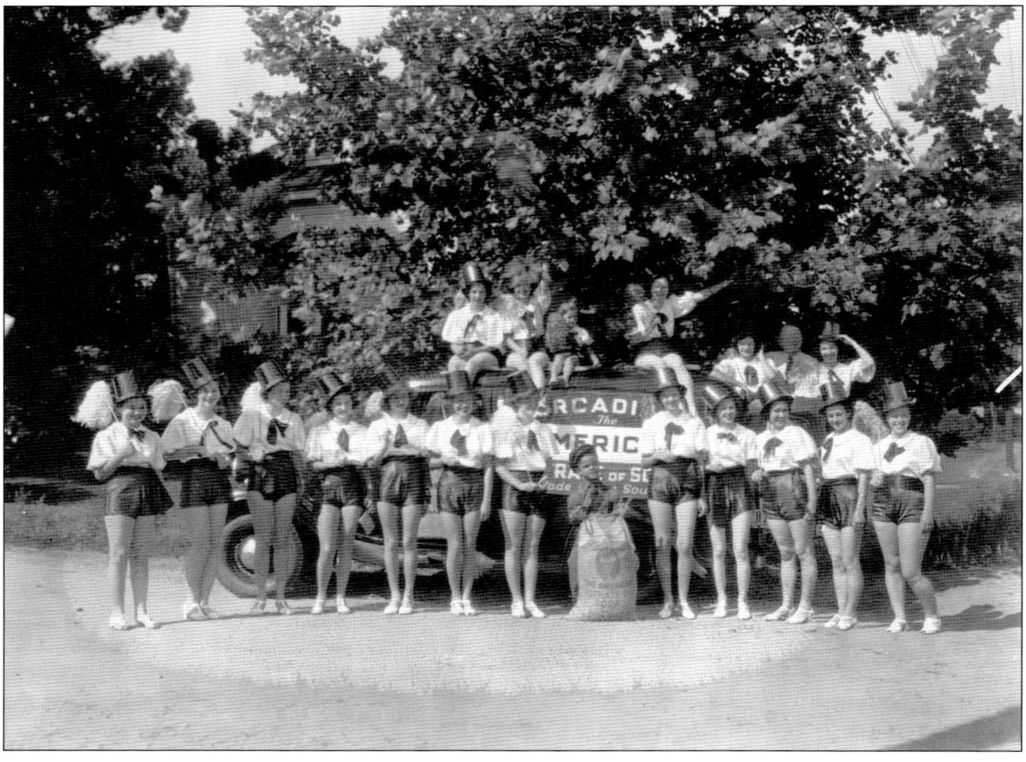

From left to right, playwright Sam Byrd directs scene designer Corwin Riff and first foreman G.E. Alphin Jr. on the unfinished set of *The Duplin Story*. Born in Mount Olive, Byrd was an actor, producer, and playwright who in the past had taken roles in performances such as *House of Mander*, *Street Scene*, *Of Mice and Men*, and *Tobacco Road*. Byrd wrote *The Duplin Story* in 1949 in honor of the county's bicentennial. Apart from his life on stage, Byrd served in the US Navy during World War II, where he saw action as a beachmaster during the D-Day invasion. He later served in the Battle of Okinawa. (Courtesy of the State Archives of North Carolina.)

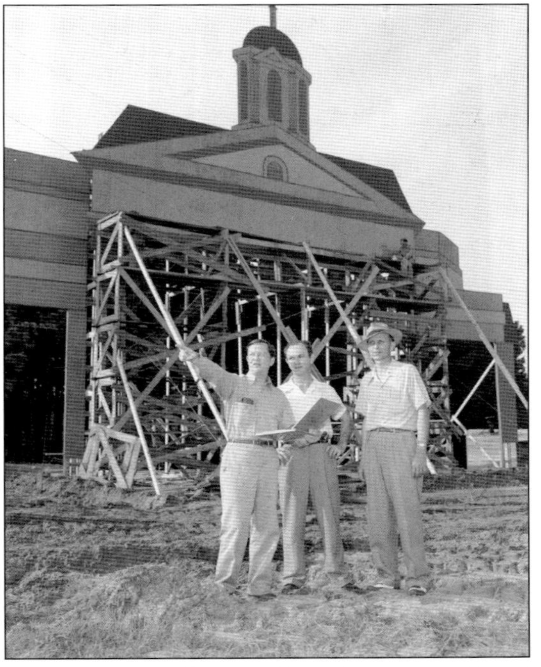

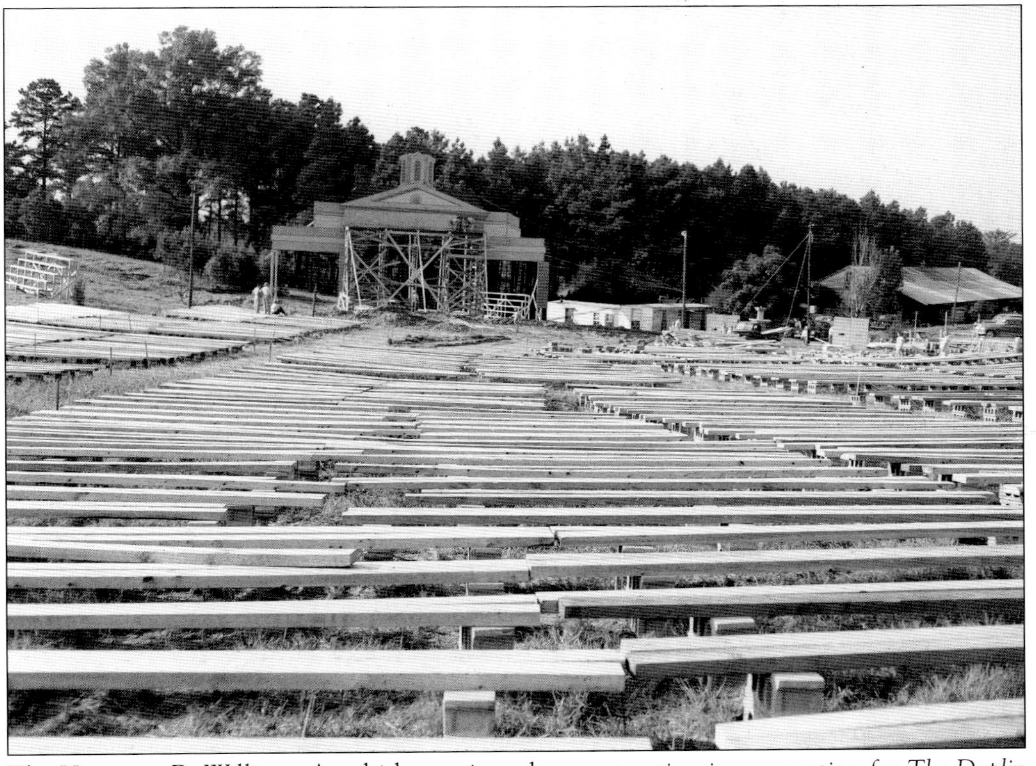

The Hampton D. Williams Amphitheater is under construction in preparation for *The Duplin Story*. The play was said to include eight different backdrops ranging from 20 feet to 30 feet in size and featured 500 actors. (Courtesy of the State Archives of North Carolina.)

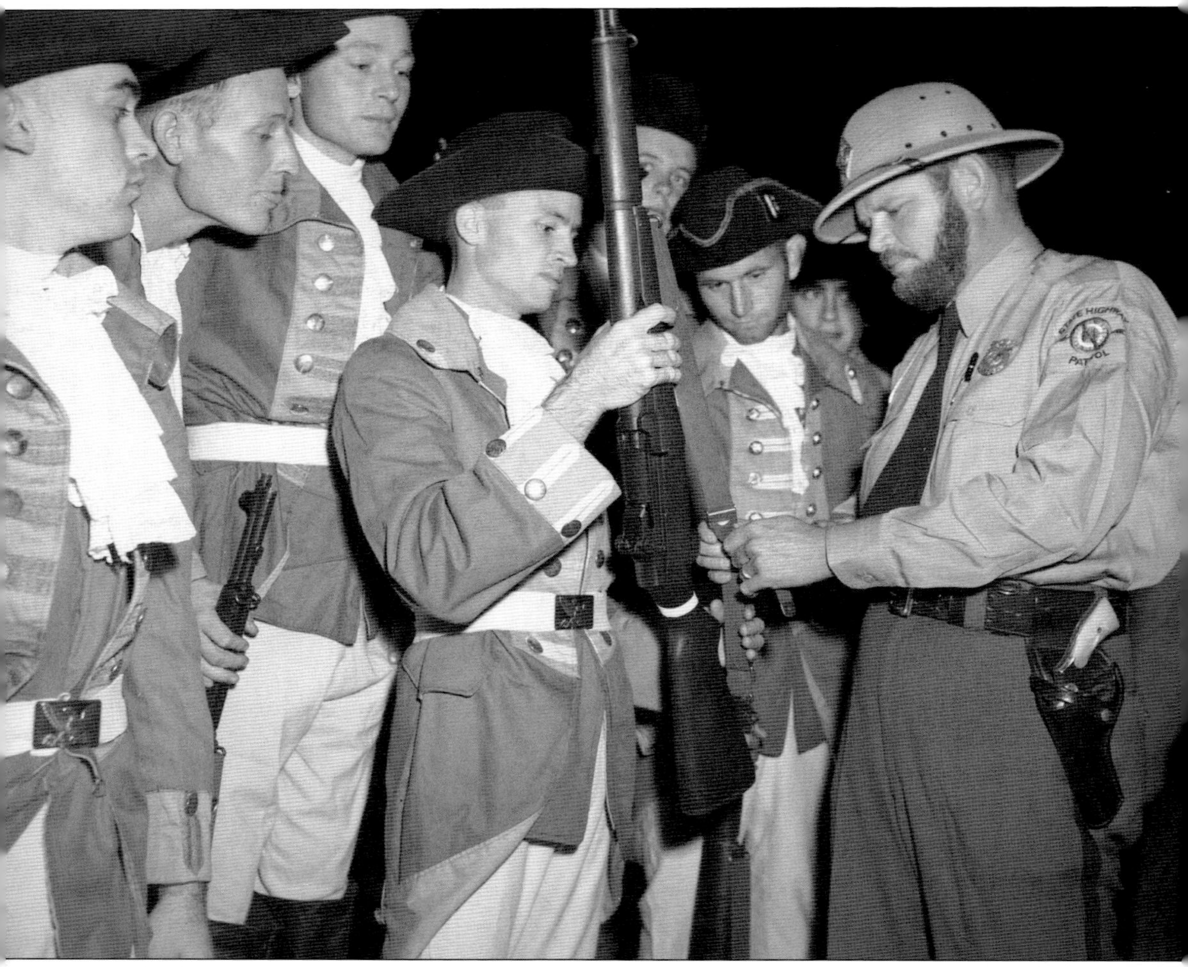

A North Carolina highway patrolman checks participants' weapons prior to a showing of *The Duplin Story* around 1949. A historical musical, *The Duplin Story* offered local audiences an upbeat yet fictionalized glimpse into the county's past. (Courtesy of the State Archives of North Carolina.)

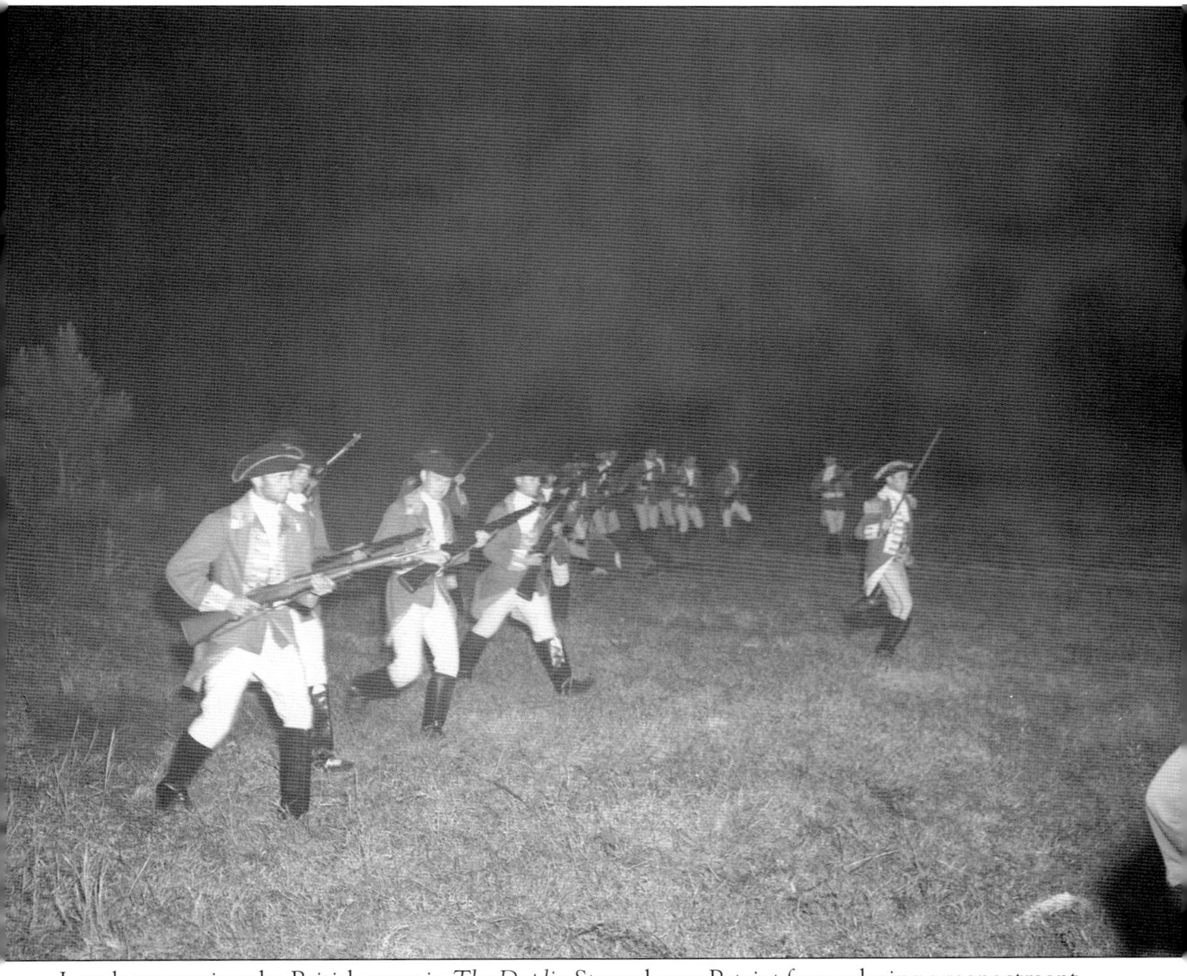

Locals portraying the British army in *The Duplin Story* charge Patriot forces during a reenactment of the Battle of Rockfish Creek. Note the World War II–era M-1 Garand rifles being used as props. (Courtesy of the State Archives of North Carolina.)

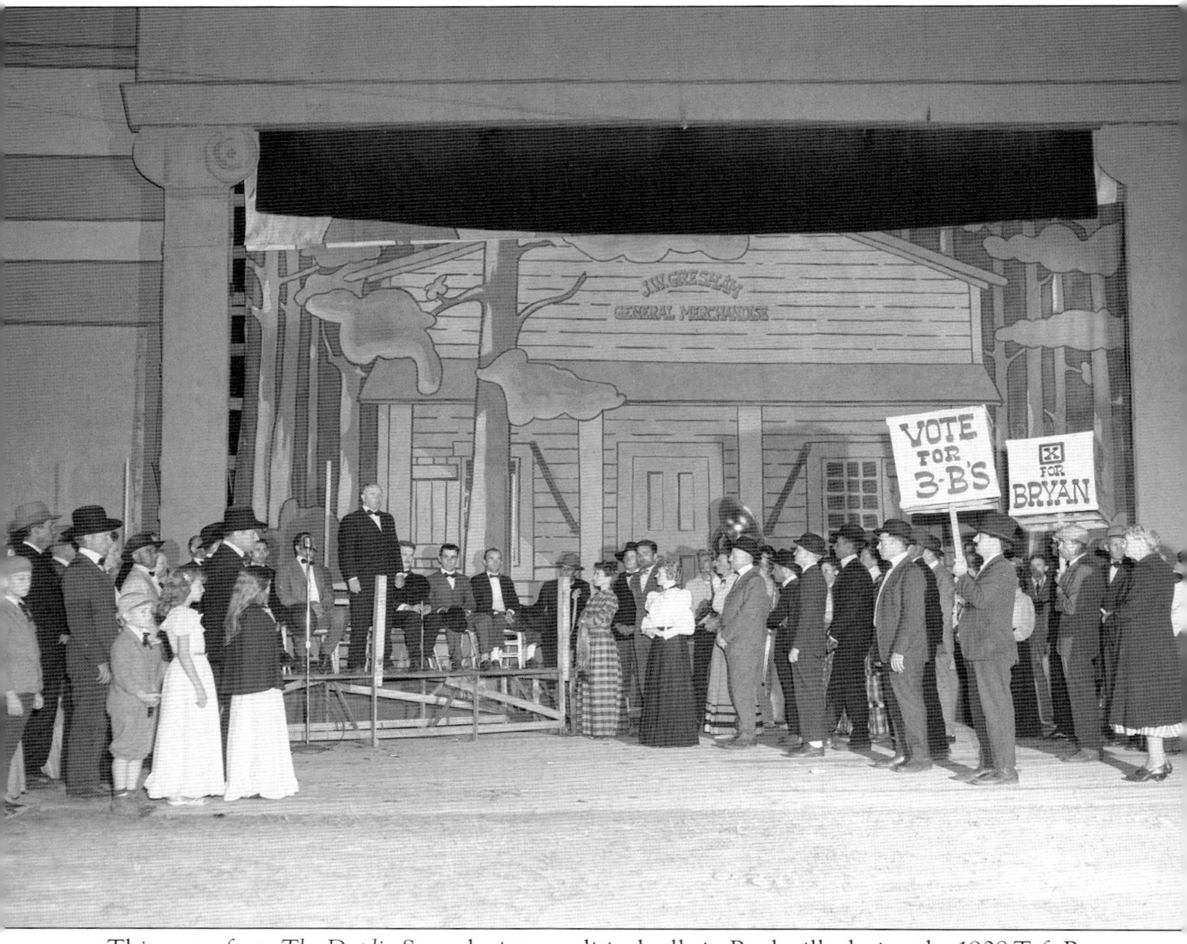

This scene from *The Duplin Story* depicts a political rally in Beulaville during the 1908 Taft-Bryan campaign. This part of the show included a brass band, square dance, and political speeches rife with humor from that era. (Courtesy of the State Archives of North Carolina.)

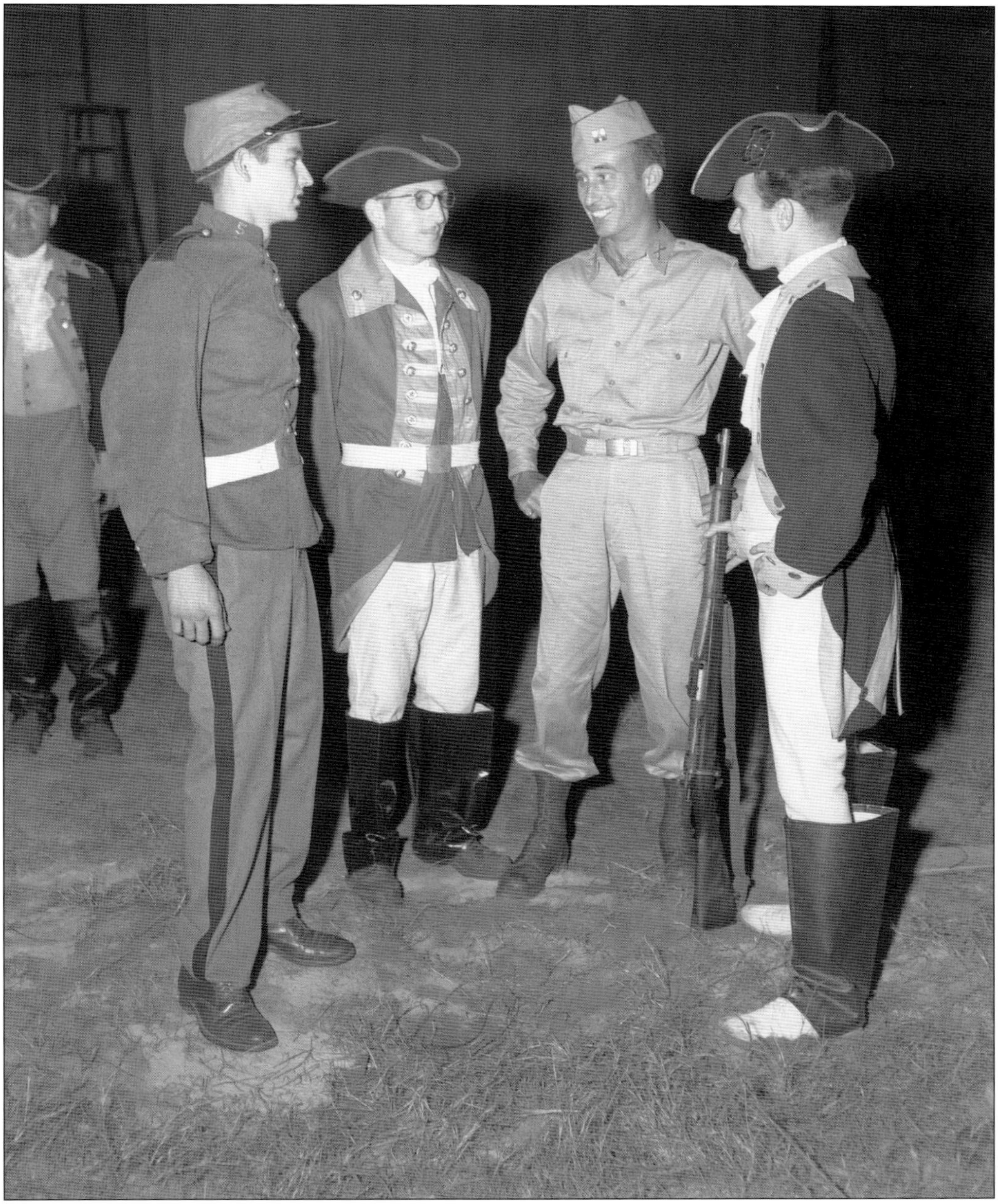

Donning military uniforms from different periods of American history, these extras prepare for their roles in *The Duplin Story*. (Courtesy of the State Archives of North Carolina.)

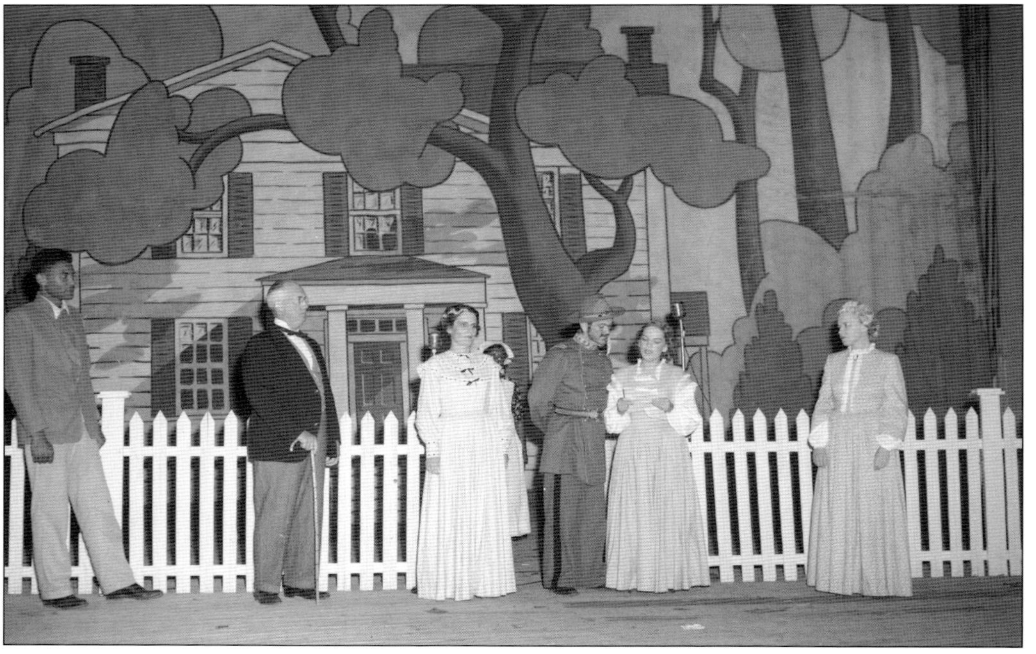

Actors reenact a scene in front of a mock Liberty Hall during a performance of *The Duplin Story*. The closing scene of the last act of the play featured a parade of war-weary Confederates making their way back to Kenansville following the Civil War. (Courtesy of the State Archives of North Carolina.)

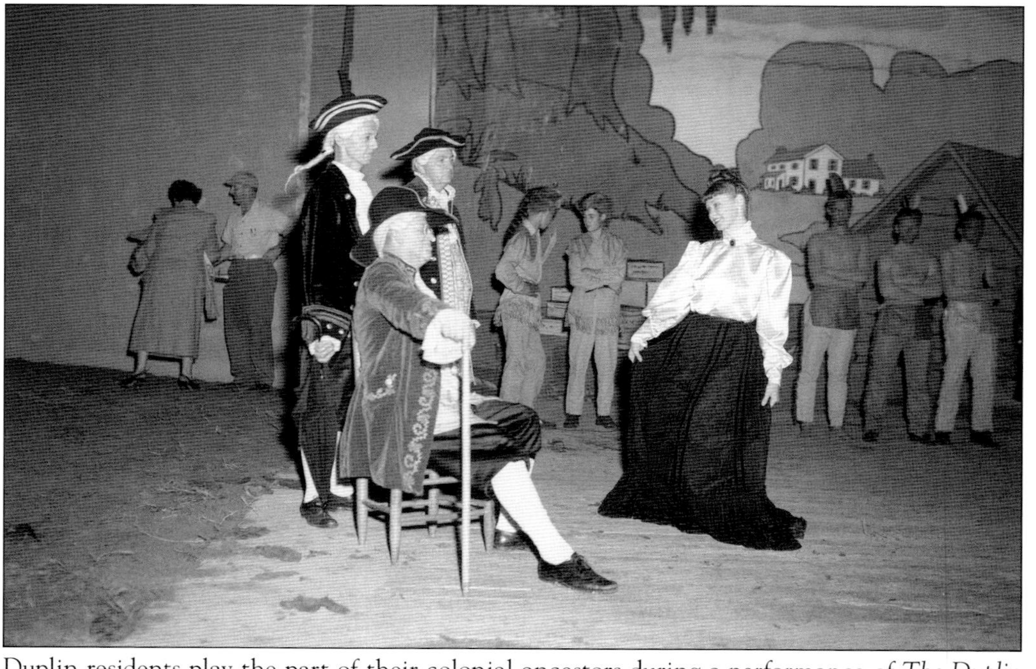

Duplin residents play the part of their colonial ancestors during a performance of *The Duplin Story*. This scene is supposed to depict an August afternoon at the river barge landing at Sarecta. (Courtesy of the State Archives of North Carolina.)

Bibliography

Duplin County Historical Association, The. *The Duplin Story: A Historical Play with Music by Sam Byrd*. Kenansville, NC: J.R. Grady, 1950.

Martin, Jennifer F. *Along the Banks of the Old Northeast: The Historical and Architectural Development of Duplin County, North Carolina*. Kenansville, NC: The Duplin County Historical Foundation, 1999.

McGowen, Fashion and Pearl. *Flashes of Duplin's History and Governments*. Raleigh, NC: Edwards & Broughton Co., 1971.

Powell, William S. *North Carolina Through Four Centuries*. Chapel Hill, NC: The University of North Carolina Press, 1989.

Saunders, William L., ed. *The Colonial and State Records of North Carolina*. Raleigh, NC: P.M. Hale, Printer to the State, 1886–1890.

Wallace Enterprise. June 1936, May 1937, June 1937.